Inside China Today

A WESTERN VIEW

ALSO BY E. GREY DIMOND

More Than Herbs and Acupuncture

Inside China Today

A WESTERN VIEW

by E. Grey Dimond, M.D.

W·W·NORTON & COMPANY
New York   London

First published as a Norton paperback 1984

Published simultaneously in Canada by Stoddart, a subsidiary of General Publishing Co. Ltd.,
Don Mills, Ontario.

The text of this book is composed in Times Roman, with display type set in Dynamic.
Book design by Nancy Dale Muldoon.

Library of Congress Cataloging in Publication Data
Dimond, E. Grey.
Inside China today.
1. China—Description, politics, and travel
2. Dimond, E. Grey.   I. Title.
DS712.D55   1983   951.05   82–14272
ISBN 0-393-30215-6

W. W. Norton & Company, Inc.,
500 Fifth Avenue, New York, N.Y. 10110
W. W. Norton & Company, Ltd.,
37 Great Russell Street, London WC1B 3NU

The map on pages 116–117 was prepared by Tom Mueller.

3 4 5 6 7 8 9 0

To

EDGAR SNOW
GEORGE HATEM
HUANG HUA
and to their adventure of 1936

CONTENTS

Illustrations appear on pages 115, 116–117 and 118.

PREFACE

On the evening of 31 January 1979, my wife and I walked from the Sheraton-Park Hotel, three blocks along Connecticut Avenue, over Rock Creek Parkway to the Liaison Office of the People's Republic of China. We were on our way to a social evening of considerable significance. The vice-premier of China was entertaining American friends in Washington, D.C.; such had never happened before in the history of the world. The United States of America and the People's Republic of China had completed formal diplomatic recognition.

Just ten years earlier, while living in Washington, we had agreed that we would use our energy to facilitate reconciliation between China and the United States. Our only resource was a keen determination that a reasonably peaceful and stable world would require the full, open participation of China.

My wife's father, Grenville Clark, had earlier reached this same conclusion, and with a remarkable ability to carry through large designs from the base of a private citizen, he had begun his effort to establish contacts with China. He died in 1967, but in the last years of his life was probing every potential, attempting in the total absence of a diplomatic relationship to find a viable path to China. He worked closely with Ed Snow, and from Ed had learned a great deal about China. Ed equally had learned a great deal from Mr. Clark, and Ed's lasting resource book, *Red Star over China*,[1] carries this dedication: "To Grenville Clark, who was taller than his time."

Grenville Clark had another able ally in his personal physician, Paul Dudley White, and the two of them with Ed's help tried elaborate routes to establish communication with the Chinese. Mr. Clark died without accomplishing his goal, but Paul White, Mary Clark Dimond, and I reached China through Edgar Snow's endorsement to Zhou Enlai.

In that initial year of contact, after twenty-two years of separation, I had a special monopoly. I was able to "expand my franchise" and, in November of 1972, stimulate the Institute of Medicine and the American Medical Association to host the first Chinese physicians to visit the United States. Now on this evening of 31 January 1979, as we walked to the Liaison Office to be received by Vice-Premier Deng, and our goal of 1969 had been essentially accomplished, my wife and I agreed somewhat ruefully that we were out of work. Our small, special beachhead of September 1971 was now absorbed into the immense highway of unfolding communication and exchanges. We remembered Grenville Clark, Paul White, and Edgar Snow, and wished they were with us on this evening.

The western observer who seeks absolutes and describes China with authority is constantly out-of-date. Missionary children born and raised in China in the 1920s, a marine stationed there in 1930, an American soldier who served there in 1945, the tourist of 1975, all saw a different act in an unending play.

For us to understand this modern China, we need to understand the thirty years of Communist leadership, but also the consistent patterns of Chinese behavior for the previous thirty centuries. Whether emperor or chairman, the Chinese leader has the essential Chinese ethical framework, shaped by the experiences of the world's oldest continuous civilization, controlling him.

In January 1979, a friend had written to me, "We are much delighted to know the United States and China have finally normalized relations. My parents, brothers and sisters are now living in China mainland and are happy and healthy. Materially speaking they don't have fancy equipment or tools to enjoy, but deep in their heart they are all happy and they understand that they are proud of their country, its independence, and to have recovered their dignity." The friend, Chinese, arrived on Taiwan with all his family in 1949. The entire family has now returned to China or emigrated to the United States. Though an American citizen and loyal to his adopted country, he can not mask his pride in China.

This pride in being Chinese and worthy of the achievements of one's ancestors is a primary truth, not a quirk of temporary nationalism. The integrity of the Chinese civilization will persist. The benefits to China from communism have come from disciplined organizational and management strength; however, the Chinese civilization is at the same time altering, changing, and guiding communism. Another invader is being absorbed by the Chinese people. Marxism, modern engineering, agriculture, science, and military attainment may be the trappings of change, but I suspect the character of the Chinese nation is unchanged and persevering, beyond Engels and Marx.

ACKNOWLEDGMENTS

I THANK the Rockefeller Foundation for the remarkable solitude of their study center at Bellagio, Lake Como, and the privilege of a scholar-in-residence appointment there. Equally, I thank the University of Missouri-Kansas City for the freedom of a sabbatical leave in 1978. These two positions: a sabbatician and a scholar-in-residence, are surely among life's happiest chances. Of course, they are also threatening. Such freedom must be justified, and therein lies the rub.

The help of Rosemary Burks, Anne Tompkins, Lea Grey Dimond, James Soward, and Betty Ann Steinman in manuscript production is acknowledged.

John K. Fairbank, Helen Foster Snow, Jack Chen, and John S. Service kindly read and criticized a draft of the manuscript.

George P. Brockway and Mary Cunnane of W. W. Norton & Company, Inc. were firm and skillful editors.

INTRODUCTION

I was fortunate in having a friendship with Edgar Snow, an American from Missouri who when thirty years old interviewed the future leaders of China, told their story in *Red Star over China*, [1] and predicted much that has come to pass. A legacy of that friendship with Snow has been to know American-born George Hatem, now living in China fifty years. George, Ma Haide, has been a kind and provocative friend, whether met in China, in Geneva, or in the United States. Much of this book comes from our conversations. I have not asked George to review the manuscript, and all areas in which I may have misinterpreted him are my own fault.

From an initial invitation given to me upon the recommendation of Snow, I have now been to China nine times and have been involved in a broad range of negotiations and exchanges. Part of this story I have told in *More Than Herbs and Acupuncture*, [2] and part of it I tell here. The subject is large, the changes great, the nuances subtle, and the bias of reader and writer significant. However, all visitors to China come home with something to say. In diaries, slides, churches, clubs, schools, and of course in books, the American home from China tells his or her version of the China story.

The traveler in China can devise several ways of assuring an unsatisfactory experience. One of the more frequent painful needs is "firstism." This has to do with an overwhelming need to label oneself the winner of a "first" label. The "firster" produces a long listing of first athlete, first actress, first physician; first black athlete, first Chinese-American professor of law; first university group of white and black medical students, first physicians who are anesthesiologists who practice medicine and do research and who are officially sponsored by an American national organization, *ad firstism*.

Two other psychological instincts characterize the American traveler. These are deeply imbedded and have long protected the American tourist's confidence in his own culture. The first is to deprecate the quality of the hotels and especially the bathrooms. Pride in America's plumbing sustains us just as Frenchmen rely on their national food and wine reputation. The second value buffering the American is the noting of all evidences of poverty and examples of human labor doing work rightfully belonging to machines.

Both of these factors, plumbing and poverty, are weighed competitively and are used as assurances of American progress, proving our "superiority." This gives the American great grist for witty writing through we-they examples of the plumbing, bedding, housing, heating, or transportation. A good example: "But nothing had prepared us for the Friendship Hotel, a forbidding pile of fortress proportions that had been built for Russian VIP's in the 1950's, and was at least a half-hour's drive from the center of Peking. Some of the bedrooms hadn't been fumigated since the Liberation (as we were taught to call it), while the bathrooms featured broken drains, inoperable paper rolls, and wooden toilets that flushed forever.''[3]

"Firstism," plumbing, and poverty are fair values for usual foreign travel. However, the size, seriousness, and significance of China's effort involves such major issues of world population, food, production, energy, pollution, and peace that the American traveler must consider the risk of pettiness of values. The world will not long remember the problems of plumbing as China races for its proper position as a premier nation. The opportunity to watch this social revolution is the remarkable circumstance. To observe and to record the problems, failures, and successes of this rising-up of the Chinese people is a large enough event of our lifetime to warrant the most careful study on its own merits, not as an issue of whether we have better cars, cameras, and commodes.

We owe it to ourselves as earth's citizens to get ourselves to China, to share and observe, to get our children there to study, to remain objective and turn away from the usual desire to compare them to us. China is a part of the world, obviously, but it is also a world in itself. It is the center of the Oriental world, and its version of industrialization, of law and contracts, of diplomacy and conduct will not be our version. No matter a Caucasian's age, profession, or origin, he is a minority person when in China. China will surprise the visitor by its lack of curiosity about his home or customs. The proper role of the visitor is that of a student or scholar, not as critic or pundit. Observe, learn, think—but don't confuse the greatness of the event with who has primacy in plumbing.

It is difficult for Americans to accept the full reality of modern China, not only because of our own propaganda of the last thirty years, but also because of the absence of an historical experience which could prepare us for the existence of a modern, vigorous China. China as a great power reality stopped with the first demands of the West upon China in 1840. From 1840 to 1949, China was never free of attack, economically, theologically, and militarily. Almost every nation, from small Portugal to massive Russia, and with France, England, Germany, the United States, Italy, Spain, and the Netherlands joining in, demanded land rights, religious rights, and trade rights. All these external forces succeeded in disabling any efforts of a cohesive government and delayed the industrialization of China.

Along with realignment of world power in which the People's Republic of China is now "recognized," there is a sudden awareness of the economic potential of China. The world's largest labor pool, intelligent and skilled, with low demands for personal salary, is entering the world's competitive production market. One hundred million industrious Japanese, without the benefit of the natural resources needed by an industrial nation, have shown the world but a hint of what eight hundred or nine hundred million, or perhaps a billion, Chinese workers with ample iron, oil, and coal will generate now that they have become a major member of the world community.

The potential influence of one billion Chinese can only be a magnification of the experience we have had already with Japan. The United States in these past thirty years has been forced to turn from an attitude of ridicule for the label "made in Japan" to one of respect for the productive capacity and quality of an able people entering the world market. A much larger number of able people, the Chinese, are now entering the world's economy.

The interesting possibility of a world in which China will have an important, if not dominant, influence is a new idea for western man. Americans do not yet perceive this and will try to submerge the reality of a world in which white, Christian men, are not dominant. The historical imperative which needs assimilation is that the 2500-year tide which we of the West identify as the Judeo-Greco-Roman origin of our culture and which swept on as Christianity to justify the colonization of much of the world, has now receded. The Dutch, Spanish, Portugese, French, and English empires have, in our own historical time, ceased.

The People's Republic of China and the United States of America arrive at the latter part of the twentieth century facing major challenges. The United States has devised a method of constitutional government which has permitted a stable transition of power, through wars and peace, for two hundred years. The degree of individual liberty, the right of personal expression, and freedom of conduct have been remarkable. But how much crime, drugs, and welfare can be justified as civil liberty?

The People's Republic of China arrives at this point with an unproved method of controlling and transmitting power. Mao's death and the immediate disgrace of his widow and half of the Political Bureau is hardly a method of stable transition. The individual citizen has essentially no personal latitude, but must be responsive to group and State. Right of personal movement, of vote, of job, of home, of immigration, have been taken from the individual.

Two nations, each with great natural resources, are testing a path of mutual respect and independence. Their needs will force them into major commercial exchange and intercourse. However, the long question of history not presented so clearly before is now to unfold: is the American concept of democracy which has had time to reach its full zenith of power, wealth, and an educated population, a continuingly viable plan? And from the other side, can a fully mobilized, regimented, stimulated, Marxist nation maintain its pace, or is the very nature of that system ultimately limiting and destructive? The citizen there and here can only be appreciative, however, that at least the options are now open for interchange and mutual influence. One definition of peace is the absence of war. If time can be bought so that the large nations of the world can discover their dependence on each other for food and materials, this awareness perhaps will force a permanent peace upon us.

Here in the United States the message is that the individual reigns supreme; in China, the citizen is committed to the good of his fellow man. Two interesting versions of a citizen's ultimate rights and duty and a challenge for the coexistence of mankind.

Inside China Today

A WESTERN VIEW

1

DOCTOR HORSE

In 1971, an American living in Switzerland needed urgent medical care. Mao Zedong* and Zhou Enlai expressed their personal concern and an entire medical and nursing care team came from China to his bedside. The team remained with him until his death on February 15, 1972. The sick and dying man was Edgar Snow, the Kansas City-born, American journalist now living in Switzerland because the witch-hunting McCarthy years had made it impossible for him to ply his trade in his home country. The head of the Chinese medical team was Dr. Ma Haide. In the days before Snow's death, a Chinese man came to join the two Americans. His name was Huang Hua.

What was the relationship among the three men—and theirs to the chairman and the premier of the People's Republic of China? What was the origin of this special friendship and concern?

The answer is hidden, in fact obscured, in Snow's remarkable book, *Red Star over China*, [1] in which he described the adventure that shaped his life, and which, thirty-six years later when his life was ending, would provoke this major Chinese expression of affection and concern.

In secret, Snow and an American physician made their way in 1936 to the Communists' headquarters in northwest China, at Paoan. There they were joined by Huang Hua, a twenty-four-year-old economics student at the christian school, Yenching University, in Beijing, who served as Snow's interpreter for that 1936 adventure.

---

* Throughout this book, the latest approved, Romanized Chinese spelling is used except where direct quotations which antedate the new spelling are used.

But none of this story is in *Red Star over China*. There is no American physician or Huang Hua in the book; Snow's narrative of 1936 does not include a mention of the other two. It was not until thirty years later in his "revised and enlarged" edition that Snow wrote: "Dr. Hatem entered the communist district with the author, but asked him not to mention it when he left and wrote of the journey . . . I . . . agreed to keep Shag's whereabouts completely confidential, even from his family."[2] Finally, in Chapter 33, entitled 'Dr. Horse', Snow tells the saga of George Hatem of Buffalo, Ma Haide of China, and Shag to his friends. "In the hot June of 1936, when I met George Hatem . . . he began a journey which entirely altered his life . . . A healthy, uncomplicated bachelor of twenty-six, Shag possessed a shrewd intelligence that had penetrated the glossy surface of society to its ugliest sores. Beneath a superficial cynicism he was serious about one thing: he wanted to find some purpose to his work as a doctor."

This description, corrected for age and marriage, is an accurate summary of the man forty-five years later. Hatem was the other American who went in to the Chinese soviet with Ed Snow, but whose existence is missing from Snow's source book on the history of those years. He need no longer hide from the pages of history. Dr. Hatem has become the famous Dr. Ma of China.

And who was Huang Hua? In 1957 Snow published for the first time many of his unused notes from his 1936 experience. On page 3, his diary for August 26 reads: "Hsu had sent a platoon of his men, mounted on little Mongolian ponies, to meet us—Wang Ju-mei (Wang Ju-mei, a Yenching graduate, came to the North-west after I arrived there. He is called Huang Hua today, and is an official in the Foreign Office under Chou En-lai), Ma Hai-teh, Fu Chin-kuei, and myself."[3]

Snow spent five months, June to October 1936, in that initial expedition to make contact with Mao, Zhou, Deng Xiaoping and the others. He returned to Beijing, began his writing, and finished his manuscript in July 1937. Later, in his autobiographic *Journey to the Beginning,* he makes clear the impact his successful book had on his life: ". . . *Red Star over China* appeared and was an instant hit in England, selling over one-hundred thousand in a few weeks. The Random House edition in New York sold better than any non-fiction work hitherto published about the Far East."[4]

George Hatem never left Red China. He became a physician to the Red armies, took a Chinese name, Ma (The Horse), a Chinese wife, Zhou Sufei, and later, Chinese citizenship. By George's earnest request, all of this remained a secret for more than twenty years, partly to protect his American family, but also to safeguard his American citizenship. He kept his American passport, had it renewed in the late 1940s, and did not make the change to Chinese citizenship until the 1950s. In fact, when Ed Snow was at the Hatem home in Beijing in 1960, George still had a "fresh green American passport."[5]

Wang Jumei changed his name to Huang Hua to protect his family, for Communists were jailed by the Chiang K'ai-shek government. He remained in the communist-held region, joined by many other Yenching University students. Over the next forty-odd years he progressed from interpreter to secretary-general of the Ministry of Foreign Affairs, to representative of the Chinese at the Korean War negotiations, to the permanent ambassadorship to the United Nations. He became foreign minister of China. Hatem's and Snow's companion of 1936 had risen to the very peak of power.

One cannot help suggesting that those early friendships with the Communist leaders, at a time when they were essentially unknown to the western world, had a lasting influence on them. In spite of the United States's persistence in claiming Taiwan's government as the true government of China, and of military actions in Korea and Vietnam, a Chinese enthusiasm for Americans has persisted. The early imprinting on the Chinese leaders by the American from Kansas City and the American from Buffalo, augmented by the importance of Snow's book and the influential foreign-affairs role of the young Chinese student from Yenching University, have had an unmeasured but positive influence on the enthusiasm of the Chinese for Americans . . . and the Americans for the Chinese.

Of course there were other latent, positive influences. Zhou Enlai's pre-college schooling was in missionary-supported schools in Tianjin. Sun Yat-sen's widow, Soong Chingling, graduated from an American college; she remained in China and served as a connecting link between the two cultures. When Americans began visiting China in 1971, and in the years up to 1976, these previous American efforts seemed lost: the missionary schools, the scholarships to the United States, the philanthropy of the Rockefellers, the American Friends' medical care teams and so on. However, once the issues of recognition were resolved, the seeds of friendship, which had been there all the time, blossomed.

The "socialization" that occurred during the twelve years of isolation at Paoan and Yanan (Yenan) brought the future Chinese leaders and a handful of Americans into a youthful, adventurous rapport, with dancing, games, conversation, and lasting friendship. As one looks at the long negative years fostered by the John Foster Dulles policy, by the Luce publications, by the churches, and all the components that make the China Lobby, one wonders why there remained a reservoir of trust and goodwill among the Chinese leaders toward the Americans. On such a small bridge as that made by Hatem, the Snows, Anna Louise Strong, Agnes Smedley, Joseph Stilwell, Evans Carlson, and a few others? Perhaps so. The loyalties and shared moments of the years of cave-living in the hard clay hills of the northwest lasted a lifetime.

A considerable demonstration of the value the Chinese place on the meaning of "an old friend of China" was the effort made by Mao and Zhou for their sick American friend. The complexity of their lives in 1971 when they were the leaders of China, did not obscure their remembrance of a trusted friend who came to them when they were living in the caves of Paoan surrounded by hostile forces.

The three men, Snow the journalist, Hatem the physician, Huang the student, who broke through the Kuomintang lines in 1936, and gathered at the end, in 1972, at Snow's bedside in Switzerland, were able to share the satisfaction of knowing the president of the United States was, finally, to visit China. Richard Nixon's visit was a direct result of the single personal tie Mao had with an American citizen. On October 1, 1970, Mao invited Snow to stand beside him on the reviewing stand at Tien-men Gate in Beijing and told him, "Please tell your president that he would be welcomed in China, either as the president or as a tourist." It was this single thread of contact, Mao to Snow, that remained as the communication link between the two huge nations, after two decades of American rejection of the Chinese leadership. No other official or semiofficial human link remained.

The common thread joining Hatem, Snow, Huang, and Mao Zedong was the coming together at Paoan in 1936. Those shared few months were sufficient reason, thirty-five years later, for Mao to send the offer and the reality of all possible medical care to his friend. Why a response of this magnitude? What could have been the value of the five-month visit by an American journalist in 1936 that would still carry such significance in 1971? There lies the question and the answer rests in Chinese history.

For the three minor characters, the Paoan visit was a mission that determined their careers. In 1936 Snow was a young journalist in search of a story and he made the trip and found his exclusive, his scoop, wrote his book, and made his career. Ten years later because of American politics, he was harrassed into leaving his own country, essentially because he had written his prophetic book. Snow's life course was set from that June day when he reached Paoan. In a certain sad sense, with the publishing of *Red Star over China,* his contribution to history was done.

And what did Paoan mean to Huang Hua? He was twenty-three, in the last year of college, but he had already become visible as a major student activist. In his junior year, he was a leader in the December 9 (1935) student movement at Yenching University. Although imprisonment or execution for any demonstration was a reality in Chiang K'ai-shek's China, missionary-controlled Yenching University gave the students a degree of protection, and to this movement Chinese intellectuals from throughout China were attracted. From them came the demand to end the civil war (Nationalists versus Communists) and to form a "united front" against Japan. Huang Hua's decision to remain at Paoan was a beacon to Yenching students and literally hundreds followed him. For himself, he gambled his life in the belief that what he saw at Paoan could provide the means of saving China. He was an educated man from an educated family, and nothing in his background made it likely that he could accept Marxist philosophy. But he saw correctly that the Chinese interpretation of it at Paoan had an honesty and vigor which would prevail.

For George Hatem, Paoan presented purpose and dilemma. His actions already showed that America's hold on his beliefs was weakened. The Depression was bitter hard for the Hatems, and George's decision to go to Beirut to medical school was the result, at least in part, because he could not get in an American school or if he did, he was not offered a scholarship equal to that coming from Lebanon. The tie to his ancestral country was considerable; his father returned there to live. His experience at Beirut consisted of two years of the basic science medical course, but once again, he could not get into an American school for his clinical years. This time he went on to Geneva to finish his medical studies. Thus, by the time he reached Shanghai, his ties to the United States were slender. He had not been there for four years; there was no family business nor girl-friend to pull him home. His medical education was foreign and the Depression was at its worst. He had his medical degree, but he had no goal and Shanghai was pure adventure. He was young, educated, but adrift between cultures. Paoan gave him a professional purpose, a fellowship, and Chinese roots. His problem was in deciding how far to go in breaking with his past. He therefore kept a foot in the door. He always had his American passport and the considerable protection it provided if the Paoan adventure tumbled in. To appreciate the significance of George's American years, one must remember that he left his native country at age nineteen.

The major historical figure, now that the story is told, was Mao. He was the true beneficiary of the 1936 meeting. Snow was a young man looking for a story, and Mao was a forty-three-year-old revolutionary, encircled, isolated, with a story and a need to have it told. The Chiang K'ai-shek censorship was almost total, and the efforts of the Reds were unknown in the rest of the world. Most importantly for Mao's purpose, not even the Chinese had facts about the leaders of the Communists and their beliefs. Snow served as Mao's amanuensis, sitting in the caves at Paoan night after night, getting down on paper the story Mao wanted to tell. Much to Snow's credit, one can now say that he got an honest story, one which stood the test of time. Mao used Snow, but Snow was not one to be fooled. The Harvard authority on China, John K. Fairbank, wrote an introduction to Snow's book when it was reprinted thirty years later.

"The remarkable thing about *Red Star Over China* was it not only gave the first connected history of Mao and his colleagues and where they came from, but it also gave a prospect of the future of this little-known movement which was to prove disastrously prophetic. It is very much to the credit of Edgar Snow that this book has stood the test of time on both of these accounts—as a historical record and as an indication of a trend."[6]

Snow waived Chinese translation rights and a manuscript copy of *Red Star over China* was smuggled to Shanghai, published and distributed widely in China under the title *Travels to the West*.[7] This book, plus many pirated chapters, became Mao's means of getting his story to the Chinese intellectuals. For the first time, the quality of the leaders, Mao, Zhu De, Zhou, their saga of the Long March, and the strength and purity of their commitment to China were learned. Thousands of students came to the Communist regions. Snow's book was available in China by June, 1937 when ". . . enthusiastic young radicals as well as veteran Party workers rolled in from all parts of China, some walking great distances. . . ." They had come to enroll at the Communists' Anti-Japanese University. By the second term of 1938, there were five thousand students enrolled. Snow broke the boycott which had obscured Mao's message.

All four men: Snow, Huang, Hatem, and Mao gained from the 1936 five-month visit to Paoan by Snow, but Mao gained the most; the Chinese empire became his. It was truly a fateful journey.

2

LEBANESE-AMERICAN IN MOTION

BEGINNING in 1971 after twenty-two years of reciprocal quarantine, Americans were able to visit China. They came by the thousands, curious, suspicious, eager to see Communist China. Some had known China in the 1930s or during the Second World War and carried images of the China they had known. But most Americans knew China as a hidden world with the view obscured by political embargo and biased news coverage. The one American who had been there all the time, George Hatem, arrived in China in 1934 and never came home. He was the only American who had seen, and been part of, the whole story: Chiang K'ai-shek, international settlements, life in the Communist-held area, Japanese invasion, civil war, Communist victory.

The Communists' conquest of China had not been easy. The campaign had lasted twenty-five years, and for one twelve-year period their forces were contained in a small area in northwest China, almost forgotten by the rest of the world. From 1935 to 1947, when the Chinese Communists, in their Yanan years, were isolated north of the Great Wall and inside the sweeping bend of the Yellow River, George Hatem was the only American who came into daily contact with the small group who ultimately ruled all of China.

Hatem was born in 1910 in Buffalo. His father, who had emigrated from Lebanon, then a part of Syria, earned his passage by committing himself to labor in a textile mill in Lawrence, Massachusetts. He saved his money, returned to his home village to find his bride, brought her back to America, to Buffalo, and raised a large family as Maronite Christians.[1] Although there never was enough money, the Hatem children were brought up with careful attention to the church. All his cousins called him Shag, his lifetime nickname among close friends. I quizzed him on the origin of Shag, but he disclaimed any memory for how it had come about. One suspects that a boy who began as a Shafik George Hatem could perhaps have had the unusual Lebanese first name "Shafik" altered to Shag by normal Buffalonian acculturation.

A move to find work brought the family to North Carolina where George Hatem grew up, and, in classic American-immigrant upward mobility, entered the University of North Carolina as a premedical student. Then came the move that showed he had an extra spark. Hatem went to Beirut, Lebanon, and entered the American University on a scholarship. From there he went to the University of Geneva to medical school, again having won a scholarship. He left Beirut without much money, sailed to Marseilles, and bicycled from there to Geneva. During summer breaks, while in Geneva, he saw most of central Europe, again by bicycle. He added to his finances by waiting on tables during vacation and learned French. In June 1934 he received his degree as a doctor of medicine.

In the summer of that year, at age twenty-three, he and two classmates sailed for Shanghai. He settled down, if a young bachelor physician could settle down in the exciting international city of Shanghai, to practice medicine. He quickly found himself deep in the seamy side of Shanghai as a physician to the police force, treating the venereal disease of the police and the prostitutes. He was not especially so motivated; certainly he had not gone to China with any missionary zeal. Soon his two classmates returned to Europe, and he found a new circle of friends including Soong Chingling (Sun Yat-sen's widow); Rewi Alley, a New Zealander; and Agnes Smedley, an American writer. He did not know Ed Snow, who had moved on to Beijing the year before Hatem's arrival. The awfulness of life for most of the Chinese soon became clear to him. He saw with what little regard labor and life were held, and wrote a medical paper on the corrosive damage to human beings from careless industrial exposure to chromium fumes.

It was in this environment that the Missouri-born American writer, Agnes Smedley, became active in a Marxist-Leninist study group in Shanghai. Smedley, Rewi Alley, a New Zealander, and Hatem became friends, and, perhaps all for the same reasons—sympathy for the underdog and a hope for a better life for the Chinese peasant—they all became Communists. Rewi Alley says: "It was around 1933 that I met Dr. Ma Haide, then Dr. George Hatem. It was in the home of Agnes Smedley in Shanghai, and I well remember him as being a stocky, breezy, wide-awake young American, interested in everything around him. Later he joined a Marxist-Leninist study group in Shanghai. . . ."[2] Manny Granich was also in that early study group, and Talitha Gerlach was a friend from those early Shanghai days. In a letter to this author, June 8, 1981, George states the case for the record: "Soong Ching-ling and Rewi Alley, together with Manny Granich and Agnes Smedley, were responsible for my going to the northwest and Paoan."[3]

In 1936, feeling inadequate as a physician and responding to an underground request by the Red Chinese for a western-trained physician, Hatem set out by train for Sian. Sian was the headquarters of the northwestern forces of Chiang K'ai-shek; Hatem's task was to reach Sian, make contact with the Communist underground there, and somehow fade away into the Red regions. He had with him half of a torn English five-pound note as his ticket of recognition. The nature of his direct contact with the Communists remains murky, but Soong Ching-ling played a major role.

At Zhengzhow, a major railroad junction, Ed Snow left his train from Beijing and came together with Hatem for the first time, and they continued to Sian together. While awaiting contact from the Communists there, they parried and cautiously developed their friendship while trying to slip through the military blockade and get to the Communists. Snow was very specific in describing his interest in this secret Communist Army: he wanted to get a good story. In *Journey to the Beginning,* Snow wrote: "I proposed . . . that I go in and try to crack the blockade around the communist-held areas in northwest China . . . The Herald offered me all expenses and a handsome bonus if I succeeded. Harrison Smith, then of Random House, also made me a small advance against a possible book. With that support I went to Shanghai, where I again saw Mme. Sun Yat-sen. I sought her help, so that at least I should be received by the Reds as a neutral, not as a spy. After I returned to Peking, in the spring of 1936, it was Chingling (Mme. Sun Yat-sen) who made the arrangements. Through her I was put in touch with a professor in Peking who gave me a letter to Mao Tse-tung, together

with other advice on how to contact the Red underground in Sian.[4]
Snow's first wife, Helen Foster Snow, later told me: "We never had
the least idea of joining any communists. They were totally helpless in
China then, including the foreign communists. We were the authentic
part of the foreign involvement in the history of that time, and we were
not artificially or secretly ordered to do anything but were entirely independent. We had only about fifty dollars a month usually to live on,
including when Ed made his trip to Paoan. I had to give Huang Hua the
household money for the month when I sent him to join Ed in Sian, just
before they went to Paoan."

The two Americans, Hatem and Ed Snow, ages twenty-six and thirty,
came to the same guest house in Sian. They quickly became friends but
with a healthy suspicion of the other's trustworthiness. It was not a good
time to find one had given confidences to a Communist agent. Or to a
Chiang K'ai-shek counter-agent. Over a period of days they were deep
into dangerous blockade running, attempting to get through Chiang K'ai-
shek's lines which surrounded and isolated the Communists. The danger was increased by roving gangs of armed bandits. Finally, by truck,
horse, mule, and on foot, they worked their way through the lines and
met a young, handsome, bearded officer—Zhou Enlai. Snow stayed
five months with the Communists, gathered his notes, then slipped back
through the lines to Beijing. He knew he had an important story and he
told it in *Red Star over China*. Helen Snow helped him and made her
own expedition to the Red area the next year. From that experience she
wrote *Inside Red China*[5] in 1939, a historical masterpiece, comple-
menting Ed Snow's report.

When Snow and Hatem arrived at Paoan, the Long March Army was
still coming in from the west, tired and in need of medical help. George
hurried on and joined them on the last leg of their journey. In that sense,
he was a participant in a part of the Long March.

3

SORT OF AN ETERNAL OPTIMIST

From 1936 when he dropped out of sight of friends and family, until he was again fully visible in 1971, what had happened to George Hatem? Snow was out of contact with Hatem until 1960, twenty-four years after their clandestine journey. In 1961, Snow had written: "I had corresponded with Alley often, and read his books, so he was no stranger even after twenty years. What had happened to Dr. Hatem since Pearl Harbor was much more obscure to me."[1] Their shared adventure at Paoan had begun with their attachment to General Peng Dehuai and his army as it moved over Shaanxi, Kansu, and Ninghsia; Hatem's medical ability was needed and he went further west to attend to the Fourth Front Army, the last group of those on the Long March.

The emotional scene when the final Long March veterans under Zhu De crossed the grasslands of Qinghai and on October 17, 1936 made contact with the troops coming out from Paoan, who had finished the journey a year earlier, is described by Hatem in his diary: "What a reunion! Men threw their arms around each other, laughing and weeping at the same time, or walking arm-in-arm and pouring out questions about other comrades. Chu Teh [Zhu De] was completely swallowed up in the crowd. . . . Chang Kuo-tao, the political commissar, is fat, tall, and smooth. I wonder how he kept so fat while others lost every ounce of excess weight."[2]

Hatem next had the task of organizing the Red Army's base hospital and a medical training system at Yanan. Until the Japanese invasion, no additional foreign doctors joined him and Hatem was the only western-trained physician at Yanan.

Hatem was incognito during all these early years. Harrison Foreman, a writer, was at Yanan in 1943 and wrote of the mysterious American physician: "Ma Hai-teh has been seven years with the communists. He has taken the name Ma Hai-teh (he refuses to disclose his American name), so that he may more completely submerge himself in the medical service of the Chinese Communist armies. He is in his middle thirties, he is full of boyish good humor and enthusiasm, and will unhesitatingly drop everything to act as an interpreter. He is an enthusiastic supporter of the Chinese communists."[3]

By the time Foreman met Hatem, Norman Bethune, a Canadian surgeon, had come, served, and died. The hospital at Yanan was called the Bethune International Peace Hospital. It was located on the outskirts of the city, in a series of caves. Foreman described the hospital, staff, and supply situation: "The hospital staff were a bright-eyed, intelligent lot, lack of proper equipment and supplies had not daunted them—really, it has spurred them to ingenious improvisations and tolerable substitutes. Chinese herbs, medicines, and chemicals were being scientifically tested. . . . Their dwindling stock of remaining western drugs were hoarded in a single drawer, and their precious few sulfa pills were dispensed in a case of extreme urgency, only after consultation by the whole medical staff."[4]

Dr. Norman Bethune, master surgeon fresh from the battles of the Spanish Civil War, had reached Yanan in March 1938 to the following reception. "In the center of the city a delegation was waiting to receive him. It was headed by a short, merry-looking American who pumped Bethune's hand vigorously. He introduced himself as Dr. Ma Hai-teh. Bethune had heard of him as an American who had come to China a few years before, had changed his name, married a Chinese, learned to speak the language fluently, and become a medical advisor to the 8th Route Army in Yenan."[5]

A year later Bethune had died from blood poisoning, as a result of nicking his own hand while operating on an infected limb under battlefield conditions. And Dr. Dwarkanath Kotnis, a surgeon from India, also died while aiding the Communist cause.

Hatem continued his arduous work as a physician until Japan's surrender. After this there was a period of almost two years during which the Nationalists of Chiang K'ai-shek and the Communists were attempting coexistence. This was the era when military, diplomatic, and medical personnel from the United States came to know Hatem at Yanan. Then, for almost a year, he was in Beijing at the old Beijing Hotel, again known as George Hatem, representing the relief organizations from the guerrilla areas in negotiations over supplies from UNRRA. By 1957, the truce and the efforts of the American ambassador, Patrick Hurley, and George Marshall were ended, and the final showdown of the civil war began. Yanan was surrounded and George, along with all the Communists, evacuated it. Yet this loss was the beginning of victory, and by the winter of 1948 Hatem was quartered with the leadership, outside Beijing, in the Summer Palace, and the Nationalists were under final siege, trapped within the walls of Beijing.

Another western physician spent fourteen years in China, from 1956 until 1969. He was Joshua Horn. In his informative and enjoyable book, *Away with All Pests: An English Surgeon in People's China,*[6] he devotes several pages to describing what Hatem did about eliminating venereal disease. Horn gives facts and figures, and credits much of China's campaign against venereal disease to Hatem.

One pauses with this skimpy collection of citations of the milestones in George's life. "Searching the literature" does not add much. Hatem has led a non-public, but important life. His demonstration that in a certain society under certain circumstances venereal disease and prostitution could be eliminated deserves more international attention than it has received. Hostility toward the Communists' political system should not interfere with an accurate analysis of what can be learned and used from under that government.

There are a few other tracks covering Hatem's Paoan-Yanan years. When he went west to join the last group of the Long March Army, he, for the first time, met the third member of the Communist leaders, Zhu De. The main forces under Mao had arrived in the northwest in October 1935, but because of leadership quarrels the Second and Fourth Front armies had delayed in the far west. Hatem was attached to troops sent from Paoan to aid their breakthrough to Paoan. In October 1936, one year ofter the main group had gained sanctuary, the remaining forces came in and George was with them.

In her book, *The Great Road,*[7] Agnes Smedley quotes at length from letters from Hatem in which he gives details of his experiences in this final breakthrough of the remaining Long March armies. Describing Zhu De, Hatem wrote, "Thin as a ghost, but strong and tough, with a full growth of beard and clad in a lousy skin coat."

She also had access to his diaries from those very early months, and one paragraph gives a sample of what the early years brought Hatem in terms of experience. "November 23–24, 1936. The battle finished. The Red Army attacked at dusk when bombers could not come. A bitter cold wind from Ning Hsia Plains swept down. Fingers of Red fighters became so numb they could not pull triggers or even remove caps from hand grenades. So they launched a bayonet charge. Many grabbed White (Nationalist) soldiers and disarmed them, and others used their potato-masher hand grenades as clubs, beating Whites over the head with them. Red Cavalry chased one White regiment, which fled in wild disorder. Dead enemy soldiers littered the paths for miles around. I saw 150 dead Whites piled up at one end of a valley, other hundreds in other places. Hundreds of Whites fell into ravines and empty wells. We have spent a day pulling them out with ropes."

In her book, *Battle Hymn of China,*[8] Smedley writes, "In Yenan, which the communists had just occupied as their main base and training center, the American doctor who had adopted the Mohammedan name of Ma Hai-teh took me to see Chu Teh, Commander-in-Chief of the Red Army since its earliest days . . . Dr. Ma also threw his arms around Chu Teh and kissed him resoundingly, then stood back to observe his handiwork."

Hatem was mocking her; she had done the same, the moment before.

Evans Carlson caught well the secret life of Hatem in those early Yanan days. He wrote, "In the cave next to Li Teh[9] lived Dr. Ma Hai-teh, who advised on medical affairs. His past, too, was unrevealed. I made no attempt to pry into the private lives of either man. Ma was short, of dark complexion . . . and sort of an eternal optimist. His cheerful, hardy way, and the fact he had learned to speak Chinese with amazing facility, made him extremely popular in the army."[10]

Scanning other books of that Yanan era simply gives little hint of a George Hatem. In a 1980 reprint of an earlier book, Helen Foster Snow added a footnote revealing one facet of life at Yanan in 1937: "All of

the top communists, as well as the three other foreigners at Yenan—
Otto Braun, Dr. George Hatem, and Agnes Smedley—had body-
guards.''[11]

One can paint but a hint of a portrait from these few sources. In fact,
all I can speak of with some confidence are my own conversations with
Hatem, between 1971 and 1982. From them, and in his own words, one
gains an idea of the mature man. From these earlier references, one
traces origins, roots, and experiences.[12] It is all so remote from the
average American's range of history that one must be reminded that the
Red forces were twelve years hidden at Yanan and Hatem was the only
American to share those long years.

4

THE HOUSE OF MA

MORE than forty years have passed since that summer in 1936 when George and Ed Snow slipped through the blockade. "This Chinese with foreign blood has passed forty-seven springs-and-autumns in our country," was the poetic description published in February 1980 in Peking.[1] His acceptance as a counselor to the high ranks of the Communist party has the allure and romance of Marco Polo's visit to China.

As a physician with the Eighth Route Army he was in uniform from 1936 until the Communists' victory in 1949. Those who see him now find a silver-haired, benign, gentle man. However, the years on horseback in the fields of combat and later, after victory, years in the fields, grasslands, and mountains, carrying through a campaign that eliminated venereal disease, makes him a veteran in all senses of the word.

The Hatem one meets today is pleasant, a man at ease. He speaks softly and offers a happy, buoyant smile. Perhaps it is the high, arched eyebrows or the slightly lopsided nature of the smile, but one sees in his face a considerable amount of devilry and impishness. A few moments of conversation confirms this suspicion and the remarks, even if serious, carry a bit of wit, a touch of irony and of sarcasm—or perhaps all the wisdom that he has acquired in his hard life, cautions him to leaven wisdom with irony.

George is intelligent, a master of reasoned conversation, thoroughly informed on world affairs, and inevitably convinced that what China is doing is right for China. He has married China; it is now his homeland. His Chinese wife, Zhou Sufei, their son and daughter,[2] their grandchildren, have absorbed him into China, as have his own beliefs and commitments. His parents were immigrants from the Lebanon part of old Syria; he was born an American but he is now a Chinese citizen, and his children and grandchildren have almost completed the assimilation of these Lebanese genes into China's life stream.

Zhou Sufei was a movie actress of considerable fame in the late 1930s. Her home was in the Choushan Islands, off the coast of China, but her career had brought her to Shanghai, the film center of China. And as did thousands of others, she elected to leave that life, to get around the Nationalists' barricades, and join the Communists in their isolated area of northwest China. Writers, professors, physicians, university students, actors, came by ones and twos, risking their very necks to join the Communists.

Sufei was one of several well-known actresses who chose to leave Shanghai and literally join the revolution. Another actress who made the same decision about the same time quickly found a new career: she was Jiang Qing. Upon her arrival at Yanan she was soon involved in romance with Mao Zedong, a romance which ended in marriage, and almost thirty years of obscurity for her which suddenly was broken by her prominent role in the Cultural Revolution, her attempt to seize leadership upon Mao's death, her trial, and today, her imprisonment as "enemy of the people." Sufei, at Yanan, also found romance. She became a member of the Lu Hsun Art Academy at Yanan in 1939; but by March 1940, the thirty-year-old American bachelor was able to convince her that there was logic in marrying a foreign physician, and Zhou Sufei and Ma Haide joined forces, an early effort, as George said to me, "in Sino-American Collaboration."

At that time, he needed to generate some ability to show he could support a marriage, and Rewi in Chong Qing (Chung-king) received a son-to-father type telegram: "Getting Married Stop Send Money Stop George." The early years of their marriage were spent at Yanan, and by 1943 George had assembled facilities and staff which made up the International Peace Hospital.

Rewi Alley made the trip in 1939 to Yanan to escort a team of doctors from India to help George at the International Peace Hospital. Their old friend, Mme. Soong Chingling, had become its benefactress and was finding international support for George. "A formal welcome awaited, for the Indians were the first international delegation ever to come to

Yenan. Among the welcomers, Rewi saw one face he knew well, and slipped up behind Dr. George Hatem to deliver him, in Rewi's own words, 'a little kick in the pants'. . . . Hatem's presence in Yenan had been kept secret, but some word of an American doctor had leaked out, and his identity was the subject of considerable speculation. His Chinese friends had reversed his surname into Ma Haide, Ma meaning horse, a typical Muslim surname, and appropriate to a man whose parents were from Lebanon . . . Hatem's first job on arrival was to check the health of Mao, which he pronounced excellent.''[3]

Ma Haide and Zhou Sufei were at Yanan until 1947, working, beginning a family, and developing the close friendships which are fostered in such isolated, high-risk emotional endeavors. George was in and out of Yanan and for a considerable period was in Beijing, advising the Communists as they attempted to get a fair share of the supplies offered by the United Nations and Red Cross to the areas of China liberated from the Japanese.

The Hatems fled Yanan in 1947, along with all the others from the Communist headquarters, as the Nationalist forces attacked. That attack was the beginning of the end for the government of Chiang K'ai-shek. Within two years he and his government were pushed off the mainland and "temporary" headquarters of the Republic of China were established in Taiwan. At the same time, Mao proclaimed in Beijing the "People's Republic of China"—and the Hatems set up housekeeping in Beijing. Between leaving Yanan and arriving in Beijing, Hatem was in active military action as a physician.

Veteran he may be, and forty years a Chinese husband smoothed by "forty-seven springs and autumns," yet he is instantly an American. His wit, gestures, slang, and language are USA. Now seventy years old and mellowed, one has little difficulty finding a twinkle in his eye and a mischievous grin. His whole life adds up to one of commitment and usefulness in complicated, very foreign, and sometimes dangerous circumstances. Yet the man one meets is not impressed by his achievement. He remains thoroughly American, and one is not surprised to learn he was one of the leading fox-trot enthusiasts of the Saturday night dances at Yanan.

I asked George about his dancing skills and he answered with enthusiasm. He learned to dance, in fact, at Yanan and his initial teacher was

Li Teh (Otto Braun) and the only music they had was a victrola with records supplied by Agnes Smedley. The selection was rather limited, consisting of "It Was on the Isle of Capri That I Found Her" and "The Daring Young Man on the Flying Trapeze." (In 1982, George and I were at a private home for dinner in Beijing. The hosts' young twenty-year-old daughter and George danced a very graceful two-step; George, a man of formidable girth, became light-footed and quite agile.) I have heard of his tennis playing, motorcycle riding, and southern barbecue skills in the early years after liberation, and all of it sounds like a very normal life, following the long civil war years.

The Hatems' home is in the north quadrant of old Beijing, one of those gray brick, one-story homes that made up essentially all of old Beijing. The home was the result of combining two original houses, and the rooms wrapped themselves around an inner courtyard. The street gate opens on a small area; upon stepping in one faces a blank wall, then a left turn, a right turn, and one is at the beginning of the long courtyard. Bedrooms are on the left, kitchen and dining room on the right, and the far end of the court is closed off by sitting rooms.

A considerable area of the court is shaded by George's pride, a grape arbor, which in the summer creates a covered area, interestingly decorated by a combination of pendulous masses of large purple grapes interrupted by paper bags swinging in the breeze. Why paper bags? These enclose George's prime grape clusters from birds and children; they are to be his entry in the local food fair.

Hou Lake in front of the house gives George a good place to swim and a length of promenade for his evening stroll. A Mongolian restaurant is a block or two to the left. The court, the sitting rooms, and the lake front walk, are all good places for conversation. A principal contestant, however, for George's attention is his number one grandson, Ma Jun. In fact, the entire house is activated by the wishes, the activities, and spirited assaults of the grandson. The earthquake of 1976 destroyed the house. For a year the family lived in a hotel while the house was rebuilt, almost a replica of the original, but this time with some space for domestic help.

Reconstruction after the earthquake gives George a delightful, spacious home. The living room is sprinkled with pictures, tapestries, potteries, old and new, of horses. Dr. Horse enjoys the symbolism. A very effective, new oil portrait of him hangs on the wall facing the door. In the portrait is a yellow Tang Dynasty horse, again capturing the message that this is Dr. Horse of China. The artist of this very good portrait is the Chinese painter, Deng Banzen.

George's Chinese given name is Haide, which in essence means "oversea's virtue," and altogether gives *Dr. Horse with Oversea's Virtue.* The Chinese sounds of Haide also are a reasonable approximation of Hatem. His daughter is a Liang-p'i, *Second Horse;* and his son is Yu Ma, *Little Pony.* George has the beginnings of his own Chinese stable, now with three grandchildren. He laughingly identifies his home as "my stable."

The Ma home is a blend of American and Chinese styles and customs. I have not explored all of the rooms, but the living room is pure USA with a Chinese heart: comfortable chairs, good reading lamps, and bookcases filled with a mix of medical books and paperback American and English mystery stories. Good pieces of old Chinese porcelain, drapes, attractive Chinese rugs, albums of family pictures, stereo recorder-player, shortwave radio, large television sets . . . all similar to a comfortable American home, but with an added touch or two. For example, the television sets are snugly covered with a cotton print "cozy." Cozy is the only logical word, for the cover is fitted tightly over the entire TV set like the ones covering teapots in Europe or, as in some American homes, toasters.

In the dining room China takes over. The odors are Chinese and the colorful oilcloth table covering is the same as those in Chinese homes and pragmatic Chinese restaurants all over the world. But a bottle of catsup declares an American eats here.

George has an interesting non-hobby, accumulating the small liquor bottles handed out on the airplanes. These came to him from American friends who, after seeing a few such bottles on a window ledge in his home, decided such was his interest. The bottles now come in, unsolicited, brought by well-meaning foreign visitors.

He left the United States before the end of Prohibition and this may account for the strange martini that he offers; a can of Planter's peanuts complete with Mr. Peanut and a tray of crackers and cheese quickly establishes the scene as American.

Newsweek and *Time* are on the coffee table and lively conversation makes clear that George is in touch with the world and not an isolated man. Then comes the call to dinner and one loses the ability to define location: an American soup in a Chinese bowl, an American lettuce, tomato, and mayonnaise salad, then sweet-sour pork are offered, and orange pop and beer. We quietly pour the orange pop and beer, half each, into our glasses, following the host's lead. Steamed bread comes, along with a slab of good sharp American cheese. One waits expectantly for apple pie with ice cream but no, fresh grapes from George's arbor—and ice cream.

George has a well-treasured culinary instrument. It is a genuine waffle iron, a hinged iron monster of some weight which is placed directly over an open flame. He has a superb waffle recipe and his longtime cook, a Chinese woman of indeterminate age, has obvious pride in her ability to deliver to the table an almost endless stream of golden, steaming waffles with many variations on waffle syrups. George has elaborated on the syrups and added mounds of soft cheeses, the sharper the better. A favorite variation is blue cheese, spread well, and filling every waffle hole.

A portrait of George is incomplete unless adequate emphasis is placed upon his appetite, or if not his appetite, his capacity for eating. Mealtime is not conversational time with George. He ties a large napkin or bib around his neck and settles down to serious, steady, sustained eating. There is nothing delicate or mannerly in his approach to food; his attention is concentrated on quantity. Long after others are finished, he is, dish by dish, continuing. One habit he enjoys, perhaps from his American youth, is lots of iced water with his meals.

The long years from 1933 to the present have given Hatem a remarkable view of the great Chinese drama. Rewi Alley sums up his evaluation of Hatem's role.

"No living American can compete with Ma for an all-round intimate knowledge of China today, for he has been a part of China for so long now, all through the years of struggle, joining the revolution when things looked so very dark for it, as a participant, not as a sightseer . . . a great internationalist in the best tradition, one of whom all Americans in particular should be proud. As the years go on and we look back in retrospect, his stature will grow ever greater as the most outstanding single person of our day in the cause of better Sino-American under-standing."

Although his fifty years in China have given him the grist for several books, George has no interest in publishing his own story. He has been asked, urged, pushed, but his intention is to follow the example of Mao Zedong, Zhou Enlai, Zhu De . . . no memoirs. Not only does George have a story to tell, but the family picture album is a treasury of snap-shots. Mao and Zhou and their Yanan days, in an enthusiastic game of ping-pong, Zhu De fox-trotting in uniform at a Yanan dance.[4] Lean, fit, laughing young men who went on to win a civil war.

George and his two special friends in Beijing, Rewi Alley, the New Zealander, and the German-born physician, Hans Müller, gather each week in Rewi's study, and with toast, marmalade and tea, have late-afternoon talk sessions. All have shared a China life: Rewi, sixty years; George, fifty years; Hans, forty years; their China knowledge, blended by their varied national origins, make this teatime one of the best of conversational sessions. The three men, Caucasians in a China sea, are tested friends, and there is a shared loyalty and affection which has carried them through unusually adventurous lives.

Rewi has written a documentary describing the experiences of six Americans in China: Edgar Snow, Anna Louise Strong, Agnes Smed-ley, Evans Carlson, Joseph Stilwell, and George Hatem. However, George's insistence on little personal publicity has dropped the title to *Five Americans in China*.

Although their adult lives have been spent in China, each has a dif-ferent permanent tie. Alley has never married but has two legally adopted Chinese sons with western names, Alan and Mike. The sons have mar-ried Chinese women and Rewi's grandchildren are Chinese, of course, so no trait of Rewi will continue in China. Hans Müller married a Jap-anese; their two children were born and raised in China, but the daugh-ter married a Swiss and lives near Basel, giving Müller Swiss grandchildren. His son has married an American and lives in Connect-icut. Hatem, too, leaves no name in China; but one can assume that the large nose of this Lebanese sire will occasionally appear in successive generations of his descendants. Of the three, George has left a "marker" to show for his life in China.

Yu Ma, his son, has George's heavy eyebrows, deep eyes, large nose, and a very non-Chinese characteristic, a heavy beard. George told me that the inheritance from the father stops there. His son has no curiosity about the world, has never learned the English alphabet, and, as George said, "He thinks Chinese."

5

WESTERN ISLAND IN BEIJING

IF one goes left to the corner on leaving the Beijing Hotel, waits prudently until the policeman gives the signal, crosses the wide avenue, passes the first building on the right, one then comes to the entrance of a large green space containing old trees, flowers, and a long, circular driveway ringed with substantial buildings. The whole is at least half a city block in area and the private, quiet sanctuary seems an improbable island, amost in the center of Beijing's eight million people. The buildings are two and three-story brick; at the far end is a steeply gabled building with a tower. All of it is very European, and so it should be: this was the former Italian Embassy compound built before the Second World War. The last ambassador was Count Ciano, Mussolini's son-in-law; the big building with the tower was the Catholic chapel, now a storeroom. The handsome edifice to the left of the ex-church had been the Italian Legation building; it is now the headquarters of the Chinese People's Association for Friendship with Foreign Countries which is actually a part of the Foreign Office and directed by the very senior diplomat, Wang Bingnan.[1] Just beyond the entrance to the courtyard is the sentry house, and next on the right is the former residence of Count Ciano, now Rewi Alley's home. Rewi used to live upstairs, and the American writer, Anna Louise Strong, on the ground floor. Upon Anna's death, Rewi moved into her apartment.

The walk from the hotel takes but three minutes, as one passes from the international atmosphere of the hotel lobby along the edge of Beijing's major shopping area. In those three minutes one sees thousands of people crowding the sidewalks and streets, and within a few steps is suddenly alone in this European courtyard.

There is a veranda on Rewi's home, shaded and cool, cut off from the heat and noise of the crowded capitol. My wife, Mary Clark Dimond, and I go up the steps, across the veranda, and knock on the door. There is no answer; we have called ahead, we know he is home, so we open the door, hear voices, and trace them to the first room on the left which is Rewi's study. We find the three we have come to join for their weekly tea and news session. Rewi bustles around and gets us seated, Hans, meticulous in his dark gray western suit, shirt, and tie, stands quite straight and courtly with Teutonic manners until we are placed. Rewi is in an open-neck sport shirt; George is in a dark blue, short-sleeve shirt, buttoned to the top. They have never adopted the Chinese style of dress. As I glance at the coffee table, I smile as I note the array of delicacies before us indicating their taste buds have never quite made the Oriental conversion either. For our "tea" we have instant coffee, evaporated milk, a can of salted peanuts, chocolates, cheese, canned meat, marmalade, butter, cookies, toast, crackers, and of course English tea.

On the side table are English-language news weeklies; a shortwave radio is tuned to the BBC. This, and the room next, are a writer's work areas; a large table has all the usual paraphernalia of pencils sprouting out of a cup, reference material, and typewriter. The walls of the room are lined with books.

We are seated along the left side of the room, where a large couch and three chairs ring the ladened coffee table. Not only are we in a European courtyard, we are also in a New Zealand-German-American coffeehouse. The conversation immediately reinforces the impression. George begins by commenting that the Dow-Jones Index was up two points. My head pops up at this bit of capitalism. Rewi nods sagely and agrees that the market looks good. He then contributes the information that the traffic control officers in the United States are involved in a slowdown and domestic air travel "is in a mess."

Hans asks the practical question of me, "Does this make air travel dangerous in the United States?" The conversation goes on and ranges over the world, and each man contributes what he has read or heard. It is quickly apparent that this is the weekly session for these three old friends when they have their gossip time. However, with we Westerners present, the current word on Chinese inner circles is omitted from this day's chat.

Rewi keeps one ear turned toward the radio, and at the right moment reaches over and increases the volume. Suddenly we are in England and the steady, baritone voice of the BBC International News broadcast comes into this Beijing room, summarizing the world's problems. The listeners in Beijing hear him through, turn down the volume, and pick up their comments. They ask me what the Americans really think about South Africa. They ask me if the American Jews will support the President's efforts in the Israeli-Arab negotiations. They ask if the continued inflation will bring on a nationwide labor strike. I feebly attempt to turn the discussion to China. After all, here I am on the other side of the earth from the United States. Why can't we concentrate on the makeup of the Political Bureau, which fascinates me?

The closest we come to China is to pool our information about which foreign delegations are coming to visit. George and Rewi each carry on a large correspondence with visitors coming and visitors who have been to China. Old friends from the Shanghai days, and later Yanan, arrive in a steady procession. The twenty-two years from 1949 to 1971 when no Americans could come have now given way to an overload of old friends. When George blames his girth on banqueting with American friends, he deserves sympathy. However, the calories offered by this coffee-tea affair are not insubstantial.

Rewi goes off to a side room and comes back with a red clay bust of himself. It is a good, strong likeness, made by a peasant. He quite suddenly gives it to us, handing it sideways while averting his eyes, a characteristic gesture of his when making a gift. In conversation, his bright blue eyes look directly at you; in giving a gift, large or small, he does it in this off-the-side manner.

Rewi Alley is a man well worth studying, and one regrets the American bias which has caused almost all Caucasions associated with the Communists to be avoided by the western press. Alley is the thread who can pull together the stories of several foreigners who had a China "influence." The significance of this influence is sometimes almost lost in the vastness of the successful Chinese revolution, or the significance is diminished by the West's desire to negate the reputation of those "westerners" who were sympathetic to the Chinese Communists' potential. Most of these Caucasians are now dead; Alley himself is in his eighties. But the United States, or its press, with the exception of one story by Lloyd Shearer in *Parade*,[2] has managed to miss him. A much earlier article by Ed Snow in the *Saturday Evening Post* is forgotten reporting.[3]

Rewi Alley came to Shanghai on 21 April 1927, in his thirtieth year, straight from a hard seven years, scraping a meager existence out of his own New Zealand sheep farm. One can find no story, from him or from others, that can glorify his reason for leaving New Zealand. He was a young man, single, looking for adventure and a job. Sheep ranching had not provided a living.

He has had many careers, including the military (he was twice wounded in World War I), sheep farming, and working as a fireman and then as a factory inspector in Shanghai. He played a major role in launching wartime industrial co-ops in China (Indusco), carried out a hidden mission as a point of contact for the Chinese Communist underground, served as headmaster of a boys' school in western China, acted as father to two adopted Chinese boys, and wrote a book a year for the past thirty years. He is the Caucasian whose travels have taken him to more parts of China than any other foreigner and . . . who knows what else? Rewi's conversation is often a series of cryptograms. As Chapple quoted him, so would I: "The trouble is . . . you are limited in not being able to say anything without getting others implicated who don't want to be implicated."[4]

The same veil of caution drops over Alley as over Hatem when one extends questions into areas which touch on Chinese Communist politics. Alley, however, has a considerable willingness to write and therefore there is much more available about him. He has never given up his Commonwealth citizenship and this, too, has made caution less necessary for him. Alley was seventeen when Hatem was born; he is Irish-English, Hatem Lebanese. However, the relationship is one of father to son and their wholehearted affection for each other is the strongest of possible ties.

In the days of Alley's initial arrival, Shanghai was also the center of the Chinese Communist movement. The founding members of the party had met there in 1921. By 1927 they were strong enough to make themselves visible and offered to join forces with Chiang K'ai-shek, to work together to unite China. Chiang K'ai-shek was, in those early years, very close to the Russian Soviets; he had Russian advisers on his staff. Earlier in 1922, Sun Yat-sen had agreed to accept Russian aid and form a united front with the Chinese Communist party.

Chiang K'ai-shek's campaigns throughout China were successful and in 1927 his forces were turned toward Shanghai with the declared intention of bringing that westernized city back under Chinese rule. The Communists came out in force in Shanghai, seized the Chinese section, and hailed the arrival of Chiang K'ai-shek's troops.

At this point in Chinese history, Chiang K'ai-shek's political orientation took a sharp swing to the right, perhaps due to the influence of the gold and the persuasion of international bankers in Shanghai. Suddenly, he ended his pact with the Chinese Communists and in the massacres of 1927 almost eliminated them. Among the survivors were those who embodied the essential seeds of leadership, but all Communist efforts were hidden after 1927.

Rewi Alley's first arrival in Shanghai was just nine days after this coup and the killings were still going on. It was "a bewildering experience for a non-political, conservative, essentially religious and totally Western newcomer." Alley saw groups of young people bound and marched through the streets to the execution area. He was told they were bandits.

With only a few pounds to his name, he got a job with the fire department of the Shanghai Municipal Council of the International Settlement. Fire prevention was important for, in essence, it protected the powerful international insurance companies. Alley was taken on as a probationary officer at Hongkou Fire Station. This meant he drove a fire truck.

In 1928 at Wuxi he saw the execution of some young silk workers who had protested their work conditions. "After the shooting of filature workers, Rewi went to see a progressive English schoolteacher—Henry Boring . . . 'I told him what I had seen and that things had become intolerable. What should and could a man like me do?' . . . a few days later he brought me some Marxist books—including Das Kapital . . . I read what bore on the problems surrounding me and . . . finally I said: 'anything we can do to pull down this rotten society—you can count on me'."[5]

George Hatem arrived in Shanghai in 1933, aged twenty-three, not caring at all about communism, a new medical diploma as his main asset. Other assets of personality and energy quickly got him involved in the whirl of an international city.

". . . [I] was guileless, good-hearted, apolitical . . . I thought I would learn a little tropical medicine in China, before completing my world tour and returning to the States to start practicing . . . nothing . . . prepared me for what I found . . . you could diagnose, write prescriptions, but the people you wanted to help had no means of paying for the medicine. It was hard enough for them just to avoid starving to death. Many couldn't even do that . . . then there were the executions all the time. It was a fashionable weekend-spectacle for some foreigners to go to the big Lunghua pagoda—where Shanghai's international airport is now—and watch young men and women being decapitated or shot . . . ''

"I used to pick up some books at a left-wing bookshop run by a Dutchwoman, Irene Wertemeyer, and there was a German, Hans Shippe . . . he was a frequent visitor in the shop. They introduced me to Agnes Smedley . . . and she put me in touch with Rewi Alley . . . [he] was Chief Factory Inspector of the Shanghai Municipality . . . [and] was indignant about conditions under which teenage boys were working over open chromium vats . . . in the chromium plating industry . . . conditions were horrifying. Chrome holes in their nostrils, chrome sores all over their bodies, the poison eating right into the bones of their fingers and in between their toes. They were living skeletons who slept alongside the vats and machines . . . I looked into this and wrote a report which was published as a monograph by the Lester Institute in Shanghai . . . it was for trying to agitate against this sort of thing that youngsters were being executed at Lunghua pagoda.''

For George Hatem it was his moment of truth. "I felt very frustrated as a medical man, surrounded by the most urgent problems about which I could do nothing. When word came through via Rewi Alley in the early spring that the Red Army needed a Western-trained doctor, I was delighted. By that time there were only two things I wanted to do—to help the Republicans in Spain or go to serve with the Chinese Red Army. Rewi's message was decisive.''[6]

The rest of the world was in a depression but Shanghai prospered because of what it did for and to human beings. White Russians and

Russian Jews founded a place of refuge from the Russian Communists. Europeans, Americans, Canadians, and Latin Americans found it a place for buying, selling, taking financial risks, offering bribes, getting favors; missionaries of all the Christian faiths used Shanghai as a safe base to carry on their efforts—but the fundamental asset upon which they all stood was the vast pool of cheap labor. Rewi Alley, who had just come from seven hard years of trying to beat a livelihood out of the sheep ranch through his own labors, soon had, in Shanghai, a three-story house, a cook, a number one boy, a coolie, and a washerwoman. A westerner, even a factory inspector without a college education, lived well, indeed.

This anomaly of an elevated standard of living for the foreigner continues today. Alley, Hatem, and Müller have comfortable, substantial homes, automobiles, chauffeurs, domestic help, summers at the seashore, and winters in the south. In a communist country, to paraphrase a truth, all are equal but some are more equal than others. In spite of their communistic convictions, one never feels that their considerable standard of living is an embarrassment to them.

6

WHEN THE CHINESE CAME

WHILE the surrounded "bandits" at Yanan broke out and conquered China, Edgar Snow, who tried only to warn his countrymen that they were misreading China's future, was unable to make a living in the United States and chose exile in Switzerland. If not exile, then survival; he could find a market as a journalist only outside his native country. Carey McWilliams, the longtime editor of *The Nation,* writing his autobiography near the end of his own life, put the story in better perspective than any other writer. He titled this section, "The 'Exile' of Edgar Snow."

"Blacklisting in the 1950's took different forms. Some journalists, for example, found themselves blacklisted in the sense that publications which long used their work suddenly decided not to—'for the time being' or 'until pressures ease up a bit.' In some cases they were blacklisted for reasons that had nothing to do with political activities or affiliations. Consider, as a case in point, the 'exile' of Edgar Snow.

"Red Star Over China (1932) was the first and best contemporary account of the Chinese revolution to be published in this country. No American journalist had better sources of information inside China or knew more about the revolution or enjoyed more cordial relations with the Chinese Communist leaders.

"But Ed was not a 'left' journalist or ideologue. He wrote for mass-circulation magazines. He had been an associate editor of *The Saturday Evening Post.* He had reported brilliantly from China, the Soviet Union, India and Southeast Asia. A large reading public had confidence in his work; he had enjoyed the respect and friendship of Roosevelt and top officials in Washington. Yet for nearly twenty years he was kept on the sidelines during a critically important period in this country's relations with China when his reports would have been invaluable. During these years—roughly from the late 1940's to the middle 1960's—the market for his work shrank in this country to a handful of publications, of which *The Nation* was one. Ironically, it was the triumph of the Chinese revolution which he had predicted, that made him unpublishable in the mass media.

"Ed and I had become friends in California, and I saw a great deal of him in New York in the years from 1951 to 1959, before he moved to Switzerland, and on each of his subsequent return visits. *The Nation* made good use of his talents; we published him as often as possible. But the editorial budget made it impossible for me to send him to China, Russia, or India, which was a major disappointment for both of us. But of all the fine journalists the blacklist turned our way, Ed was the prize catch. (One of his pieces, 'Nationalism—Colonialism: the New Challenge' won a top prize in the Second National Mayor's Peace competition.) That such a gifted journalist, with such unique insights and experience, should have felt compelled, as he did, to join a year-long world "study abroad" safari of high school students in 1959–1960 is a sad commentary on the know-nothingism which then beset the American press, the academic world, and official circles in Washington. Of all persons, James Reston referred to Ed in a front-page piece in the *New York Times* as being part of a 'mixed bag of Communists and liberals,' a grotesque statement for which he later apologized, but the damage had been done. Equally grotesque was the blacklisting of Lois Snow, a fine actress, whose career was blighted by an idiotic and utterly erroneous reference which had crept into the files of a blacklisting agency.

"I never ceased to marvel at the philosophical way in which Ed put up with the unpleasant consequences the tacit blacklist had imposed. After he moved to Switzerland, his writings were more widely published, but by then his life was nearly over. Fortunately he was finally able to revisit China, in 1960, 1965, and 1970. Yet when he returned from China in 1960, Dean Rusk was too busy to see him or had only a few minutes to spare. It was a hint dropped by Chou En-lai on Ed's last trip that "the door was open" which resulted in Kissinger's initial visit to Peking. Nothing could be sadder or more ironic than the fact that Ed should have passed away on February 14, 1972, just as Nixon was preparing to leave for China. At least someone in the President's entourage had the tact to prompt Nixon to send a letter of condolence to Lois. Ed was scheduled to have preceded the President's party to Peking as a correspondent for *Life,* which after twenty years of thumb-sucking had decided it was again safe to make use of his remarkable talents and unique credentials."[1]

I had met Snow in the early 1960s. I visited him in Switzerland on several occasions in the following years and he knew of my interest in making contacts in China, even if my American passport prohibited travel there. His interests and mine coincided after his visit to China in 1970 for, upon his return, he wrote a series of articles for *The New Republic* which described what he had seen in China concerning birth control, a health care system, and surgery done under acupuncture. The usual negativism about such "positive" reporting on "Red China" had followed and Snow was criticized for attempting to analyze subjects outside the field of international journalism. We corresponded about this criticism and agreed I would accept a chance to go to China and look at the same events and give an opinion. Snow, through Zhou Enlai, got an invitation for me in August 1971. After my visit I wrote a series of articles and spoke widely about what I had seen, verifying all that Snow had said, and carefully noting the hesitation and even fear I found among the Chinese physicians under the pressure of the Cultural Revolution.

Snow had not been well during his 1970 trip. Upon returning to Switzerland he found his energy low and suffered a constant back pain which kept him from productive writing. He tried rest, baths, and a vacation on the Mediterranean. When I saw him in early September 1971 he was haggard but in good humor, and concerned only that he could not "get the kink out of my back." In November, an exploratory operation at Lausanne was done, and a cancer of the pancreas was found. The physicians gave the right answer: this was an incurable problem, chemotherapy should be tried, it might slow things down but the end result was only a matter of months. But they gave this information in a cold, technical manner which left no margin of hope and only the chill of modern, impersonal, medical care.

Ed's wife, Lois, reached out as we all would, and asked for help and alternatives. I contacted the White House and Mr. Nixon's physician gave the president my letter pointing out the appropriateness of bringing home this American and doing the best that could be done at the National Cancer Institute. Mr. Nixon's first visit to China had already been announced, and in my letter I suggested that no gesture could say more to the Chinese than this action by the American president to show the concern of Snow's native country for the journalist whose lifetime message had been that the two countries should be friends. Mr. Nixon elected to write a letter to Snow telling him he was sorry to hear he was sick.

The Chinese responded differently. Within hours, the Chinese ambassador to Switzerland extended an invitation to the Snows to come as China's guests to Beijing for medical care. However, in delivering this message, the ambassador saw for himself that Snow was too sick to make such a trip alone. Within the week, the message came from China that a complete health care team would come for him and escort him to Beijing.

The team did come. It was led by Ma Haide and was sent with the expression of personal concern of Mao Zedong, Zhou Enlai, and Soong Chingling. All the friendships of that summer of 1936 were at work.

The Chinese physicians immediately saw that there was no possible means of moving Snow, and that what needed to be done was to give him comfort and to sustain his wife. Lois Snow described the months from November to February 1972 in a book with the subtitle, *When the Chinese Came*. The title of the book, *A Death with Dignity,* defines the strength given to the Snows by the Chinese when they found him too sick to be moved. They stayed with him, made his home his hospital, and escorted him to . . . a death with dignity. Lois wrote the following concerning their visit.

"They came as friends as well as experts, these Chinese citizens; they came with individual commitment. They saw at once the inroads of the dreadful disease and they knew the trip to Peking was no longer feasible. The evening after they arrived Shag said, 'We had made a home out of a hospital for you in Peking; now we'll stay here and make a hospital out of your home.'

"Shag Hatem stayed with us at Eysins, occupying the small library at the back of the house where light filtered in through the winter-bare fruit orchard beyond our garden. Soon his room turned into a miniature pharmacy, the bookshelves cleared to accommodate a jumble of jars, bottles, liquids and pills—Chinese calligraphy mixed with Latin inscriptions . . . Shag's fluency in French and Chinese the means of communication.

"Shag dressed Western-style, usually in slacks and sweater. On a rare visit to Geneva one evening, he donned the sports jacket he had worn on arrival in Switzerland. It was eye-catching, a thick, handsome, multi-colored tweed, different from any I had seen in China.

" 'Where in the world did you *get* that, Shag?' I teased. 'From Chou En-lai,' Shag replied seriously. 'When I saw him the day before we left Peking, he asked me what I was going to wear in Europe. I had on my nice old padded jacket and told him that that was what I was to wear'.

" 'You are not!', said the Premier. 'You'll disgrace us all in that.' He called a tailor and I had this the next morning.

"Shag turned around for inspection. A black beret perched on his head added French zest to the general effect.

"It was Shag who relished the cooking he hadn't had in years. It was fun to watch him down a pizza on which Chris (Snow's son) had heaped a mound of golden Gruyere, or Mme. Granger's apple tart, or a break-fast of pancakes, bacon and eggs. Would his "Chou coat" button in the front? We wondered. But Shag was not deterred; he is a gourmet in several languages."[2]

American food had never lost its appeal for George. In the early 1950s, when life settled down in Beijing for the new government, old food habits were quickly remembered by the expatriates. Shapiro wrote, "I was a member of a small amorphous group which met every week or two at a bar and grill . . . it had beer on tap and served steak and French-fried potatoes . . . most of the time the quorum consisted of George, Rewi [and myself]."[3]

Lois' book continued.

"Shag hardly ever left the house; he was the last of us to go to bed, the first of us up in the morning. In his easy way he was available to everyone, yet always ready in a corner of the room whenever Ed wanted to talk, to turn, to get out of bed . . . he was constant and so was his strength and wit. It was clear what a perfect companion he had made in those far-ago days when he had gone with Ed in search of the 'Red bandits' in China's forbidding northwest.

"Word spread that George Hatem had come with the Chinese doctors; he would have been deluged by callers if he had responded to all the telephoned messages. He answered a few from old friends of Geneva days and finally, after special pleading, he agreed to talk at an evening meeting with the medical personnel of the local hospital . . . I did not attend and regret not seeing him, with his round girth enclosed in the bright tweed jacket . . . Though Shag is not a proselytizer, he is a dedicated worker who knows more about present-day Chinese medical practice than almost anyone else in the world, and his behavior bears witness to the good possibilities of man.

"Of course, the presence of the Chinese among us was extraordinary. Since neither of our children had been to China then, they had no personal way of measuring to what extent (these) few people reflected their society in general. This came to them, a lot through Shag Hatem. Their father had written that '. . . not Marx but life experience had made an emotional radical of Dr. Hatem before he reached China. An emotional radical is not that unusual; what is unique about Dr. Hatem, is his more than usual desire to be of service to mankind, found terra firma in a social base that nourished and guided him when young'."

All of this loving care helped Ed die gently and brought his family through, even strengthened. Ed died on 15 February 1972, just as Mr. Nixon was beginning his flight to China, a flight which in essence was an apologia for American past attitudes. John Service, a former member of the American Foreign Service, also hurt during the McCarthy Era, wrote Lois Snow and said what all the rest of us wanted to say.

"Ed would certainly have savored the historical significance (and irony, after all that had happened in the past twenty-three years) of an American president, shaking hands with Mao Tse-tung and Chou En-lai. But what could be done with a 'correspondent' who was much more than that, who was really a ghost at the banquet? How could he be expected to be one of the hoard of confused and frustrated news and television men, watching from afar, and gleaning little? He could hardly be a member of the President's party (though that might be fitting). And his presence could only have posed awkward problems for the innate courtesy of his old (and very important) Chinese friends."

Ed's service was at the John Knox Foyer in Geneva. Lois described it. "Friends from around the world sat in soft shadows as Ambassador Chen read the messages from Mao Tse-tung, Chou En-lai and Soong

Ching-ling. Dr. Grey Dimond spoke for those in the United States who had known and loved the man; Gilbert Etienne for Switzerland, our second home; K. S. Carol and Han Suyin for Europe and the East; and Charles Harper, Director of the Foyer read the words I couldn't bring myself, yet, to speak aloud. George Hatem's brief words represented two worlds.''

Later, George escorted Lois and her children to Beijing and there, on 19 October 1973, on the campus of Beijing University where Ed had taught in 1936, one-half of his ashes were placed and a white marble block was put over them with Ye Jianying's calligraphy, in gold lettering, simply identifying Edgar Snow as an American friend. Later, a few of us joined Lois at Sneden's Landing on the Hudson River above New York City, near the home they had shared before leaving the United States. On a day in May 1974, we found a large stone at the river's edge and carried it up the hill to a wooded glade, and dug a small grave for the lacquer box brought by Lois: the other half of Snow's ashes. The rock has the simple brass initials E.S. as its sole identification. The neighbors knew and admired Snow and they understood why one day a large black limousine brought a Chinese man who stood there, head bowed, by the river stone. It was Huang Hua.

7

LUNCH WITH GEORGE HATEM IN
BEIJING, MARCH 1976

I FIRST met George on the steps of the Tung Fang Hotel in Kwangchow in September 1971. I had with me a letter of introduction to him from Edgar Snow, and I had looked forward to delivering it in Beijing. But I was in Kwangchow, just twenty-four hours in China, and here on the broad steps of the hotel we met by chance. We next were together in Switzerland at the services for Snow in February 1972, and in Beijing in 1972, 1973, and 1976, in Beidaihe, China in 1977, at our home in Kansas City in 1978, Beijing in 1979, Beidaihe in 1980, and Hainan Island in 1982. Does all this add up to a friendship? Of course it does, but the friendships of one's later adult life are different. There is a guarding and yet a compassion. There are no antecedent confidences, no shared planning or dreaming. However, there is real wit and a high level of intellectual give-and-take. What is told is said because it passes one's screen of judgment and indiscreet remarks are rare. We share our American birth, the English language, medicine, and a similar style of humor. He is a four-plus communist and I am a modest capitalist. I can criticize freely and enthusiastically those things American that I regret; his criticisms of China and China's leadership are nil.[1] Between these facts, we are able to pick our way through good conversation.

Nineteen seventy-six was a special watershed year in the history of Chinese communism. All three of the founding leaders died: Mao, Zhou, and Zhu De. Within weeks of Mao's death, his widow and her associates were under arrest. My conversation with George, in March 1976, occurred while Mao and his Cultural Revolution were still the law of the land. It was not the end of the Mao era, but the beginning of the end.

In Beijing, March 1976, we were enjoying a Chinese meal and probing our way into a good talk. George asked me if anything seemed changed on this trip compared to earlier visits. I replied that I noted no differences in the attitude of the people, or in the hundreds on hundreds of Chinese we saw only in passing. Their attitude was always one of curiosity and never hostility. However, in our contacts with our individual hosts, the physician contacts, there was a distinct difference. I noted that they were more relaxed and able to visit with me more openly, coming into my room at the hotel for example, and having tea and chatting informally. However, there was still a "regulated" friendship and never a conversation of depth.

My first China visit in September 1971, had been a stilted, stiff experience although the physicians had been courteous and considerate of our well-being. It was obvious that they were ill at ease, and although I would not want to use the word unwisely, I had wondered if they were "afraid." As I thought about it at the time, I had decided there might well be that quality in their attitude, but a more exact description might be to say they were very guarded, cautious, and maintained a "security" for themselves by never being alone with us. They had stayed clustered and, quietly, had made certain that interpreters were always present.

George smiled and said, "You realize, of course, that your coming here at that time had not been a decision of the physicians. Your invitation was a political decision, and the physicians were directed to be your hosts. Several of them had been through a very unpleasant time in the Cultural Revolution, and one or two of them were brought back from their May 7 School especially for your visit." I began listening carefully because I had a considerable curiosity as to the May 7 School concept, which I had suspected was a form of concentration camp. Here was a good chance to learn of its significance.

George was busy with his food but he kept on talking and eating. "I know you do not yet fully understand our concept of a May 7 School. In your book, *More Than Herbs and Acupuncture,* [2] you make it sound like a version of a Russian concentration camp. That simply is not our way. A May 7 School, when run the way it should be, is considered a desirable experience by the majority of those who are there. Many of our people ask to go and there is a waiting list.''

I groaned, ''You sound just like the mother who tells a child that a spanking will be good for him. The question of 'good' and 'for whom' seems to be glossed over by you.''

George has mastered the eating style which makes chopsticks efficient: both forearms on table, leaning forward, distance from dish to mouth reduced. He used the chopsticks as a gentle baton and gestured at me as he spoke.

''Here is usually how it works: men and women of responsible positions, often brought up in the old society, realize they do not really understand Marxist teachings. A May 7 School combines group discussions, reading assignments, and classroom work. The subject matter is not only the writings of Marx, Lenin, and Mao, but also a group analysis of some recent world affair, using Marxist theory. If you insist on calling it indoctrination, that is an acceptable word. After all, that is what the Catholic Church teaches: how to view the world you live in, based on Catholic beliefs. As I understand it, every successful American business has constant meetings of management to discuss company policy, sales campaigns, the effect of new legislation. A May 7 School is a place to learn national policy, national sales campaigns, and national legislation Chinese-Communist style. It is combined with a period of clean living, kind of like the two-week reservist experience in the United States but without any booze. Everyone does some manual labor, helps in construction, or fieldwork. There are also calisthenics and sports. I don't claim it is a picnic, but it is not a punishment time.''

I responded, ''But I definitely have heard of people being 'sent' to a May 7 School. That certainly sounds like more than free will.''

George nodded pleasantly, giving me my fair share of the dialogue, then he continued. ''Yes, there is that aspect. If the director of a hospital or, let us say, the provost of a medical center, is doing reasonably well in his administrative work but is not accurately thinking toward our socialist goals, then he might be assigned to a May 7 School. Take yourself, for example, I would think a few months reviewing your political thought and a physical fitness program might be good for you!''

I laughed and accepted his analysis of my politics and health. ''George, my political thought would have me in a permanent May 7

School. Another reason I suspect a punitive element is involved is the time one spends at the school varies. I have heard of some who have been there for years."

George nodded, heard me out, and helped himself to a liberal amount of a peanuts and pork dish. He responded, "The length does vary, but I don't believe there are many who have spent 'years' there. Here is how it really works. Let us say that Mr. Li, who works in an organization with several hundred other employees, will simply have his rotation come up for the May 7 School just as will all of the other management-level employees. It is not punitive. All will go, over a period of time. The period of time varies and may be from three to nine months. Mr. Li will not go just one time, but will again go, perhaps, in three, four, five years when his rotation comes up again. Some people are singled out and sent; that is true. For the majority, it is a planned part of their socialistic education. You know, it might be a good idea if your own government had a July 4 School, where everyone had a chance to review your Constitution and get reconditioned. Instead of all this jogging I read about, why not group-reading of the Bill of Rights in the morning and group-jogging in the afternoon!"

These remarks pleased him and he smiled, savoring his wit, and I watched with interest his attack on the new snow peas with water chestnuts. I offered, "You may well be right that we Americans should keep on repeating the Bill of Rights until we all live by them. At that, we come closer to it than we are given credit. It's a world hobby to fault the USA, but we have not found it necessary to put a wall around the place to keep us in, to prohibit free coming and going. And before you criticize our physical fitness, let me slip a tape measure around that tummy of yours. You are a very well-fed Marxist."

George smiled happily and placed appreciative hands on his abdomen. "I have lost my figure because I am kept busy going to elaborate banquets for foreign guests, especially Americans. It is a sacrifice I have had to make."

I felt we had talked enough about the May 7 Schools and I changed my direction. "What about the question of freedom of movement? Can Chinese move about their own country freely? Can a Chinese citizen go on holiday abroad? Can he emigrate?"

"Those are three large questions, Grey, you know? Each has a dif-

ferent answer, not simply yes-no. First, we have watched the experience of much of the world, where the farms have been abandoned and
the people pour into the cities. The cities become slums; vast numbers
are on welfare; there is idleness and crime. We are making a determined
effort to hold down the growth of the big cities and even decrease their
size. Our plan is to hold the farmers in their rural areas and keep them
gainfully, honestly, earning a living. As we industrialize, we are trying
to put new factories in those villages and small town areas, and as
mechanization replaces manual labor on the farm, we will try to provide
factory work there to absorb this labor pool. We are trying to populate
areas that do not have enough people to exploit fully the natural resources
in the area. I know this is hard for you to understand because westerners
believe China is vastly, even dangerously, overpopulated. That is only
true in the 500-mile belt on the eastern seacoast. Many other areas are
very thinly populated, and a great deal of the government's planning is
going into creating entirely new, self-sustaining cities in these areas.''

I asked, ''But when you say you are 'populating' an area, that certainly indicates you are gathering people up and shipping them there.
Do they want to go?''

A large bowl of clear soup with thin mushrooms came to the table
and we each ladled for ourselves. George kept talking. ''The large
majority are anxious to go. If you were a youth in Shanghai, without a
good job prospect and with a long wait for housing, would you not
prefer to go to a new area with a whole new prospect of opportunity?
Essentially that is how you settled the entire West of the United States.''
He paused, raised an eyebrow at me to indicate my turn. I responded,
''But I read that the young people have resented this compulsory movement to the farms and to the underdeveloped areas. We hear that they
gradually drift back to the city and hide out until they can get a local
job. Also, because they are hiding out in the cities they steal, and therefore, there is an increase in crime.''

''You are reading, obviously, Hong Kong experts, the China Watchers. That, Grey, is one problem you Americans suffer; your news is
often biased. Their specialty is to find one example out of a thousand
and announce an epidemic. We are talking about millions and millions
of young people. Millions. Without a doubt, there are young people
who don't like what has happened to them. They 'fight the system', as

you say. I can offer you no figures, but the facts speak for themselves; millions have gone to the countryside or to new areas and have stayed. Some have not. Many go home after two years. The same thing is true with another favorite China Watchers' statistic: the number of Chinese who flee to Hong Kong per day, per week, per month. I once read that hundreds per day were fleeing. Then we hear that so many have fled that the Hong Kong authorities can't feed them and are sending them back. Then we read that they are still fleeing, that they are hiding in Hong Kong so that the police there won't find them. What is the truth? Well, I am sure that some Chinese youths are getting to Hong Kong. They are primarily those who are from the Kwangtung area and have had an easy access to western television and radio shows coming from Hong Kong. They also have a geographically easier way to the border. I do not know what numbers we are speaking of, but out of 800,000,000 people, it must be a very small percentage. Something that is never mentioned, however, is the number of overseas Chinese who are returning to China. For accurate data that figure should be included too."

The tureen of soup was almost empty. As George tilted it to get the last mushroom, I asked my next question, "But I have heard of these returning Chinese from overseas, and I thought most of them were Chinese who had been expelled from Indonesia or were under pressure in the Philippines or other places, and simply had to return."

"That certainly is a part of the story," George acknowledged. "I am referring to the continuing, almost daily return at the present. You see, there is one major factor that you must not underestimate, and that is the pride almost all Chinese here and throughout the world feel in watching the recovery of China. When Mao said, 'China has stood up', that expressed a totally non-communist emotion. Chinese all over the world are proud to see this return of China to its historical role. The largest number of visitors are overseas Chinese coming home to see family. They come and go freely, through Canton, by the hundreds everyday."

"What about the Chinese in China going overseas to visit or to be tourists? When is that going to happen?"

"In asking that question, you are also asking about the basic economy of China. China is still extremely poor. There are absolutely insufficient resources here to underwrite the sending of people out as tourists.

On the other hand, there are people coming and going constantly; for example, where the children live overseas and they pay the travel cost for their mothers to come to visit. That is a regular affair.''

"But no tourists go from here?''

"No, not for the Chinese. I repeat that this is essentially because of the total lack of cash resources. Those of us who are foreign-born and have family abroad may go at our own expense. Last year Hans Müller went back to Europe for an extended visit.''

I shook my head and criticized his answer. "You make all this sound more open and easier than it really is. There is a lack of 'freedom' here, and it shows itself in every briefing, every day, every place. The constancy of a repeated 'party line' is alienating to a visitor. I have now been here often enough to know that whatever is the current Peking pearl, that I am going to hear it at every commune, every kindergarten, every hospital. Why the incessant hammer? Won't this heavy-handed, almost non-thinking, method eventually alienate the people?''

George held his chopsticks, one in each hand, raised in front of him in defense. "Perhaps you are right. There is no doubt that in these first several decades, as we were working with essentially an illiterate population, our main objective was to drive home a single concept: 'Swat that fly'! If you had been here then you would have heard that in every briefing. There is another factor that you overlooked; part of this whole thing is but a part of the Chinese way. Slogans, mottos, campaigns were not invented by the party. That has long been a part of the 'communication' system here. The Kuomintang had their 'campaigns' too, you will find, if you read about that era. However, I am inclined to agree with you that it does get a little excessive and boring. I tend to turn off my thoughts during the briefing and think about flowers, birds, etc . . .'' He raised his eyes and tried to look dreamy.

I turned to another topic. "What about defectors from delegations that go out from China? Soccer, ping-pong, basketball, and various athletic teams? Those are all young people who are likely to want to try the outside world. What has been the defection experience?''

"Well, I am certain that if there has not been a defection, that there will be some day,'' he answered and shrugged. "Just by the matter of the numbers involved, something should certainly happen. If there has been such an event, I have not heard of it. You probably already know it, but I was surprised a year or two ago when one of our senior doctors who was assigned at WHO in Geneva up and left. He even left his wife, I believe. I have heard he is in the USA. He is just about the only one I have heard of.''

"Are the overseas delegations very, very carefully screened? As 'tight' as I feel things are here, I would think the members of a delegation would really be under double-scrutiny.'' I asked this question, knowing part of the answer for I had traveled with several delegations in the United States and knew how very carefully the members had been chosen.

"Well, of course,'' he answered. "They first are screened by the selection process which has proved that they are expert in their field. If we send a ping-pong team overseas, I think it is fair enough to assume that they are really experts at ping-pong, and they have not been chosen simply because they are 'dependable'. That does not mean, however, that considerable emphasis is not made upon 'trustworthiness'. By that, I do not mean that all must be party members. That certainly is not true. But a careful review is made of their background, their family situation, and as I say, their trustworthiness.''

"What do you mean by their 'family background'? Do you mean that it is well to be certain that they have parents or wives and children remaining here, to assure their return?''

"I would think that such factors all figure in. Obviously, Grey, the Chinese government does not seek to be embarrassed. I would think most countries are embarrassed when one of their citizens hijacks an airplane and flies away—or when several citizens kidnap and murder prominent fellow-citizens. China is perhaps even more emotionally vulnerable in these areas than many nations. Perhaps the years of being treated by foreign nations as if the Chinese were naturally 'inferior' has made them extra sensitive. The idea of a Chinese citizen hijacking one of our passenger planes and flying to Taiwan certainly would give the party leaders a headache.''

"What about the fighter pilot who took his plane to Taiwan fairly recently.'' I asked this with honest curiosity, not in an effort to irritate.

"We, of course, have heard about that, and it may well be true. It may equally be true that it never happened, and that the affair was staged by the Kuomintang government for the obvious publicity value.

I read the interviews he gave in *Time* or *Newsweek,* and he certainly seemed to me to be poised, articulate, and at ease. I could not keep from wondering if he was not remarkably well rehearsed.''

"You have not asked my advice, George, but I do have a suggestion to make regarding the selection of American delegations coming here.''

"I have not the remotest idea how that choice is made. I enjoy most of them. What is your suggestion? I won't do anything with it, but let's hear it!''

I made my suggestion in good faith, for I had found myself occasionally surrounded by left-leaning Americans who seemed more activist-minded than the Chinese hosts. "I think too many of your USA visitors are avowed leftists and fringe-communists. This is bad because I assume one of the primary reasons for allowing so many Americans to come here is that your government wants to influence public opinion in the United States and improve the image of China versus Taiwan. You do your cause no good by bringing over flocks of people who by their behavior alienate most Americans. If anything, you should concentrate on our conservative fringe!''

A mound of rice had been set on the table in case we still had unmet hunger. I was relieved to see George was willing to let it pass. He responded to my suggestion: "Your point is perhaps a good one. I say, 'perhaps'. I frankly think we are having a full mixture of everything that makes up the American population. Senators, congressmen, ministers, doctors, athletes, nuns, old ladies, kids, leftists, sexists, racists, black-power advocates, bankers—I can't think of anyone who has been left out. I think the mixture has been total. Why should we veto an American because he is a Communist? Or a Republican? Or an ex-president! Remember: 'China has friends all over the world'! That is my slogan for the day.''

"On my trip in 1971, the fact that we were among the first Americans to be here since 1948, and the fact that the Chinese official attitude toward the USA was one of hostility, certainly did make some of our hosts, guides, and interpreters a bit reserved and guarded. I would describe that as a very tense adventure. The party line, or indoctrination, or approved phrase book, was remarkable and frightening. The intensity of propaganda by our Chinese contacts was unreal. The Little Red Book was everywhere. Now, five years later, the Book is unseen.

I suspect that there are more copies in the United States brought back by us eager tourists than here. Every American lecturer worth his salt is telling his United States audiences that all the people of China carry and quote this Little Red Book constantly . . . not knowing that the Book no longer exists!''

George smiled benignly and said: ''Well, perhaps it served its purpose? The whole question of how far to push the image of Mao should never be overestimated by you. It will wax and wane, but he will remain honored. The Chinese are not likely to make him a god or to give him the Stalin treatment.''

I responded: ''I suspect the Book's disappearance is closely related to the fact that the frontispiece was a photograph of Lin Biao, and that my first visit here in September 1971 exactly coincided with his attempted assassination of Mao. I'll bet those Little Red Books were collected by the millions and have been burned or reprocessed into pulp paper!''[3]

He winced, grinned, and said: ''It is true that Lin Biao's conduct ruined a best seller. Hang on to your copy; you may have a collector's item. But what else do you notice has changed since 1971?''

''Then there was 100 percent wearing of Mao buttons, and now essentially none. In fact, I was surprised to see my good friend the surgeon wearing a tiny one on his left pocket. Practically no one else has one.''

''Well, you see that has nothing to do with Lin Biao,'' he chuckled. ''You can't relate the button's disappearance to Lin's disappearance. The button is just the manner in which the Chinese express their respect and endorsement. The Mao buttons were a way for the Chinese to express their backing of the chairman's efforts to fight those within his own party who were against him. In the United States you wear campaign buttons, and while wearing a Mao button had some of that significance, it really meant much more. It actually meant for many of these people that they were declaring their willingness to fight and die for their chairman. As the Cultural Revolution unfolded, it really was a war between two lines of thought, and the wearing of the Mao button was your way of not only showing how you would vote, but more impressively, how you would fight with your hands, rocks, or sticks, if necessary.

''One small problem developed,'' said George with a bright smile. ''Essentially all the Chinese people considered themselves to be true followers of the chairman, and actually *everyone* was wearing Mao buttons, including leftists, rightists, Maoists. It was very confusing, but there was also a certain feeling that no one was going to be caught without a button! Finally it sorted itself out, and by the time you were here in 1971 all of us wanted to wear our evidence of affection and support of the chairman. You see, it means much more here, for example, than your wearing a Hoover button in the States!''

I yelped, "Hoover button! Good God, George, you need to come home once in a while. You are behind in your buttons.''

He continued to smile and said, "Is that a nice way to tell me I've begun to lose my buttons?''

George's wit is always of this type, both an arrested, well-aged version of America circa 1930, and at the same time fully up-to-date on the American scene. He faithfully keeps up with *Time* and *Newsweek,* and of course after 1971 he was on the "must visit" list of many American groups coming to China. He not only enjoyed this contact with visiting Americans of all ages and backgrounds, but I suspect it was a part of his official assignments.

Whether it is Dr. Spock of baby fame, or Ann Landers, or a United States Senator, or a college group, George is available for a talk session with them; in fact, he is a master at give-and-take dialogue. Without ruffling a hair he leads the most stubborn exponent of conservatism into a verbal trap of "contradictions" until the conservative is propounding Mao Thought as the way of the future. I saw two such performances which were classic examples of Hatem in action. One experience was with a member of my travel party who was a thoroughly honorable, practicing Catholic and prosperous Republican. After two hours with George, my friend was telling one and all: "These Chinese are tremendous! They take care of each other, the kids respect their parents, the old folks are part of the family, you don't see any messy, long-haired, guitar-playing punks. If you don't work, you don't eat! This is the way it should be.'' Atheism, Communism, Maoism were no longer an issue to my friend. The fact that people worked hard, paid their way, put money in the bank, kept the family together . . . what did a little atheism matter if it got that kind of result! Two more weeks in China plus George's guidance, and the Pope would have had to fight to reclaim my friend's soul.

The other experience was a full-fledged session with a group of American physicians, one of whom had been loudly proclaiming his faith in democracy, capitalism, Taiwan, and the disgust he felt in this Red China where mankind was being held prisoner by a ruthless dictatorship. We were all in a hotel room and I had had tea, beer, and the usual orange pop sent up. I think my good, staunch, conservative friend was first weakened as he watched George calmly pour himself half a glass of beer and then fill the remainder of the glass with orange pop. The conservative American doctor exclaimed, "What in the world is that? I don't mind a straightforward, honest boiler-maker of whiskey and beer, but what are you doing mixing that impossible orange-fizz Nehi with good beer?"[4]

George took a delicate sip and said, "It's really quite good. The malt, hops, and orange help each other bring out the flavor."

The conversation then began and our group was led most skillfully through a discussion of Vietnam, Taiwan, and Mr. Nixon's problems, with George asking just enough questions each time, so that the only answer must be the one that my colleague did not want to give. George would never let the questions be more than one at a time, never hurried, and would end his own answers with a carefully placed question that further engaged the hook in the mouth of my now slipping colleague.

A year later I received a hardback book, a privately printed memoir from my American friend, who after his lesson with George in dialectics, plus three weeks of observation, was able to write: "I left China with the firm conviction that the United States has been backing the wrong horse since the days of Roosevelt, and that the best interests of the people of China have been served by the incumbent government . . . Frankly, I was fascinated by the literally tens of thousands of friendly people that I saw who only a few years ago would have looked upon me with contempt as a 'capitalist running dog'."

Quite a statement for my friend to place in print. Had he been brainwashed? Perhaps not, but he certainly had been put through the very effective Hatem laundering process.

To return to the Mao buttons, I told George that to my eye the buttons had left the Chinese wardrobe, and I was therefore quite surprised to see the small one on the tunic of the Chinese surgeon. George replied in an even voice, "There are some who have had an exceptionally bad time in the Cultural Revolution, or who have certain undesirable class relationships; for example, they may have been educated in western missionary schools, they may even have been so-called Christians at one time, or they may have had some of their advanced training abroad. For such individuals the struggle to prove their sympathy with the proletariat must be constantly maintained. You might say that our good friend is wearing his Mao button to show his respect for the chairman and as just a little additional cushion against any possible criticism of his conduct.''

I agreed that this was evidently a small bit of insurance just to stay a step or two ahead of trouble. I asked if he himself had been singled out by the activists at the height of the Cultural Revolution? He gave a wry laugh and said, ''Oh yes, I was honored too! It was not too bad for me, but I certainly was not ignored.''

Although these conversations of March 1976 may now seem dated, they are the ''real-life'' as it happened in China and as Hatem tried to interpret what was happening. I never felt he was being a propagandist, nor have I felt that about Rewi Alley, either. They are men who are close to the sources of power, but they are not initiators of Chinese policy. Their skill depends upon accurately reading the ''tea leaves'' of politics and they are sustained by their true affection for the Chinese people. In March of 1976, no one knew of course that Mao would be dead in six months, and that George would have a new set of rules to endorse.

8

CHATTING WITH GEORGE, APRIL 1976, BEIJING

AGAIN we were alone and this is the conversation as it happened, not corrected by later events or "policy change."

I tried to probe, and because we were alone I felt I could be fairly direct. All American travelers try to unravel the message of the Cultural Revolution. George was there through the entire decade. I asked him if he had had to seek special help from the chairman in order to secure his own safety. He replied: "Well, not directly. He was very busy, and as one small citizen of this vast country, I hardly felt that I should point out my personal concerns."

I replied: "If I translate that smooth answer correctly, someone did see to it that you were not terribly imposed upon, even if you did not go over to the chairman and say 'Tse-tung, *Lao Peng Yu* (old friend), we have been friends a long time. You know how I feel about your Thought. Can we arrange for a little peace and tranquility around my home'?"

"For several months," George nodded sagely, "at the very height of the activities while the contending forces were sorting out their differences, there was an actual danger from excited, even armed, young people, some just children. Even though I am a Chinese citizen, I am also a foreign-born . . . For several months many of us found it best to not go out publicly, and thus ask for problems."

"Is that an Oriental phrase for telling me you were under house arrest?"

"Oh, no! Just as we doctors have vaccinated against disease by either active or passive immunization, my staying out of public places was a form of personal, passive immunization!''

"Were our other friends hurt by the Cultural Revolution? How about Rewi[1] and my friend, the chest surgeon?''

"Rewi is not a Chinese citizen, and he is a very respected friend of China.'' Here George gave a brief smile. "Armed soldiers were placed around that compound where he lived to assure that he was not disturbed.''

"What about my friend the surgeon?'' A prominent Chinese surgeon had been my host during several visits and I wanted to hear George's analysis of the surgeon's experience.

"He had a very hard time, and it was very difficult for him. It was also difficult for us who wanted to help him, but you see, he was almost a perfect collection of all the targets of the Cultural Revolution. He came from an upper-class family, which alone was one of the separations between good and bad as far as the Cultural Revolution was concerned. Further, he was educated in a missionary-directed public school, and he went to the United States for his advanced medical training. He directed a very specialized hospital which needed expensive, foreign equipment. He was assigned a chauffeured automobile. His clothing was of a better quality cloth, he frequently went out of the country to attend foreign medical meetings . . .''

I interrupted. "Those are not faults. Those are but the biographical events of a very loyal, highly placed Chinese medical leader.''

With a shrug that said he felt sad I was so characteristically elitist, George added: "My friend, you do not understand the contradictions of class. The whole purpose of the Cultural Revolution was to make those of us who had, even unconsciously, acquired attitudes and styles of living that were too removed from the peasant's way of life realize our error and bring ourselves back to a socialistic equality. Even if it was hard on our friend, I have heard him say that the whole experience was good for him, and he came out of it with a new socialistic class consciousness. He freely admits that previously he was still 'thinking like a mandarin'.''

I picked up the conversation and agreed. "Yes, he has told me that he was required to go out and live in a commune and do manual labor, digging trenches, making bricks, and building his own shelter, in order for him to understand the miserable life of the peasant. Do you honestly think it is the right way to help the senior surgeon of a national hospital become aware of national priorities? Does education require a heavy-handed treatment?''

George sipped his tea and gave me a long look with his eyelids half-way over his eyes, a characteristic expression. ''You forget how huge this country is, and how for three thousand years a very small number of people really lived well. Chairman Mao will perhaps be remembered in history not only because of his successful establishment of the Communist government in China, but because at the remarkable age of seventy-three, he was willing to rebel against his old comrades whom he thought had forgotten the objectives of their own revolution.'' Making this point with earnest emphasis, he continued: ''At a perfectly legitimate age for honorable retirement, and with every possible evidence of success, he carefully evaluated the result and through his own personal investigations, he decided to explode the whole thing and leave behind him an entire new generation of young people who understood what the revolution was all about.''

''I agree with the remarkable fact that at that age he still had sufficient 'fires of spring' to tear down his own administrative structure. However, as I read the western reports on the Cultural Revolution, there is regular agreement that the whole affair got out of his control, and he had to call in the army to run the country. We would call that martial law and not exactly a success.''

''You underestimate the objectives and you, of course, do not know the extent of the problems. Don't forget, you first came here in 1971, and by that time the factors that had caused the chairman to call for the Cultural Revolution were essentially resolved. During your visits you have seen some of the early explorations of new approaches in education, and you have seen the three-in-one management committees. All of this is but the end, the resolution, of the serious issues of the early and mid-1960s.''

''I accept the fact that I got here too late,'' I replied. ''If I had been here in 1966 I would have been a prime candidate for the general Red Guard treatment. I do not believe in dollar-elitism but I certainly believe in intellectual-elitism. Call it the 'thinking man's aristocracy' if you wish, but I do not see success coming from a deliberate sacking of your best-trained people, medical or technical. Intelligence is a prime national resource, communism or not."

George hurried to answer. "Oh, I agree with you, but you are over-simplifying your analysis of the objectives of the Cultural Revolution. And let me agree that our surgeon friend is perhaps one example of where the masses in their enthusiasm were too harsh; but one does not nicely contain, all parts tidy, a full revolution especially in a country as complex and large as China. But still, don't forget that the surgeon, in evident sincerity, acknowledges that, overall, it was an important experience for him, and he came out of it far more aware of the absolute need to improve the way of life of the poorest peasant."

"If I were the surgeon and had been put through what he has been put through, and I knew that my wife, my children, and myself were here to live for the rest of our lives, I suspect I could become a very convincing enthusiast. The alternatives are not exactly numerous," I replied, trying thoughtfully to put myself in the Chinese situation.

"Well, you persist in seeing all of this from a very personal view-point, and I think I now understand the reason. You Americans continue to extol the merits of individual, personal rights. You emphasize this *personal* right as if it took precedence over the right of any other individual with whom you had to live. Is that not selfish? How can we each live in a family, a house, an office building, a town, a world, if first above all comes a personal, selfish, guaranteed, protected 'right' of our own? And what have you done with your precious individual civil liberty in the United States? The right to be unemployed? That automatically proclaims the right to welfare. The right to welfare automatically means that all the rest of the citizens give up some of their personal liberty and must pay huge taxes to pay for the other person's welfare check. And the right to medical care? What kind of personal civil freedom is it, if when sick, you cannot afford medical care? I call that first-degree and second-degree personal freedom: first-degree is you are completely free to be broke, out of work, sick; and second-degree freedom is that hopefully you can find some form of charity, public or private, that will help you."

I replied: "You have a certain amount of truth in what you say, but in fact you here do much the same thing. You claim there are no personal taxes, but you have a 100 percent tax: you take all the produce of all factories, own all businesses, and you simply spread the revenue out over the country. But from traveling here, it is obvious that equal amounts of money are not getting out to the poor peasant pulling a heavy cart with his own muscle power, as compared to the men in authority in Peking, whipping around in their chauffeured cars.''

George lifted his glasses, perched them on top of his head, and then replied, ''It is exactly that fact that the chairman wanted to drive home to every single person. Once the country was liberated in 1949 and the Communist party was in control, we experienced an exciting ten years in which industry was launched, roads, railroads and canals created, and production leaped. All of us who had shared the earlier years when we were fighting, felt we had achieved our goals and that the objectives of the revolution or civil war were in hand. We felt the revolution was over. But Mao could not accept that. He insisted that the real objective of the Communist party was the life-condition of the peasant. At that time Mao essentially disappeared for almost five months. He went into the smallest villages; he sounded out the peasant. He did his own field-study. And he did not do it as your president does it, by taking along the newspaper and television people and wearing iron hats at the factory and Indian feathers on the reservation. Mao simply disappeared and carried on, in person and without publicity, a thorough investigation of what were the facts.

''This was always Mao's way; beginning in the 1920s, he always did his own analysis of the situation and drew his own conclusions. Incidentally, you were speaking of personal liberty in the United States! How much personal liberty or even safety does your president have? Could he dare go out on a five-month field trip! How big an army of secret service guards would he need? Wasn't it President Johnson who couldn't even *leave* the White House, for fear of demonstrations?''

I smiled, accepted this bit of truth, and asked, ''You exaggerate a little. It is true that during the height of the war in Vietnam, President Johnson was careful about public appearances, but let me point out to you that that is exactly what I mean by civil liberty. All of the Americans who opposed his Vietnam policy felt free to speak out, raise hell, and in fact make it clear to him that he could not possibly be reelected. How much action of that sort would your own government tolerate?''

''I didn't set this trap for you, but you have nicely walked into it.

Here in China the chairman was at a level of such respect that I can give you no example of a similar person in the United States. Your president gets elected essentially by fifty-one percent of the people voting for him, and forty-nine percent voting against him. That hardly places him in a venerated position. Now it is true that in atheistic China I cannot claim that Mao is revered, but he certainly stands completely above any need for a popularity contest. For a number of years he did not worry about the daily management of the country. Our very trusted and competent Premier Zhou Enlai did those very hard, exhausting duties. The chairman is free, more free, I should say, because Zhou Enlai also had broad vision; but anyway, Mao had the perspective to appraise what had been accomplished since liberation: what was good, what was bad. He confirmed his impressions by an extensive tour of the country.''

"You nicely leave out Liu Xaoqi, who was said to be running the country. Fit him into your analysis, George. What about his 'civil liberty'?''[2]

"You are being slightly harsh, but I will admit that you sound exactly like Ed (Snow). Here is how I explained my feeling of all this to Ed. You must remember that I am just a very low, very small citizen, and I am not close to the inner workings of the power structure. However, just as one observes a play and especially when one knows all the actors, I have formed some opinions. I may be completely wrong, and I will willingly accept that! Now, first you make a mistake in asking about Liu Xaoqi's personal liberty. When one reaches the very high level of the Political Bureau, one must accept that he is an interdependent part of a group-decision-making body. One may certainly advance arguments, engage in debates, and above all, be objective. However, once a group consensus is reached, you as an individual become a part of that consensus. Therefore Liu, to a considerable extent, loses a degree of personal liberty. Interesting, isn't it?'' George arched his eyebrows high and indicated it was my turn. Conversation with him is satisfying, an even give and take.

"We are both talking ourselves into corners, George. I appreciate the explanation of the Political Bureau's method of debate leading to monolithic policy. However, the issue that shook Ed, and the issue that excites all of the old China hands, is that the policies of China were proceeding in a very orderly manner, and the Central Committee, the

Political Bureau, and the Chinese Communist party were all functioning in full harmony. It was evidently Mao who found himself on the outside looking in and not happy with what he saw. In fact, he had been honored 'up and out'. I realize our view of what goes on here is through a very murky window. It must be a miserable life to be assigned to Hong Kong and told to make intelligent interpretation based on the skimpy rumors and facts that come out of China. But between the Hong Kong bird watching group and the Tokyo reports (which often seem reliable) and from the *Peking Review* which I read, boring as it is, one gets some idea of what the facts are here.''

"Grey, the western idea that everyone must know everything everyday, always amazes me. None of us would want such widespread broadcast of the latest conversation or quarrel we had with our wife! Why can't a government have at least some of the same privacy over its own affairs? Ultimately, of course, it must explain what it seeks to do, but no really good analysis and hard reasoning can be carried out with the whole world listening in.''

"That is one of the few times I caught you not using effective analogy, George. What happens between a man and his wife affects them and is their own personal business. But we Americans don't believe our form of government was set up to hide from us. You know that. It is *our* government, and there is some place in our Declaration that says something about the fact that the power and right of the government rests with the people. I have read that China's Constitution says the Communist party alone runs China, and it is the people's duty to support whatever the Communist party decides. That is a substantially different definition of who is in charge. We poor, overseas China-watchers have the distinct impression that here in China the official Communist party with all of its administrative framework displeased the chairman of the board, and evidently he owned enough stock in the company to fire just about everyone but Premier Zhou!''

"No, Mao fired no one. The people did. After Mao finished his thorough study of the conditions and flaws in what was being done, he did try to reason with Liu Xaoqi and persuade him to make the necessary changes, but with no success. I remind you that we are talking about a quite old man, and I think it is remarkable that he had the energy to take on what he did. When he was ready to make his move, he made no national TV proclamation as your president would do. He simply swam ten miles across the Yangtze River! With ten thousand youths and a barrage of cameras.''

"Those pictures appeared in our news magazines, George, and the interpretation was that someone had glued his head on top of the water. Do you really believe he swam those ten miles? Or did he take a dip, smile, picture taken, and out he came?''

"You were complaining a moment ago about the unwillingness of the Chinese government to give the world press all the tidbits of news that it wants. Now when a major item is released, an event recorded by hundreds of cameras, and by at least ten thousand other swimmers, you label it a fraud and say someone must have pasted his head on the river. I can honestly say that when a specific news item is officially released by the Chinese government, it can be trusted. Can your good friend, Mr. Nixon, make that statement?'' George made this query with a happy smile.

"Mr. Nixon is not my friend, and other than his first trip to China, I have no kind words for him. But when Mr. Nixon does try to bend the news to his favor, then the American 'system' protects us. I mean not only the press, but the other people in elected offices, such as congressmen and senators, and finally, the courts. Mr. Nixon could swim the Potomac if he wanted to, but he couldn't turn around and fire the entire government!''

"What was it I read about the Saturday Night Massacre? I thought he did fire his government.'' George raised his eyebrows and looked appalled at this conduct.

"He certainly tried, and I have no idea where he would like to have gone with his personal cultural revolution, but at least our system protected us and he is now peacefully at San Clemente, California.''

"Yes, so we know. I suppose you would say that he in a form of house-arrest? But wasn't your whole CIA and FBI a part of his plan? Weren't houses and offices being burglarized and mail being opened and . . .''

"We are not a very old country, but in our two hundred years we have had only one Mr. Nixon. I really don't have enough facts about Mao's China, but in the fifty years or so that he has been in action, the literature suggests that one of the most risky jobs in the world is to be the second-in-command to Mao! I go back to the fact that before I came here in 1971 I went to Edgar's home in Switzerland for a briefing on what we would find. He had just come back from a five-month trip here and had seen and talked to everybody: Mao, Zhou, Lin Biao, Zhu De, all of his old friends and their wives. He and Lois had stood upon the Gate in Tien-men Square on 1 October 1970 with Mao and Lin Biao. They showed me the photograph and laughingly pointed out that the real picture had included Lois, but the official one cropped her off and left Edgar with Mao, and Lin Biao holding his Little Red Book. Edgar was absolutely complimentary of Lin Biao, and said that he now felt Mao had accomplished the missing piece of his masterpiece: he had arranged for a fully accepted heir to the party leadership, and the whole party had made clear the harmony of this decision by writing it into the Constitution.

"But you know what happened. We both were bombarded by Edgar with questions when Lin Biao suddenly disappeared in 1971. You and I met at the Tung Fang Hotel 'by chance' in Kwangchow early that September, and you agreed to sit down with Paul White, Sam Rosen, myself, our wives, and give us an informal briefing.[3] I have my notes from that meeting. After all, it was our first day in China, we were excited, and here was a remarkable chance to talk with the one American doctor in all of China. Incidentally, now that the time has passed and it is no longer too important: were you sent to Kwangtung to screen us and let Peking know if we were 'O.K.'? I must admit it seemed a little suspicious that George Hatem should be standing on the steps of our Kwangtung hotel, a couple of thousand miles from his home, just as the first group of American doctors in twenty-five years arrives. Were you checking us out for the powers-that-be?"

"You are imagining goblins where there are none. Hans [Müller] and I were on our first vacation in years. We were sightseeing just as you were. I had my son with me. Hans had been ill, was feeling better, and we thought a trip would be good for all of us."

"I accept that answer at about the eighty percent level. It was just a bit too coincidental. Perhaps even you and Hans did not know that you were being manipulated by your own system into being there at just that moment. I have learned that a very little happens by coincidence in the schedule of the foreign traveler here. But let me get back to my attack.

I will wager that when you went to Switzerland to be with Edgar in his final illness, that sick as he was, he grilled you on just what had happened to 'Chairman Mao's most trusted comrade'. What did Edgar get out of you?''

"He could only get that which I know, and I know very little. In spite of your glamorizing my status, I am a very tiny pebble and have no remote relationship with the Central Committee nor with the Political Bureau. I am a dermatologist who sees people, peasants and workers, with itchy skin everyday at the Fu Wai Hospital. I only know what I read in the paper and hear on the radio. Sometimes I even learn more from reading the foreign news magazines, but this is always risky simply because they have so many inaccuracies.''

I raised my hand in defense and interjected, "When I lived in Washington, D.C. and had no relationship to the high echelons of government, I discovered that the gossip circuit, the evening dinner circuit, was essentially 100 percent reliable. In fact, without that unofficial communication link, I suspect the government could not run. Isn't that true here?''

"It is true that the Chinese are great talkers, and there is a very lively and constant analysis of all political events. I suspect the average Chinese citizen is better informed about world affairs than the average American. I know you won't trust that statement, but you see, we have weekly news analysis sessions, no matter where we work or what we do. One of the primary aims of the Cultural Revolution was to raise the level of political consciousness of every citizen. Very detailed analysis is carried on about the imperialistic actions in Africa . . .''

"Let me interrupt your small bit of indoctrination, and get back to what must be or has been one of the hottest news items to come along: what happened to Lin Biao?''

"I will answer you in general terms, but don't hold me to exact dates or even names. First of all, to understand the downfall of Lin Biao you must analyze it in relationship to the whole range of events happening in the world at that time and here in China. You want quick answers, and there is no quick answer. Also I must remind you that this is only my own very personal interpretation. There was an official statement made by Premier Zhou Enlai, and I am sure you saw that. Let me give you my own understanding, and again, don't hold me to exact dates.

All through the history of the Chinese Communist party, there have been episodes of what we call 'two lines of conflicting thought'. In fact, as a part of Marxist teaching, we encourage that as the best means of analyzing, discussing, and reaching consensus. Such conflict is basic, and it is why the Political Bureau is able to be an effective, top administrative system. You Americans enjoy underestimating the democratic methods of the Central Committee and the Political Bureau. You lump all of their shared efforts under the label dictatorship, and yet you know very well that all members of the Political Bureau are members because they each represent a real political constituency. Someone speaks for the railroad workers; another speaks for the strong unions; another for the communes; another for press and communication, and so on.''

"Evidently quite a few speak for the army! There certainly seems to be an adequate number of generals.''

"That will be true in these early years of the new government. Liberation of China was won by the army, the leaders of the army were the leaders of the Communist party. They are one and the same. But if you read the list of the present membership you will find younger people beginning to appear. The young Wang from Shanghai, Yao, Chiang Ch'ing, and others . . .''

"Return to your point about 'lines of conflicting thoughts'.''

George laced his fingers over his abdomen and in his quiet, expressive voice continued. "Those ideas or issues which are satisfactorily resolved within the discussion framework were defined as 'internal contradictions', and everyone is encouraged to speak out in support of his viewpoint. Then when the consensus is reached, those who have opposed the prevailing vote are expected to fully endorse the ultimate consensus opinion. There is no stigma or penalty for taking an opposing opinion, arguing vigorously for it, but when the final vote is in, this 'internal contradiction' is ended, and the ultimate action is unanimous. The argument is ended. There is no rushing to the press and putting out your minority opinion and attempting to promote public opinion on your behalf. Nor are you permitted to go 'behind-the-scenes' and try to convert others of the Central Committee, the Political Bureau, or the leaders of a province to your way of thought. Such an action is very bad, and is labeled an 'external contradiction', and that carries with it the designation that you are an enemy of the people and essentially a traitor.

Throughout Mao's career he faced numerous situations where there were two lines of thought, and each time his correct analysis proved right and prevailed. In each of those episodes, there was a direct opponent, pushing an incorrect line of thought, an *external contradiction,* and each man thereby lost out.''

As George paused, I exclaimed: "It would seem that another way of saying it is that Mao always won, therefore he was always right. It is a game where the winner takes all.''

"The Chinese people have studied these points of contradiction, continue to study them, and there simply is a national, unanimous endorsement that Mao was right each time. It is the fruit of each of these events that have become Mao Zedong Thought, you see.''

"Pick up the thread and explain how this relates to Lin Biao. I won't ask for it now, but one cannot help but wonder how Liu Xaoqi went from being Mao's successor to being labeled 'a running dog, a scab, and a triple traitor'. That's pretty harsh language to use for an old buddy who has been with the party through thick and thin. I still think there is merit in our American system where we simply vote the man out.''

"Oh, come now. Of your last three presidents, one was murdered; one couldn't even be seen in public; and one had to resign. I won't even mention Mr. Agnew and a few other assorted murders and shootings of national figures.''

"But since the beginning of our country we have had every election on time, war or peace, and evidently the system has strength or it would have folded under the problems of these recent years. I know China is ancient and has endured, but you still have not found out how to find a successor for Mao. I still want to hear the facts about the last choice— poor old Lin Biao!''

Much that George presented as the gospel back in March and April 1976 was changed drastically by Mao's death, and the May 7 Schools had not only altered by 1980 but in fact, one could not find evidence that they existed. Yet much of George's interpretation about how the Chinese feel, act, and do, has been right. The after-Mao deluge was an unforeseen swing toward moderation. Somehow the new leaders managed to bring Mao down in size, rehabilitate his enemies, and still keep him as the honored founder. But back in early 1976, all of this was unforeseen. But by 1982 there was evidence that the more things change, the more they remain the same. The new, conservative government had opened special study schools for correcting the thought of those who still carried too many Maoist characteristics!

But back in early 1976, all this was unforeseen, and we continued our conversation, two men without a crystal ball.

9

CHINA RECONSTRUCTS

GEORGE smoothed his way through our conversation, ignoring my strongly pro-American remarks. His dark skin, gray hair, tinted glasses, western-cut jacket, dark blue open-neck shirt, all reminded me, strange as it may seem, of Aristotle Onassis.

George began his Lin Biao explanation by saying that Lin Biao had been with Mao all the way. From the original Chinese-Soviet effort at Jiangxi, on the Long March to Paoan and Yanan, to the leadership of the Eighth Route Army, on the Central Committee at all times, and on to the Political Bureau itself, Lin Biao had been the dependable general-plus-political commissar that Mao sought when he realized that he had to repoliticize the full army if he was to have a force prepared to fill the void after he had succeeded in driving the existing party bureaucracy from power.

I said, "But were they not really old friends, and true allies?"

"Yes and no. Lin Biao had certainly been committed all the way, although there had been one time when he had not fully backed Mao, and there had also been a period of time when he had been hospitalized in Russia for what was considered to be tuberculosis. It was many years ago, during the period when going to Moscow for medical care was fully accepted. Others had gone, and one of Mao's own sons had been a patient there. The real problem with Lin Biao probably was related to the American invasion in Vietnam and the bombing close to the Chinese border. Many of the best Chinese generals were convinced that an invasion of China by the United States was coming soon. All of them had been through World War II and remembered the American backing of the Kuomintang. Almost immediately, in 1950 in fact, after the Communists had liberated China, U.S. troops were on the Korea-China border and threats were made of the possibility of bringing Kuomintang troops into Korea to get them back on the mainland. Now, in 1970–71 with the Russians gone and the Chinese weapons outdated and inadequate, all reasonable military leaders pushed for turning again to Russia for new weapons.

"Although Lin Biao was already guaranteed by the Constitution that he would succeed Mao, he and his followers became convinced that Mao had gone too far in the disruption of the country through the tactics of the Cultural Revolution. Lin Biao and his men felt they could not wait for Mao's natural death. Even though they had agreed in the beginning to Mao's philosophy of guerrilla warfare, they now felt, with the American forces bombing immediately against the Chinese border at Hai Phong, that military resources must be sought from Russia. Russian help had to be arranged and Mao himself deposed.

"This was probably not a sudden decision. Over a substantial period of time, in fact for several years, prominent members of the army, air force, and navy had made strong statements concerning the probable intent of the United States to invade China from Vietnam. Both of the army men who had preceded Lin Biao as head of the military had spoken against Mao's policy. One of these had been very outspoken, not only about the need for weapons to match those of the United States, but also about the need for shared action with Russia. They each carried their arguments beyond the level of internal contradiction, and in each case were pitting their opinion against the belief of the chairman. Both men had been put out of office by Chairman Mao."

"Did you know them? I would assume you must know all of these old-timers."

"There are degrees of knowing people. Of course in the Yanan days, I had some kind of acquaintance with most of the old-timers, but often only because I was one of the few doctors; I did a little bit of doctoring for almost everyone. We were there for a number of years seeing each other, but don't forget that those were busy years, and we were at war."

"But did you know Lin Biao?"

"Yes, of course. He was one of the best generals we had."

"But still, there came a time when he evidently decided that his old leader was making wrong decisions, and must be eliminated. That certainly is a considerable contradiction. What were the specific events?''

"Lin made detailed plans, and we believe he did so in league with the Russians. We believe he was prepared to kill Mao by making it appear as an accident or sabotage, perhaps by the Kuomintang. Lin would then have automatically been the new leader. He was prepared to do then what the satellite countries had done in Europe; namely, declare a state of emergency, call for Russian aid, and allow the Russians to fly immediately into our major airports with full military divisions. All of this would be in a friendly role, but it would have reduced us to a subordinate place in Russian-dominated communist countries. Lin was willing to pay this price because he felt we were in great risk, not only from the military actions of the United States in Vietnam, but because he considered the beginning negotiations with Kissinger and Nixon a real sellout. Remember the dates? Kissinger and the ping-pong team had already been here. Nixon was coming. Lin thought this was all wrong, poor judgment, bad for China, bad for communism, and he decided he could not wait for his natural inheritance. He and his military associates felt the need to have the security of the nuclear weapons of Russia behind them. There is no doubt that Lin Biao had a clique of officers with him, representing a true military coup. He probably could have won if he could have carried out his single need, the removal from the scene of the Chairman. This he could not do. He gambled, lost, and died.''[1]

"I did read the statement made by Zhou Enlai, George. One can only assume that what he said is exact. I must admit, however, I have been impressed on several occasions when we have been to museums presenting the historical facts about the Chinese Communist party, that the data and photographs were being changed in an effort to keep up with the current 'story' of your government's policy. It is activity such as that which makes any of us chary of trusting even official government statements from China. You have a handsome magazine that we see in the United States. It is called *China Reconstructs*. I sometimes think that would be a suitable name for the Chinese historical museums . . . there seems to be a great deal of 'reconstruction' of history, almost with each year's events.''

George responded and agreed that there was no need at all for the rewriting of history. However, he did feel that history is simply that which is written by so-called historians who are peripheral to the facts. "What is important is that Mao did what he did; the results are what should be history. Those problems that he overcame, whether they were a stubborn Liu Xaoqi or Lin Biao, are not his monument. Let the historians record the fact that China was almost ruined by outside invasions from 1840 to 1950, and now it is back with a healthy, well-fed, happy people. Who even remotely knows all of the truths, all of the mistakes now called history? For me, history consists of the ultimate, large facts that cannot be argued by some professor digging away at obscure rumors. Mao made history. The time was right for someone to rise up here and bring the people back together. Many tried but one succeeded, and I simply cannot be very critical if the winner seems to want to tidy up a few of the facts. I personally don't think they need to, but they do, and they are in charge.''

"I think this constant manipulation within the very top leadership of the party itself undermines not only the confidence of the people, but places a shadow of intrigue over the party. Intrigue, coups, and casting down of former loyal colleagues are dangerous acts to present to those who are governed," I countered.

George was silent; he looked down without speaking, then said: "Grey, you and I both were raised in the United States. That has certain advantages and disadvantages. Additionally, I have Lebanese Oriental genes, and that plus my fifty years here has perhaps made me a little more able to understand this remarkable world called the Orient. You cannot, and you are not here enough to gain any finesse. Keep trying. But above all, keep your mind open. Just because the western world thinks and acts by one set of rules does not guarantee that the truth rests there. If you really want to take something that is a masterpiece of manipulation and make a story, take the whole fundamental explanation of the origin of the Christian religion. Immaculate Conception? God's Son? Until the West gets that sort of mythology and make-believe out of its daily life, it will certainly have to be cautious about criticizing the government here. The missionaries' defeat here in China where they poured on every possible pious method, including food, money, clothing, and education if one would join up, is something to be remembered when judging Chinese society.''

I nodded my head in agreement and responded, "I agree the tide has turned. China is on its way back to a world leadership role. Sometimes when I am speaking in the United States, I try carefully, deliberately, slowly, to explain to my audience that a huge historical event is now ending and that we are all watching the return of China to the world scene. When I give this impassioned talk, I try to judge whether my audience can stand my final shot. If I think they are strong enough and my chances of getting away alive from the speaker's stand good enough, I then suggest that in the next century the leading industrial nation will be China, having captured the markets of much of Asia, Africa, Central and South America. While the United States will remain the world's great agricultural resource, it will be essentially unable to compete with China in most industrial areas. My last suggestion is that the audience reflect on the number of Toyotas, Datsuns, Hondas, etc. on the American highways just thirty-four years after we had thoroughly defeated and bombed Japan."

George's expression did not change. His comment was a pure Hatemism: "That's a very interesting thought. It deserves analysis."

What seemed to my ears at first a Hatem endorsement, upon reflection, was but a suggestion to 'send it to committee'.

10

A VISIT WITH GEORGE HATEM IN BEIDAIHE, JULY 1977

I HAD been on a lecture tour in northeast China, and after a week on the train and in hotels from the oil fields to Harbin to Tianjin, I was able to get a break and join George and Rewi at the seashore. For more than twenty years, my two practicing communist friends have managed to summer at Beidaihe, a lovely village on the Sea of Bo-hai, a sheltered extension of the Pacific Ocean.

As the train came into Beidaihe Station, I was looking forward to non-medical holidays and interpreter-free talk with two good conversationalists.

On the platform was a relaxed, smiling group. The dominant sight was a very pink-faced, smiling Rewi. He had on khaki shorts, just below-the-knee white socks, plastic sandals, short-sleeve white shirt, and perched on his head an embroidered cap, a cross between a fez and a yarmulke. This headpiece was embroidered in bright colors on black and red velvet. It was his anti-sunburn equipment, he announced. The hat, which he wore to protect his sensitive, fair, English skin was something he cherished from a visit to Xinjiang.

Rewi could be described as a pair of huge legs supporting a completely packed torso, all in rose and white. George was a matching counterpart, a dark version, without the Xinjiang cap. He was in knee-length, dark green shorts, which in the West we would have called Bermuda shorts. His deep tan was accented by white teeth and silver hair; his bare feet were encased in leather sandals. He too had a substantial torso, but his arms and legs were not of the tree-trunk dimensions of Rewi's, although every shirt button was at maximum tension.

They have each acquired a gentle, benign worldliness—two old revolutionary firebrands now in snug harbor, and although not capitalists in a monetary sense they are certainly rich with experience and shared events. With neither man can one ever find the slightest crack in their full commitment to the Chinese cause. Both are always astute, very astute, in knowing exactly what is winning in 'internal contradictions' at any given instant. Their political, internal, weather-sensing systems are operational at all times. Both men could spend a perfectly happy, bland hour talking of nothing but George's successful grape arbor, or they could spend an hour, voices equally bland and gentle, discussing world revolution and the awfulness of life in the famine areas of the 1930s. Each man has an unshakable calmness; Rewi in particular often speaks with a final dropping of the voice, ending in a sigh—a sigh saying: "Yes, yes, so it was, and so I have seen it. . . ."

George's wife, Zhou Sufei, was in a cool blouse and long trousers, and I felt a keen sympathy as she maintained a bright, alert smile while we all excluded her, with no malice, as we launched into a stream of give-and-take good-humored English. For myself, it was therapeutic to talk freely, idiomatically, casually, after days with an interpreter. Sufei used the international language of giving us great hugs and pats.

My wife and Rewi took off in one car and George, Sufei, and I in a second car. George asked if all had gone well with our trip, and then immediately we became involved in our comparative versions of world affairs.

He said our secretary of state's trip to China was anticipated with enthusiasm. The fact that the Carter Administration was sending Cyrus Vance to China as almost one of its first international actions was very encouraging.

The return of Deng Xiaoping to power was the best possible thing that could happen, as far as George and Rewi were concerned. This meant that the government was in good, steady hands. Rewi said he and George had "breathed a sigh of relief when Deng took over."

I said I had a thousand questions to ask and was counting on him to educate me while I was in Beidaihe. George volunteered that unless Mr. Carter could understand the absolute uniformity of Chinese opinion about Taiwan, then Mr. Carter would find no useful purpose in sending

Mr. Vance. I told George that I had supported Mr. Carter for the pres-
idency and had high hopes he would move rapidly on resolving our
relationship with China. Also I thought that he had a problem of equal
importance, specifically, getting the United States to define its energy
program so that we could use these next twenty years to end our personal automobile era and our vast consumption of the world's petroleum.

George said he had some facts to share with me on the prospect for
China's oil and that China was now quite confident that it was a major
world reservoir of petroleum. He believed that Chinese industrial development would now be the main action of the Chinese government and
would be beyond any present world comprehension. He felt that it would
be a very few years before Japan was essentially dependent upon China
for oil.

George pointed across the field and said, "Over there is the airport
where Lin Biao took off on his fatal flight."

I was surprised and said I had assumed Lin Biao had been in Beijing
at the center of things when he attempted his coup.

"No, almost all the top brass were down here on holiday. Part of
their plan was to look innocent by being here at the seashore, relaxing."

I shook my head and groaned, "I arrived here seven years ago when
I thought all was well within the dictatorship. I have now been in the
country a week, and from the moment I landed at the airport in Beijing
I have heard nothing but Gang of Four problems. These are the same
four who were declared to be among Mao's closest personal colleagues
each time I have been here. You owe me some serious guidance; we
have been in the car for five minutes and you indicate the airport from
which the chairman's closest 'comrade in arms' made his dash for Russia, you tell me how delighted you are that Deng is back because he
will really get the country organized, yet he was one of those most
thoroughly put down in the Cultural Revolution. How can Mr. Carter
and Mr. Vance have any confidence in who's on first, what's on second, and he's on third? Come on, George, you have been here for fifty
years and you are too clever not to have figured out the system. What
is the story?''

George was sitting in front, beside the driver. Sufei was beside me
in the back. George turned around and gave me a smile and said, "You

are always looking for simple answers here, but you never seem to realize that your political system at home is not at all logical. There is no dictatorship here. There are political facts of life here just as in the United States. You suggest that what goes on in China is highly irregular. You have no idea the problems I have in trying to explain to my Chinese friends how American political leaders rise and fall. They ask me to explain the ups and downs of Muskie, McGovern, Wallace, Brown, Reagan, and what happened at Chappaquiddick and Watergate, and how come the most important congressman is related to a dancer who jumps in a fountain, and another congressman has a high-priced secretary who cannot type, and a thousand other questions. China has its own political problems and solutions. Frankly, they make more sense than some of the things we read about in the United States!''

We were now coming down a shaded street and many old, frame houses, some huge, were among the trees. We turned into a widened road and stopped in front of a green and white framed house, screened with full veranda, looking very much like a Cape Cod summer place. We were in the heart of what had been the foreign summer settlement in the old days. Many of the lovely old homes had been the summer homes of the missionary families.

Rewi was already out of his car and rapidly taking over. In Chinese, he was getting our luggage organized, telling the drivers what to do, at the same time telling us to be ready for an ocean swim in thirty minutes. Rewi Alley was in charge, and we were on a tightly conducted Rewi tour. In fact, Rewi changed nothing of his own daily schedule and simply structured us to fit it. It was delightful, and I could have stayed all summer.

Our time in Beidaihe was a pure nugget of living. We swam together, saw the Great Wall burrowing down into the sea at Shanhaikuan, had low tea, high tea, dinner together, listened to the world news by short-wave radio, bought German pastries, snuggled George's grandson, walked, and talked together.

We drove the eighteen miles to Shanhaikuan to stand silently in front of the First Gate Under Heaven, the initial gate above the sea of the Great Wall. To the west the Wall performed its unbelievable task of climbing the backbone of the precipitous, jagged mountains; and to the east, the builders brought the Wall to the water's edge, ignored the water, and carried the masonry out into the sea. To pass it by sea needed a full sea-going armada; to pass it by land required an assembling of men and weapons made impossible by the terrain and the Wall. The logical invasion route was through the gate itself, with the cooperation of traitors from within the Wall. George knew a great deal about the Chinese history, and told that the Manchus had found their way through, their way eased by help from behind the Wall.

I used this bit of history lesson as my access to pick up the question which was first on my current list of China mysteries. I asked George what I felt was the most difficult question of them all, the question which is not answered but simply overridden. "We are receiving a steady barrage of propaganda at every briefing. Every problem is blamed on the Gang of Four. Even issues that in recent years have been presented as great successes are now presented as near catastrophes. How can all of this activity be isolated to a foursome? How does one so skillfully remove the chairman as the leading member of the Gang? Is it not really the Gang of Five? It must have required a very skillful operation within the Political Bureau to somehow remove the chairman from his own companions."

George was silent. He looked at me for several moments. Finally he said: "Let us not underestimate what the Chinese have learned in their five-thousand-year history." Nothing more was said. The car slowed to a crawl as we drove through a six-inch flooding of the road. In an effort to reclaim the salty marshes and bring them into arable use, great ponds of freshwater are collected above the marshland. Periodically, carefully regulated purges of fresh mountain water are poured across the area, with just enough intensity of flow to lift up the salt and carry it to the sea, but not with so much agitation as to loosen the all-important earth. The separation of Mao from his companions was the matching history lesson.

Another five minutes passed and George said, "When my ancestors were crushing shells to make a purple dye in the eastern Mediterranean, the Chinese had already mastered the variations of diplomacy and management. There is no perfection when one must work with the imperfections of man. But the Chinese are wise enough to know that Mao was indeed a special man, a man big enough to bring together 900,000,000 people and admired enough to have acquired whatever remained of the significance of the 'Mandate from Heaven'. Mao is the essence of New China, and although much of what he did in recent years was resented, his old comrades understand that it is not necessary to have more than a Gang of Four. Let's talk about it more tonight?''

Dinner was early and the July sun still visible when we began our walk. Rewi and my wife, arm-in-arm, walked down to the entrance to our compound of houses. George and I followed. Even the phrase "leisurely pace" would be excessive. With imperceptible motion we somehow moved forward. This promenade had been described by Rewi as his daily "afterdinner constitutional." American jogging enthusiasts, with their commitment to exercise that must increase the heart rate, would consider Rewi's walk as a form of passive resistance.

The pace was perfect for conversation or momentary chats with neighbors, for window-looking, and to study the movements of a group of Chinese women mending fishing nets. They were seated on the curb or on small wooden benches, a cluster of a dozen women of all ages. They were wives and children of the men who netted in the Sea of Bohai each day. George volunteered that they were members of a nearby commune charged with this task of fishing. The men were rewarded by "work-points," and here in the evening the women were fulfilling their own "work-point" quota. Rewi commented that these same families had lived here for centuries and had been a self-sufficient, independent, sea-going people. He said that it had not been easy for them to adapt to their new role as commune members with the area farmers, all planning together, accepting production quotas, and acquiring a responsibility as work-team members of a large communal governing unit. Rewi added that it required a "lot of give-and-take on both sides," and that the fishing village still remained essentially a self-contained way of life; but they had gradually discovered the value of a steady market for their fish, a ready source of fruits and vegetables, and perhaps, above all, the advantages of assured medical care.

I found my eyes focused on the hands of the women as they moved through a repetitive pattern of looping, tying, looping, tying, making each unit of the net. I gradually lowered myself until I was sitting on my heels, my eyes within inches of the flying, blurred hands. With all concentration I could not separate the motions into separate parts; the hands *were* quicker than the eye. I looked back at the group chatting animatedly, earning work-points, yes, but also sitting in the cool of the evening being useful, and with every evidence of happiness. I hoped for them a long, continuing pattern of their life, and a postponement of the day when a factory and machines would take away this dusk-time combination of gossip and useful work.

I rejoined George, and after a few moments of further sauntering and easy hailing in Chinese of neighbors and friends, I suggested we continue our Gang of Four analysis. How had they become so powerful? How was Chairman Mao exempt from criticism?

Off in the distance one could hear the music of a simple wood flute. A slow-paced but happy tune serenaded us as we walked along. The notes were Oriental and mellow. The combination of the cicadas' drone, the flute, the occasional tinkling of bicycle bells, the clusters of children, men, and women gathered on the sidewalk, playing games, talking or sewing, gave one a feeling of total removal from the twentieth century's mechanized, urbanized, even terrorized, life.

George began his remarks by straightforward, doctrinaire words. He often does this, and I do not believe it is a defense weapon. George is far too facile to need Marxist dogma as the basis of his vocabulary. At the same time, because he is very intelligent and has made himself a master of the Marxism-Leninism-Maoism logic, and because he is attuned to every shade of reasoning handed down by the Chinese Communist party, he usually makes his opening gambit by citing a fixed fact. From there the conversation moves. George is not an opportunist who finds security in China by "following the Party line"; he believes thoroughly, cerebrally, in the Chinese approach. Fortunately his natural wit and excellent sense of humor make possible true give-and-take sessions. Through these years of matching wits with overseas visitors, including reporters, he has remained thoroughly convinced that his native United States is on the wrong course.

He began. "The present action of the Third Plenary Session of the Central Committee was a high point of China's national policy; in fact, the most important action of recent years. Although the present action included the reaffirmation of Hua Guofeng as chairman and the announcement of the endorsement of the downfall of the Gang of Four, these were items of but secondary importance. The real message and the one that brought forth such spontaneous happiness from the people and caused them to pour into the streets was the return of Deng Xiaoping to power. Deng is highly respected and trusted.

"On Army Day, Deng appeared at a sporting event in full army uniform and the crowds stood, cheered, and applauded for a full ten minutes. The return of Deng means that the solid policies of the past will be picked up again, and the near disaster of recent years ended. His appearance in uniform must not be underestimated; he was clearly reminding everyone of his authentic revolutionary past and his role as an army general."

I asked the question, "Is it possible for him to return from years of house confinement and embarrassment and not have a collection of vindictive plans?"

"There is no vindictiveness possible if you have made a careful analysis of the contradictions and have arrived at the right conclusions."

I have no idea what such a phrase conveyed to George, but for the sake of smooth conversation I let it pass without comment. I continued my attack, attempting to understand the fluctuations in Chinese policies.

After listening thoughtfully, he continued. "Chairman Mao identified eleven crises of authority in his career as chairman of the Communist party. Each of these eleven times there had been dissatisfied elements in the Political Bureau that had challenged or threatened the chairman's leadership, and each had failed because the opponent of Mao had stopped using the procedure of analysis, discussion, and consensus. Each had resorted to physical attack, which automatically made him a traitor to the Communist party."

I understood, but tried further: "By that definition Mao himself in the beginning was a traitor. He certainly turned away from the ruling decision of the Chinese communist party. Perhaps having an army and winning makes one right? The one who has the least guns also earns the title of traitor," I suggested.

George shook his head and then, thoughtfully and slowly, gave a substantial answer. "The whole essence of the Political Bureau is based upon compromise and management by consensus. Each individual in the Political Bureau is a member because he has enough constituent political power that he has to be accepted on the Political Bureau. This system functions only when the full membership of the Political Bureau is functioning, because only then are all interests of the country heard.

In past years there have been seventeen to twenty members, and this gives a sufficient range of discussion and analysis of problems for the Bureau to come to a reasoned opinion. This is not management by a central dictatorial person, but management by, for example, a seventeen-person authority, each of whom speaks for a vast political power base, but each of whom has no power base unless he is willing to give enough so the other sixteen members of the Political Bureau can find sufficient harmony to endorse a given plan. The number of members may vary, but it must remain large enough for all views to be heard: large enough so that the stalemate of recent years may be avoided, yet small enough for close personal relationships and cooperation.

"In the last four years there have been many deaths among the Political Bureau, not only Zhu De, Zhou Enlai, and Mao Zedong, but several others. As a result, its numbers were finally reduced to eight or nine individuals. The balance of decision became extremely precarious and opposing opinions were hesitant to suggest a call for filling the vacant positions. Among the eight or nine still remaining, however, there was a solid voting block of four, all of Shanghai origin, and all representing the power base of Shanghai. This group had a shared philosophy: one of communism based upon the absolute common equality of all, measured at the lowest level of peasant structure. The group from Shanghai felt that true communism must be absolutely free of any social strata or intellectual elitism, and the only way to gain this was by leveling all prerogatives, salaries, titles, certificates, qualifications, etc., to the level of the largest number of people in China: the peasantry." Using both hands in frequent gestures, he continued: "Their theory had been that from the most common denominator would rise the future of China and that talent would be identified and assigned to its correct role. But there would also be a true common man, with no differential between the uneducated and the educated in terms of standards of living style, quality of clothing, access to reading material, and no salary bonus or inducement. The other half of the Political Bureau held the same basic philosophy of socialization and communization, but they maintained that one cannot compete in the existing industrialized world without fully utilizing the intellectual capacity of the best talent of the country. They also insisted that such talent must be recognized, measured against international standards, and given every encouragement. They argued that basic research cannot be deferred while waiting for the entire nation's common man to catch up.

"Throughout Mao's life, his method of administration had been one based upon personal observation. He believed in finding the facts for himself, of not only accepting reports, but going to an area, studying the issues, talking with the people involved, and then deciding on policy. As he became old, and especially in these last few years, he found himself cut off and his traditional sources of information and method of operation became lost to him. Zhou Enlai was hospital-bound, and here again a dependable source of information was lost. Marriage alone gave his wife the greatest access to his time and attention."

I remained silent for I recognized I was hearing the best analysis I was ever likely to hear of what had happened.

"The Shanghai group took on positions of unusual power. One of them, for example, became the political commissar of the army and was responsible for the political indoctrination of the military. Another became responsible for production of movies, television, and use of the arts in carrying information to the public. Another was responsible for the use of the printed word, editorials, and the utilization of the newspapers. The fourth one, a young man, Wang Hongwen, was brought in to capture the goodwill of the so-called Red Guards, who were the youths activated during the Cultural Revolution. The Red Guards had been Mao's instrument of attack when he found himself cut out of his own party's bureaucratic administrative structure. He successfully aroused them to be his new agents and comrades, *his* Red Guards. This fourth member of the Gang of Four was Mao's token payment for this Red Guard help.

"Mao was simply caught short by age. He could not quite get done what he set out to do when he began the Cultural Revolution. But he almost did! And he recognized the problems that were building around him. I do not think Mao was misled. Perhaps at the very end, in his last few months, he was not fully responsible. But he personally advised the Political Bureau in 1974 to be aware of his wife's political ambitions, and to be prepared to contain her; he even gave her at least three distinct warnings and reprimands. At the very end, with the deaths of Mao, Zhou, and Zhu De, there was certainly a period of danger in China. There was too much contention within the Political Bureau to gain a consensus. Important decisions were tabled. There was an inability to gather a central body of cooperative people, and in fact, there was a 'standoff' between the two equally divided factions in the shrunken Political Bureau. With a Political Bureau at full strength and with all members of society having representation, the validity of consensus and compromise will be again apparent.''

George went on to comment that the physical removal of the four dissenters, the Gang of Four, from the Political Bureau, was somewhat similar to someone not being reelected in the United States. I was not prepared for this analogy and pointed out that the method of making leadership changes in China seemed to be very risky and harsh. I commented that Liu Xaoqi had been placed under house arrest for the last seven or eight years of his life and his wife still remained in permanent disgrace, that Lin Biao took the extreme step of attempted assassination and died trying to flee to Russia, that Mao's own widow, rather than being voted down, was being humiliated by the leaders' ''calling upon the public to show anger against her'' and that she herself was under house arrest.

George very calmly said, ''Well, I have already explained to you that the basic premise of communism is that there are always alternate views, and that this is the basis of dialectical materialism. These difficulties are good examples of contradictions, and for any issue there are two views. These two views should always be handled by mutual discussion and analysis. When one member of the discussion and analysis resorts to hostility and physical threat, then that person becomes an enemy of the State and must be dealt with. That individual moves to a position of external contradiction and becomes a traitor.''

George concluded our walk by saying, ''I hope you can make your government leaders fully aware that the contradictions here have ended. The present make-up of the Political Bureau fully reflects the mood of China. Do not be misled into assuming that any further disruption of any sort will occur from the Gang of Four.''

George spoke with unusual, absolute finality, just as he had when he had spoken with such enthusiasm of the return of Deng Xiaoping. I felt that I was hearing the direct voice of the Old Guard, reaching back to the days of Yanan and before.

We had just about reached the far point of our walk down near the village center. A few drops of warm summer rain began to fall, and George commented that often at this time of day a very sudden, heavy downpour could occur.

Quietly, undetected, the young Chinese girl from our cottage appeared at our side, smiled, handed us each an umbrella, and gently scolded George for being away from home unprepared. We popped up the umbrellas and turned back toward our base when the rain came in huge, bouncing drops. I was in sneakers and cotton pants; George was wearing leather sandals and knee-length shorts. The umbrellas protected our heads, and the slanted rain felt good on our bodies.

The people sitting on the sidewalks and curbs had disappeared, and the only sound was the ripple of the raindrops on the street and the gentle kettledrum effect on our oilpaper umbrellas. We walked at a leisurely pace, each under his own protected little world, the width of our umbrellas keeping us apart. We felt no need to hurry and no need to talk.

We came slowly up the hill, past the old home of Anna Louise Strong, up to the veranda of Rewi Alley's house. All were there, and the evening cooled sufficiently for Rewi to have a blanket wrapped about his legs. George's grandson was waiting for his goodnight bear hugs. Rewi said, ''They were worried about you, but I said, 'Let them walk, they are probably talking medicine'.''

George chuckled and said: ''You are right! We have been considering the prognosis for the largest private practice in the world . . . 4,000,000,000 people! The whole world!

We sat on the veranda talking until 9:30, a late evening in China, and then George, Rewi, and two young girls, with flashlights, escorted us to the door of our house, a full forty feet away. They all looked in to see if we were comfortable, checked the beds, the bathroom, the thermos for boiled water, the tea caddy, and with final hugs, handshakes, and felicitations, they left us. The two men have acquired a marriage of manners and combine the best in amenities of the East and West. They are indeed comfortable to be with.

11

NARCOTICS, PROSTITUTES, AND VENEREAL DISEASE

GEORGE is usually identified as the man responsible for the elimination of veneral disease in China. This is a large statement and there were undoubtedly other prime characters who had large roles, yet it was in this area that George made his major contribution to the Chinese people. A brief reminder of his early years sets the stage for a review of this massive social purge.

George was at Chapel Hill, North Carolina, for three years of premedical education. Then a scholarship took him to medical school at the American University in Beirut, Lebanon; another scholarship enabled him to finish his medical degree at Geneva. A free ticket to Shanghai made it possible for him to go there after graduation. Necessity creates responses; in the exuberant, international life of Shanghai in 1934 and 1935, venereal disease was reality. In his position as staff physician for the Shanghai International Settlement police, George became a specialist on venereal disease. He had a massive postgraduate course in the social logic of prostitutes, police protection, power, and V.D. What was to be a short visit to learn something about tropical medicine, turned out to be a lifetime.

In the 1930s venereal disease was treated by the skills of a dermatologist, perhaps because a skin rash is one of the clues to a blossoming syphilis. In the world of skin and sexual disease which was generated by crowded, complex, exotic Shanghai, George rapidly acquired an encyclopedia of knowledge. The years at Yanan and in the Chinese army added to his professional view of what a social system can do to morals, skin, and economics. When the Communists won in 1949, the first order of business was the elimination of addiction, prostitutes, and venereal disease. George quickly became responsible for the medical attack on all these interrelated problems.

Among the real accomplishments of modern China has been the elimination of narcotic addiction, prostitution, and venereal diseases. No travelers to China omit these observations from their diaries, and equally, all who have returned from the "China trip" repeatedly faced the challenge, usually as a distinctly antagonistic question: "You tell us that there are no drug addicts, no prostitutes, and no venereal disease in China. Just how can you make such a complete examination of a whole country in twenty-one days? What is your proof? Is it not likely that they led you through a carefully screened route, and you were allowed to have contact with only healthy examples?"

Such questions are fair, and the thoughtful answer has to be a qualified one. The "believer" presents observations carefully made but carefully qualified. There is little to be gained by a wholesale endorsement based upon shallow examination. Sufficient time has passed, however, and enough observers have, with varying degrees of initial skepticism, confirmed the elimination of drug addiction and venereal disease. The same confidence is held by most travelers regarding prostitution, but here there is such a multitude of unobserved human moments, covering such a variety of degrees of willingness, commerce, and definition, that one prefers to maintain a margin of latitude in one's opinions.

The last sentence is sufficiently ambiguous to allow me some margin of escape. However, to be definitive: Those business activities known widely as solicitation, streetwalking, whoring, pimping, along with the brothels, cribs, love-for-sale, tricks, madames, white slavery, and ladies-of-the-night, do not seem to be present in China. An ancient trade, considered to be among the oldest areas of commercial endeavor, evidently has stopped. I had the opportunity, with seven other American physicians, to sit down with George Hatem for an entire afternoon with the agreed-upon agenda: "Drugs, prostitution and venereal disease."

The American physicians included articulate males, females, conservatives and liberals. George was at his best—thinking, explaining, seeking to make the reality of what was done understandable and not obscured by slogans and Maoisms.

The opening question from our group was clear-cut: "George, how did China get rid of narcotics?" What follows, almost without interruption, is Hatem's verbatim response.

"That is a very good question, and I hope you do not expect me to give a very detailed answer; but I will tell you what I know about it, partly from experience and partly from what I heard.

"Opium in China has a definite history of coming from abroad, but not exactly at the time of the Opium War nor from the British. It must have come in from Persia and probably in the Tang Dynasty, before 900 A.D. It is recorded in the medical pharmacopoeia as a medicine at that early time, but there is no record of its being used by the population for smoking until the late Ming Dynasty, which puts us in about the sixteenth and seventeenth centuries.

"The first real account of its being used as a narcotic for nonmedical use, being abused, is at the time of Emperor Ch'ien-lung, which was about the time of the American Revolution, about 1770 or thereabouts. At that time it was brought in from Java in the form of opium water sprayed on tobacco and smoked as tobacco. That is the first time it is mentioned in the Chinese literature as being used by the population for a nonmedical use. At that time opium was not made into this opium 'extract'; instead, it was opium 'washings'.

"Then comes the time in the story of how the rest of this problem started. It was during the time of the early traders, which the British led off at the beginning of the early nineteenth century.

"As trade grew, China would accept only silver for its silks, porcelains, teas, etc. Soon, however, the amount of trade had increased to such an extent that there was not enough silver to pay for the exports from China. So the British started bringing in opium. The British had the Indians in India plant the opium, would not let them use it, and exported this to China instead of silver as their means of payment. This went on until the time of the Opium War. You are all familiar with that.

"Up until the beginning of the twentieth century, the old junks and ships were lined up in the middle of the Whangpoo River at Shanghai as depots for storing opium. The Chinese government would not allow it to be warehoused on Chinese soil, and the foreign traders got around that technicality by simply sinking junks out in the river and using them as fixed warehouses beyond inspection. The opium was sold directly from them.

"This was the period when the Sassoons, the Hardoons, the Jardines, the MacLesans, all the early opium traders made their fortunes.

"A lot of efforts from many angles were made, but the trade was never stopped. At one time it was suggested that the Chinese government buy all of the opium and confiscate it. This attempt was made and the government began to buy all of the opium chests, $20,000,000 worth, but the foreign merchants quickly saw this as an opportunity to import major quantities with a guaranteed market.

"Various attempts continued until the Kuomintang period, the era of Chiang K'ai-shek. There had always been an outcry against opium from a population of well-wishers, foreign and Chinese, missionaries, etc.— and so Chiang K'ai-shek set up an Opium Suppression Bureau which turned out really to be the government monopoly for distributing and selling opium.

"Then came the war, revolution, liberation, etc.; this is but a little background to describe the problem.

"The amount of smoking that went on was pretty universal and by quite a high percentage of the Chinese. It struck at both ends of the spectrum: those who had a lot of money, and those who were extremely poor. The extremely poor, the rickshaw pullers, the heavy carriers, some of the soldiers, for example, got their supply from the dregs in terms of quality, but they got it as pay from their masters.

"At that time, to give an example, to live would cost about five or six silver dollars a month. However, the opium habit could cost $2 a day. That was the percentage ratio in the early 1900s. For the rich this was possible; for the poor it obviously caused crime and prostitution.

"In our own liberated areas, I am speaking of 1936 and afterward mostly, opium was completely prohibited at all times. Opium was not allowed to be grown, dispensed, etc. By the time of liberation in 1949, we already had a little experience in handling this problem, and we had worked out some methods.

"The technical methods that we had worked out were basic. One of them was withdrawal, as it is said, more or less 'cold'. In severe cases we used magnesium sulfate, twenty-five percent, by injection as a muscle relaxant. When we would take over a city, this is what our clinics would offer, and it was just about all we had. As we liberated areas behind the Japanese lines we would, of course, stop the growing of opium.

"Did we have citizens who wanted to go back to the drug or stay on it? Of course we did. The real solution came with the attitude the new government took to this whole problem. Fundamentally, the government decided to eliminate it.

"After liberation one of the first things that was issued was a directive, a circular, prohibiting the growing, manufacturing, distributing, and smoking of opium. This was one of the first communications of Zhou Enlai. This was in February 1950 and was issued by Premier Zhou as head of the government Council.

"Once it was decided that it was to be cut out, and it was an honest decision with every intention to carry it out, we mobilized the people. Obviously, the best of governmental decrees get no results unless the people support it. In each block, each neighborhood, each city area, each village, township and county, the circular was explained to the people, along with the reasons for it and the objectives behind it. All means of communication were used. Thorough discussions were encouraged. Time was spent in small groups to gain the people's understanding and cooperation. The influence of the narcotic problem on their welfare was explained. This is what I mean by mobilizing the people. We did not make the newspaper or radio our only means of communication, nor did we simply nail the directive on a wall.

"Experienced, carefully trained, sensible leaders made personal contact with all citizens. Every neighborhood has natural leaders, and one must earn their support; we did this not with money or bribes, but by carefully and logically making clear the wisdom behind the directive.

"The people were then asked voluntarily to bring in their supplies, and to come in for treatment if they felt they had to break the habit and could not do it on their own. They were offered gradual medical treatment for it; pretty primitive, I must admit. Actually the majority quit cold. They stopped the drug and then suffered through a preliminary period. Opium smoking is different from heroin. Except in about a third of the cases, it is never a very extreme habit. But heroin is entirely different.

"Well, the first circular was that: mobilization and education. It was quite effective and gave us a dependable communication framework with the people.

"But there were also legal measures that were equally carefully explained. For example, if after you had had this considerable opportunity at self-rectification, then if you were caught with the drug and had made no effort to bring it in, you were made into an example with a lot of 'fanfare' and held up to the community as quite a nasty character and practically an enemy of your own friends and society. You see, one thing we have learned is the value of moral persuasion, or as it is called abroad, peer opinion or pressure. In the western countries when one violates a serious rule, he is immediately removed from his peer circle, and instead of society having the opportunity to influence the wrongdoer by the very neighbors with whom he must live, he is removed and the government is made into the punisher. He is put into a criminal environment, a prison where all peer influence is criminal! Our technique assumes that one does not want to be embarrassed or publicly displayed as an enemy of his own brothers, sisters, fathers, mothers, and children. Someone might say that the idea of putting someone in pillory is cruel and has been abandoned in civilized nations. But you and I know that penitentiaries are cruel—and not only cruel, but train minor wrongdoers to become major ones. We believe in the value of encouraging the block or apartment building in which the person lives, or the factory in which he works, to be the most important place for correction of bad behavior.

"We have jails, of course. Some people are dangerous to others and must be confined. But even in our jails we try to persuade through periods of education, reward, punishment, and the punishment is often a form of humiliation.

"With narcotics, we allowed the local pressures of the citizens to mount, and this action could not only become psychologically very supportive for the ex-addict, but also could serve to single out and isolate the noncooperative person.

"Then we had to solve the problem of the opium growers. In the course of land reform when the land was taken away from the landlords and then redistributed to the peasantry, the elimination of opium growing was added to the objectives. Very early we found out that in land reform, if we just said, 'Well, all of this land now belongs to the peasantry: we will divide it for you and hand each one his share of it!', then that land reform was not effective. A lot of the peasants said, 'We don't want it!'. They were still afraid of the landlords. They hadn't liberated themselves; it was being done for them and such an action, even though it was a good intention by the government, was suspect to the peasant.

"So, in many places the land distribution had to be redone. One of the ways this was done was the same as I have described: to mobilize the people by educating them. This meant that again we went into each village, into each small unit, and examined the role of the landlords in the community. We looked at the things that they had done, which included a great deal of recapitulation of the life of the poor peasants in those areas, 'they speak bitterness meetings . . .', that is, a peasant got up and told what had happened to him and what the landlord had done to him. The causes of this were explained, and the collective decision that the landlord's land must be confiscated and divided up by the peasants was made. They went out and measured it, evaluated the productivity of each piece, and made a uniform, agreed-upon decision. One lesson we have learned repeatedly: a central government cannot carry out actions which are not understood and supported by the people at the base level.

"In the course of these procedures the problem of opium was taken up. Opium was grown quite openly in Szechwan Province, Yunnan Province, Fukien Province, and many other provinces. Growing of opium became forbidden.

"Next, the Ministry of Health initiated a series of regulations at the end of 1950 concerning the use of narcotic drugs in medicine.

"Since 1953 or 1954 I have never heard of the problem again! I only think of it now because so many people ask about it. You see, it has been twenty years since it was *heard* of here!

"Now don't try to paraphrase my remarks or make them fit the American scene. The entire situation is different and a solution that fitted the Chinese people cannot be transferred blindly to the United States. I have lived long enough to believe that the solution to a problem usually begins with agreeing that it is a problem, and that the real solution comes only *from* the people. A good leader gains a consensus for both parts of this equation: agreement on the problem's existence and agreement by the whole people to solve it. When these two agreements are in hand, then the people will accept and implement strong declarations by the leadership.

"Basically, it is all a matter of mass education, but not by dependence on mass media. The real education is right at the person's doorstep, neighborhood, and factory unit.

"The economics of opium was defused. At the present time, as I understand it, in the western countries that do have a drug problem, the United States, Britain and France, it is a *billion*-dollar industry. And under that system and those rules, where money has a logic of its own, so to speak, which is alienated from man and his well-being, an industry that counts in the billions is not something you cut off under your capitalistic system. But if you do not cut its economic roots, you're never going to stop it.

"Of course, as we made our progress in this field we also reached a point where those who still wanted opium would make greater efforts to find the drug, and those who supplied the drug for profit would push to ignore our rules. That is why I spoke of the legal phase that lasted almost four years. The opium addict was treated more leniently than the 'pusher'—and the 'pusher' was treated more leniently than the smuggler.

"As soon as we got the people on our side and got them organized, we then could begin isolating the pushers and the smugglers. Once the majority of the people dared to speak out, then the problem people were either reported or caught red-handed. By this time it was clear that the pusher and the smuggler were major enemies of the people, and a variety of measures of persuasion were used.

"I know you have difficulty in understanding the social censure which the Chinese utilize. A pusher, for example, would be brought before the citizens of his own block, seated in the center, and surrounded by them. Personal, direct interrogation would take place right there without court or lawyer. The very people whose lives or whose children he was jeopardizing would castigate him and warn him in very clear terms. He would be encouraged to analyze his own misconduct and, there before his parents and his children, be guided into identifying what he was doing, why he was doing it, why it was wrong, and then, after this period which we sometimes call 'struggling' which could become very excited and personal, he would perhaps over a several-day period offer his own 'self-criticism'. You see, here in China this is a very effective means of neighborhood persuasion, and we find it far better than the elaborate court process of removing the person to jail, at a distance from his reality, and putting him into a situation where the jailers actually become the enemy. Even the pusher's family gets confused and begins to think of all punishment as 'vague' and something alien, if you use the jailing technique.

"For smugglers there was reform by labor, real labor, but, again, also steady conversations in which the message was not so much one of friendly persuasion, but a more clear-cut reminder that further involvement in a criminal act would be dealt with by shooting.

"This final solution was done openly and with a full declaration to the public of the crime involved. This sentence was made by an appropriate court, not by the neighborhood, and once made, was carried out promptly. Long, technical delays were impossible because the circular issued by Zhou Enlai had been very specific, and the individual had almost always been given at least one clean chance for reformation of his conduct.

"Such executions were not done on any large scale. Extreme physical violence, such as an execution, is used reluctantly and with restraint, and then only as an educational measure for the rest of the population. You see, we feel without reservation that the death penalty does have a major deterrent role for personal misbehavior and is an education to others who may be finding it difficult to be good citizens.

"Capital punishment was used but only in a very limited sense. Let us say a fellow would be caught pushing narcotics once, twice, three times, and was thought to have been fully reeducated. Then if he was again found selling drugs we would consider him irredeemable. We found that if you had fifty such men, the execution of one was very likely to reform the remainder.

"I personally never saw such an execution. I only remember reading in the newspaper of such executions occurring about 1951 in Canton. I purposefully have tried to make it clear that such violence as executions played only a minimal role. It was one of the small factors. If you grade the measures used according to importance, execution would come at the bottom of the list. But it must be there, declared, and definitive.

"Also, the very clear declaration of Premier Zhou Enlai's contained a distinct statement: a cutoff date. The defined cutoff date was preceded by ample national discussions and evidence that the public had endorsed the message. And there was no equivocation.

"Now in solving the problems of prostitution and venereal disease, many principles were the same. But of course it had its obvious differences. Basically, it still remained a question of having the people on your side, to get them to agree that this thing, this goal, is a group thing. We've said that in our concept of the New World we were going to build, a moral world, there was no place for these things. That kind of education and propaganda was much easier because it fully fit the basic moral instincts of the people.

"Here again the process was through penetration into the very neighborhood, with thorough, adequate dialogue and endorsement by the people. The government then adopted the formal commitment that such social diseases were to be eliminated. Once this decision was made, the job was given to the medical services to work out the method.

"I must stress again that this decision was one that reflected the general demand of the people. The foreign press enjoys explaining or excusing China's success in this area by categorically assigning the result to a 'dictatorship'. That is not an answer; that is but an excuse for the failure of programs in their own country. There are a few true dictatorships in this world where the word of one man can eliminate the lives of thousands. But that same dictator cannot eliminate venereal disease unless he and the people share a moral climate in which there is the public desire to eliminate these social diseases. China has been successful in these areas, but it has been by the power of education, of public endorsement. Then the central government is not dictating; it is carrying out the wishes of the general population, and the population has already expressed its willingness to work for this general demand.

"Now you may twist my words and think, 'He is a clever old fellow, slipping this bit of communist propaganda into our conversation.' Well, I am able to answer your questions only upon the basis of what has been China's solution and given the characteristics of the Chinese people plus the methods of the Chinese Communist party. Let us agree that I will give you factual answers, and you of course will hear my words, but your own emotional computer will translate them into whatever political orientation controls your bias.

"Let me tell you what we did in Peking. The first job I got after liberation was the elimination of venereal disease. When we first came to Peking the logical way to begin was to investigate all houses of prostitution, open and secret ones. We moblized our women's association and our women leaders who, in our old liberated areas, had had previous experience and training in working with women, and some who were what you would call social workers.

"A detailed investigation of the whole of Peking was made, and all open and clandestine prostitiution was identified. The location of the houses, the numbers of women, the owners of the property, and the managers of the system were all recorded. After all these data were collected over a period of a couple of months, within forty-eight hours they were all completely closed.

"The women remained in their own place of 'work', and the house became an institution for education, treatment, retraining, and handling the problems of the women. The first thing that was done was to separate the owners of these homes who were running the prostitution racket, the racketeers, and pimps and so on, from the women and eliminate further contact.

"We then did a regular medical investigation including serology, smears, etc. . . . We found sixty-seven percent were infected. These were treated. That part of the solution was straightforward and medical. The entire house was their reeducation unit, and they remained there. Of course at the same time, so-called streetwalkers and their male organizers had been identified and housing arranged for them. You will note that no jails or courts were used.

"Of course much of the data were already known, and as in almost every city in the world the police can provide very accurate information as to the individuals, the locations, the bosses. But for the women, we did not make them criminals, and we did not herd them down to a night court.

"In the original investigation very little police activity was involved. Again, we gained the cooperation of women's organizations, helped them with leadership, and events moved surprisingly easily. When we actually closed the houses and detained the women on the premises, we again mobilized neighborhood groups to bring in food and to be sure there was no coming and going. Intensive neighborhood involvement

At Yanan, 1945; American Field Service Team. Hatem in front row, Margaret Stanley on right. (Photo courtesy Margaret Stanley)

Hatem at Beidaiho, 1980. (Photo courtesy Mary Clark Dimond)

The map of China, without the offshore islands, depicting the two man-made landmarks of history, The Great Wall and The Grand Canal and two journeys of contemporary times, The Long March and the route of Edgar Snow and George Hatem to Paoan in 1936. As a reference for distances, The Long March was six thousand miles.

GREAT WALL

GREAT WALL

Beijing

Shanhaikuan

Tianjin

Paoan

Yanan

GRAND CANAL

Zhengzhou

Xian

Shanghai

Hangzhou

Long March

— — — Great Wall
· · · · · · · Long March
● ● ● ● ● Journey to Paoan
- - - - - Grand Canal

The author and George Hatem at Hainan Island, 1982. (Photo courtesy Mary Clark Dimond)

and women's group involvement went on at all times. The girls lived there, ate there . . . this became their home. We simply removed the top management.

"Then we began the whole peer process of education. The female political and social workers would sit down with these women, day in and day out. They would lead the discussion and review the prostitutes' past lives; how did they get into it? These causes were interesting: poverty, destitution, floods, ex-concubines sold by the warlords, the need for money for drugs, etc. Upon hearing their stories, the social workers used them to explain why the women were in their present situation, so that the causes of prostitution in a great majority of cases were seen as an economic problem or some fault with the social setup . . . the system.

"This was used to give the girls a political understanding of the forces of society, and how and why they had moved to trap them, and how such forces can make a person into a prostitute. It was explained that there was no stigma attached to them for having gone into the profession. It had been done to them or forced upon them by the old society.

"There is sometimes always a certain willingness to accept the existence of prostitution by saying it is: a) a necessary safety valve for society; b) the girls really enjoy the work; or c) it is a private activity and not an affair for an outsider or busybody.

"We began with a basic belief and morality that accepted none of these phrases. And, as I have said, we were able to assure ourselves from our contact and discussions with the masses of the people that the population really did not agree with these age-old excuses, either. Most of our people truly believed that the women were caught in a trap of poverty, racketeers, pimps, and fear. And that most became so cutoff from any normal way of life or normal contact with parents and family that they essentially were prisoners of the system.

"Now you may want to take some exceptions to my declaring that it took a new society, a revolution, a sweeping away of the old to accomplish this. I ask you to remember our conversation the next time you are in Hong Kong. There you have the very same race, the Chinese, with all the merits of the Chinese in terms of intelligence, frugality, family ties—but with narcotics, rackets, murder, and prostitution.

"Yet here, a very few miles away, we do not have these social problems. You will always want to say we have done this at rifle-point or by brute force. I remind you that I lived in the United States during the years of the Volstead Act and that all the government guns, police, laws, and jails failed because the people did not want Prohibition. Major issues of change involving the whole society can only be accomplished by an educational process. And the educational process must be at the level of every single citizen. We call that the 'mass line', and that phrase does not happily translate into English. The word 'line' in America has become synonymous with a form of selling, almost as a falsehood. 'What a line!', you will say about someone who is overstating his case. That is not how we use the word. We mean that the message has become the fully endorsed public message.

"To return to the reeducation of these women. We would say to them, 'There has been a revolution. You are now liberated, and it is your job to practice a trade that will be useful to the new society'. On that basis the woman has a whole new cooperative concept to work with.

"I need to emphasize that the women leaders we counted upon to lead these reeducation programs had been through long training and study and had gained experience by severe seasoning. The right kind of woman leader is one of the keys, of course.

"On the basis of such discussions, a day-in and a day-out process, the women were taught how to read and write, their venereal disease was eliminated, their self-education moved along, they were taught how to earn a living, and thus did not need to go back to their old trade. They were offered help in going back to their own villages. Some of the girls had come into the towns because they were starving or because they had been sold by warlords, or they had been married and sold by their husband just to keep them from starving. That type of case was often given the chance to go back home, and work was done at the other end for her reception. Close cooperation between the women leaders at both ends was necessary. It is obviously not easy to arrange such things, but this was considered to be of primary importance in solving the problem. Unless you work on every facet of it, you would leave ragged edges.

"Those who had no chance of going back were taught a trade. The women remaining in the house, for example, were formed into a cooperative to knit stockings and socks by hand with those little round machines.

"In 1959 I went back to one of the 'houses'. It was now a full-fledged factory. Most of the women had married. It was no longer a closed community or any such thing. We did our last health survey there in 1959 as a final study for our record. There was a zero-positive serology. It was simply a normal community. Some of the best venereal disease workers with me were the youngest girls we got from these houses, and we trained them as lab technicians and field-workers. Very excellent people. Some became nurses.

"Your thought about all this, I know, is to wonder if we were not simply hoodwinked. Did not the 'hard-core' girls simply open up shop in a new place? Well, we came back again to this problem which my friends from abroad have difficulty understanding, and if not understanding, then believing. You keep asking where was the 'enforcement', the police force, etc. Well, that is not the solution. You must begin with public endorsement and cooperation. No new house of prostitution could open because the very neighborhood itself would single it out, identify it, call for help of trained leaders, and the process was thus cut off by the people.

"I might point out that all the Americans, the hundreds of Americans that I have met here in Peking, have enjoyed telling me that they leave their hotel rooms unlocked and nothing is ever stolen. I asked them if they have ever seen anything remotely resembling a policeman, uniformed or secret, any place near their hotel floor. The answer is always one of acknowledgment of their absence. You see, *morality* is a state of behavior; we believe the general code of public morality can be raised by a general policy of public education. We do not believe an individual should be allowed to exercise his own personal liberty if it is against the wishes of the whole people or the people with whom he must live and work. And I realize that much of this morality is Chinese and not something brought by the Communists. Nationwide peace and stability, plus strong leadership, allowed the innate morals of the Chinese to solve these problems.

"It may sound to you like some very early form of Christian message, but we believe it is more important to do good for others than for oneself! Have you perhaps heard that thought before? We do not need policing because we have taken the time to discuss these issues fully and to educate every household. You see, things must be achieved without the coercion aspect. Coercion, in the final analysis, represents failure. All of these problems that have a social evil connected with them, things you call a social problem, in the final analysis will have to involve a change in the relationship of man to man. Revolution, in our sense of the word in China, meant first of all changing the relationship of how a person earns his living and how that person related to his fellowman. Do not try to understand what we have done without at the same time understanding the conditions of China when we began our revolution. By changing the economic basis of life here . . . man was no longer allowed to be in a position to flaunt his fellowman.

"Now please remember that I am only telling you part of the story. If the whole story of what we started out to do is ten fingers, I am only giving you nine fingers. The tenth finger is all the negative aspects: where we failed, where we didn't make it, where we used other measures.

"In this area of prostitutes again . . . I can truthfully say I have never seen a single woman put in prison. But I have seen our women leaders sit down in that room of the former house of prostitution for hours and hours and hours, discussing with a prostitute, 'Why do you go ahead with this life?' And you know, for most of these women, no one had ever done anything but scoop them up, book them, fine them, jail them. No one had taken the time to talk it through, offer solutions and not just big solutions, but every detail of a solution. One thing we did not do was to put them on a welfare check. We did support them during the rehabilitation period, but from the beginning they were working . . . either cooking, or cleaning, or fixing their house, or going to class, or making an honest product for sale.

"Now speaking of man's relationship to man, that is a continuing, unremitting education. It is never achieved or finished. We do not believe man is perfectible—and once perfected there he remains. We do believe that good in all men can be the primary objective of society—and that then the personal liberty that America has offered its people can become a reality. But unless you combine personal liberty with an equal personal responsibility to your fellowman, you may well find that one man's personal liberty is accomplished to the harm of the personal liberty of others.

"There truly is no way to use force in China by the military, the police, or terror; it won't work on a population of 800 million . . . it is self-defeating. So all of this has to be done, one way or other, by education. I'll give you another example in the area of venereal disease: how we worked in the countryside.

"In 1958 I went to a county in Kiangsi Province, an old Chinese Soviet area. We used one county to set up a model. We had perfected a questionnaire system for finding patients with venereal disease. For example, the questions were: 'Have you slept with another man's wife? Have you visited houses of prostitution in the past? Have you broken out in any skin disorders?' . . . a total of ten questions.

"We took this questionnaire to that county to see how we could most effectively apply it to find two percent or three percent of the population which we expected would be zero-positive. In rural populations in China proper, we had never found more than a three percent positive serology.

"So instead of screening the whole population with all the complications and expense of blood-testing everyone, we chose this one county to see if the questionnaire method could not give us an adequate accuracy and economy.

"These ten questions would give us about a thirty percent harvest of the whole population. That is, enough answers were positive to warrant a blood test. And from this thirty percent, we found our two-to-three percent positive we had anticipated. And thus ultimately we found a way not to require the blood examination on seventy percent of the population, a huge factor when you are dealing with millions of people.

"Now, how do you get the people to discuss the questionnaire and fill it out honestly?

"What we did may sound Sunday Schoolish and Boy Scoutish, and it may sound anything you want . . . but in the environment of old China, when you talk to these people and give them the chance to talk of the old life that they had suffered, and they already know from this new life that they have enough to eat . . . you can begin the conversation on a basis of some confidence. My friends from the West have great difficulty sometimes in understanding the constant reality of near-starvation and starvation that was the peasant's way of life during the years of China's near-destruction. I sometimes must remind my western friends that the fundamental freedom that any living thing seeks, from bird to man, is freedom from hunger. We, through coordinating the country's resources and distributing the food honestly, perhaps made no one fat in those early years, but also we allowed no one to starve.

"It was from this basis of confidence in us that we were welcome in the villages and could explain in frank and open discussions the purpose of our questionnaire. We based our approach upon calling for a meeting of the heads of the families, and in straightforward language telling them what we were trying to do and that our only desire was to give medicine to those who needed it. Also we would have with us farmers from other villages who had been involved with the questionnaire and who had been found to have a positive serology and had had treatment, and who were willing to give testimony on our behalf.

"From this start, we did nothing more than what people call 'plain talk' or 'bitterness talk'. We encouraged dozens of small groups to talk out the things that had happened to them. Things that had not really been their fault. The only way to break out of their old life and the awfulness of it was to cleanse themselves of all of its evils—including venereal disease.

"There are little bits of this approach sometimes in your own society, for example, Alcoholics Anonymous. As far as I understand it (I don't really know much about it), there your fellowman is on tap: he will come and sit with you and hold your hand and give you support.

"Again, however, I repeat that China's solutions are based upon China's customs. Throughout China there are villages and villages and villages that only have one family making up every household. The vast majority, not all, but the very large majority of the people living in the Chinese village have always lived there . . . By that I mean there simply is not a time in history in which the people of a certain village have not all been of the Shen family, for example. At some remote time, 1,000 or 2,000 years ago, it was there that a man named Shen broke the earth and gradually a cluster of buildings had become a village of Shens. The sons go out to other villages and bring home wives. And the village endures, I can say, forever. Unless you understand that this is the basis of Chinese society, you will never understand why cooperative farming has been logical, or why no one is really rootless, or why we have so little need for psychiatrists. The family is therapeutic. It is a continuity. If you are bright or dumb, a genius or, and I mean this, a moron, you are still a member of a specific village, a village that has gone on forever and into whose life you fit.

"That is the cohesive strength that is China, and it is that strength that this new society is based upon. All we did with our revolution was to let these huge parts of society have the freedom to run their own country. Those elements: landlords, foreign influence, Confucian rules, that trapped the majority into a peasant's role, are what the peasants threw off through the revolution."

George's words of 1973 reminded me of something I had read of Edgar Snow's in *Red Star over China*. In 1938, Edgar had described the Communists' use of propaganda:

"You know in one sense you can think of the whole history of the communist movement in China as a grand propaganda tour, and the defence, not so much of the absolute right of certain ideas, perhaps, as of their right to exist. I'm not sure that it may not prove to have been the most permanent service of the Reds, even if they are in the end defeated and broken. For millions of young peasants who have heard the Marxist gospel preached by those beardless youths, thousands of whom are now dead, the old exorcisms of Chinese culture will never again be quite as effective. Wherever in their incredible migrations destiny has moved these Reds, they have vigorously demanded deep social changes—of which the peasants could have learned in no other way—and have brought new faith in action to the poor and the oppressed.

"However badly they have erred at times, however tragic have been their excesses, however exaggerated has been the emphasis here or the stress there, it has been their sincere and sharply felt propagandist aim to shake, to arouse, the millions of rural China to their responsibilities in society; to awaken them to a belief in human rights, to combat the timidity, passiveness and static faiths of Taoism and Confuciansim, to educate, to persuade and, I have no doubt, at times to beleaguer and coerce them to fight for a life of justice, equality, freedom and human dignity, as the communists see it . . .

"What this 'communism' has amounted to in a way is that, for the first time in history, thousands of educated youths, stirred to great dreams themselves by a university of scientific knowledge to which they have suddenly been given access, have 'returned to the people', turned back to the deep soil—the base of their country to 'reveal' some of their new-won learning to the intellectually sterile countryside, the dark-living peasantry, and have sought to enlist its alliance in building this 'more abundant life'. Fired by the belief that a better world can be made, and that only they can make it, they have carried their formula—the ideal of the commune—back to the people for sanction and support. And to a startling degree they have won it. They have brought to millions, by propaganda and by action, a new conception of the State, society and the individual."[1]

George, speaking to us in Beijing forty years later, made clear the success of this "propaganda" approach. He told us he had summarized much of this in an article.[2] Propaganda in its best sense is public education for the public's good. How poorly that logic is utilized in much of the world. My group of American physicians were, in the main, impressed by what George had told us about the elimination of these "social" problems in China. One member of the group, however, kept coming back at George and, shaking his finger, stated: "You are not telling us all. There is a club here someplace that you used and you are not telling us about it. Someplace you were using more severe tactics than you are telling." George could only shrug and say, "I am telling you what I know and what I saw." When our session ended, my American colleague stayed in his chair, shaking his head and muttering, "There is something about this I don't understand."

12

A VISIT WITH GEORGE HATEM IN
KANSAS CITY, AUGUST 1978

TIMING is everything. This brief warning covers all fields and was the essence of George's decision to make his first visit in fifty years to his native United states. The timing was certainly wrong for all the years between 1949 and President Nixon's visit in February 1972. From 1972 on, George was thoughtful and cautious. Invitations came from a multitude of American medical professional societies. Special visiting professorships and guest lectureships were offered him. With courtesy he thanked them all, but always with the message that the time was not right. In Beijing he was extremely active, and unending medical and nonmedical visitors had a good visit with this exotic, transplanted American. George was walking a very careful path during these years of the Cultural Revolution, and his sensitive antennae and thoughtful analysis of the Chinese scene kept him aware that the time was still not yet right for his visit to the United States. This precarious timing was made real to me in February 1974. My mail on February 18, 1974 had included a typed and accurately addressed letter with the following message: "Dear Dr. Dimond: All the reactionary forces in the world always harbor fiendish hatred of our revolutionary people highly raising the great red banner of Mao Tse-tung's thought, and our significant socialist revolutionary achievements. *China,* an anti-Chinese film photoed by an Italian director, Antonioni, represents the psychological excitement of the extreme hatred of all the current international imperialists, revisionists and reactionists in China.

"There are some kinds of People who pretend to be ostensible friends to us. They come to China not for promoting the understanding of China, but for possessing enmity against the Chinese people. They take the meanest and the most elaborate methods with a vain attempt to realize the anti-revolutionary restoration in China, and pave the way to reduce China once again to a colony or a sub-colony to the imperialists. The ghost of Dulles, Antonioni, who were mistaken as our friends by us, has done some shameless and dirty anti-Chinese activities. We never forget that the anti-Chinese force is always existing all over the world.

"If your purpose asking for developing our friendship and exchanging medical students is simply paving the way for the imperialists and the social-imperialists in their attempt of crimes to isolate the subvert China, you are just moving a stone to smash your own feet; if you want to incite the Chinese people to be discontented with socialistic system by using the bourgeois lackey Ma Hai-teh to do some dirty tricks in the inner of our country, you are destined to failure disgracefully." Signed: "The Opposing Current Faction, Chinese Medical Association."

This was obviously a thoroughly hostile letter. It carried a message of real threat to George, and certainly did not express any enthusiasm for the two and a half years of effort that I had committed to establish contact with the Chinese medical profession. The title of the authors: The Opposing Current Faction, Chinese Medical Association, was clear evidence that all was not peace and harmony in Beijing. Whether George was under direct criticism by some group internal to the Chinese Medical Association or not, I do not know. The Chinese Liaison Office in Washington suggested that the letter could have been initiated and forged, by a Taiwan source and inserted in the mailbags in Hong Kong. I am inclined to think that it was valid correspondence and an accurate expression of events in China. With such opinions being expressed by "The Opposing Current Faction," the timing was certainly wrong for George to even hint about a possible visit to the United States.

However, the change in the government gave George new confidence. By the summer of 1977 he was making plans for coming to the United States in the spring of 1978. Not only was his position well stabilized in China, but he was assured that he could travel freely and safely in the United States. This question of safety had been a major issue when I had first negotiated for the Chinese medical delegation to tour America in November 1972. At that time there had been angry demonstrations over the question of Chinese athletic teams coming here, and diverse groups including those led by the fundamentalist, rightist, Reverend McIntyre had staged volatile, anti-PRC demonstrations. To insure the safety of the Chinese physicians we had needed full-time security agents, police-escorted transportation, and guarded hotel suites. All of this activity had perhaps been excessive and unnecessary, but still, both the Chinese and the Americans had willingly accepted this shield of protection. But now, five years later, Chinese delegations were traveling throughout the United States, without problems and without tension.

The unexpected finding of cancer of the pancreas in the fall of 1977 suspended all of George's plans. Intensive X-ray therapy and general debilitation stopped all thoughts of possible travel. George spent the entire winter of 1977 and early 1978 in the hospital. However, as winter came to an end, the timing for his long-delayed trip "home" became imperative. Now was the time. All of us recognized the irony of the fact that George was suffering the same incurable disease that had taken Ed.

George, at the lowest of times and with the bleakest of prospects, simply held to his plans. Once he had admitted that he was planning to come to the United States, he never wavered. Letters from China carried this message and at the same time reported on his dismal condition. Tenacity and attentive care helped, and in early spring, 1978, George and Sufei arrived in the United States. He realized his trip could end at almost any moment; his reasonable life expectancy was six months.

He felt that the hazard of his personal illness was no reason to cancel the trip; rather, it increased his awareness of the need to capture the fleeting moment. And it was a time when such a return home was possible, indeed, the first since he had joined the Communists' forces in 1936 that he could feel secure from harassment from congressmen or journalistic attack here—and perhaps the first time he felt comfortable in having the understanding and approval of the Chinese leaders.

Ma Haide, Chinese citizen, had the harvest of the fall of a full life . . . a return to the land where George Hatem was born, schooled, and had grown up fifty years ago. A long journey, a long, long time.

For George it was the first view of the country that he had left when it was in the depths of the Depression, and for Sufei, a first experience

in her husband's homeland. George was not daunted by the unpredictable risks of his condition and had come for a full and lengthy visit. He
arrived in April, spent a month with his brother Joe in Roanoke Rapids,
North Carolina; then on to Washington, New York, Buffalo, Cape Cod,
Los Angeles, San Francisco, Tucson, Kansas City—a full half-year.
There were leisurely gatherings with relatives, friends, classmates. It
was a mellow time, a time for reflection, comparison, mending of ties,
a time needed to complete one's life cycle, and a time which had had
to wait its moment of opportunity.

On the day of their arrival, George's brother, Joe Hatem, came up to
Washington's Dulles Air Field, and other old friends and relatives
assembled there for his return to America. They did not have a clear
idea of what to expect. How sick was George? They prepared for the
worst and had provided, just out of sight, a wheelchair. In addition, a
private plane was obtained to move George to his brother's home in
Roanoke Rapids, North Carolina or to a hospital medical center, which-
ever was needed.

With a mix of anticipation and dread they waited for the plane. When
it landed there was a slow straggle of passengers coming from the plane.
And then there was George, fully agile, in fact, keen and lean. He was
smiling and there was almost forty pounds less of him than when any
of them had last seen him.

Concern over the complications of passport control for a man who
was perhaps both an American and a Chinese proved unnecessary.
George had never adopted the Mao tunic of the usual Chinese professional and was wearing a gray suit, gray sweater, and what I would call
blue hush puppies. A large button in his lapel, indicating that he had
been a delegate to the recent China national conference which had
launched China's science and technology drive, hinted that he was not
just another American coming home.

George and Sufei went first to his brother's home and reunions with
his family and his Chapel Hill classmates. Then on to Washington, D.
C., where word soon spread that the famous George Hatem was in the
city. The National Institutes of Health, all of them, hosted him and he
stayed with it until they tried that special American torture, the 7:30
A.M. breakfast meeting. He was invited for a long chat by Senator Ted
Kennedy; he met with the Assistant Secretary for Health and Scientific

Affairs, Dr. Julius Richmond; George Washington University and Dr. T. O. Cheng made ready to "give him the works," which meant a complete medical workup including the ultimate new altar of equipment, the total body scanner. George persuaded them to settle for a sample of his blood and skillfully avoided the physical exhaustion of a modern, total medical work-up. He did have a thorough examination at Duke University, arranged by his brother, Joe Hatem.

In June, they were in New York City to stay with Helen and Sam Rosen, who had been with the Paul Whites and ourselves at the time of our intial 1971 trip to China. George, Sufei, Helen, and Sam have become close friends. In late June he had a reunion with six classmates from his American University days in Beirut, complete with pictures, slides, and toasts.

The Rosens had first met George in 1971 when Sam Rosen finally had been able to visit the People's Republic of China. I say "finally" because Dr. Rosen had every possible optimistic hope of being in China much earlier when he had received an invitation to come and demonstrate his stapes operation for deafness. This skillful inner-ear surgery had been developed by Dr. Rosen and he was the world-recognized authority on the operative procedure. But overeager press releases from the United States State Department had declared that Sam's going to China was an example of how the United States was willing to help backward China. At that point in Chinese history such remarks were considered examples of imperialism's patronage, and China withdrew the invitation. It is a reminder that yesterday's mistakes can be today's catechism. In 1964 China's attitude was one of doing only what they could do themselves. Viewed in relation to other events and especially in terms of Russia's total abandonment of commitments to China in 1960, the Chinese response to the State Department's bit of American chauvinism was perhaps logical. However, the swings in mood and acts of a country are just as volatile as in an individual. Then a helping hand was an insult; today, of course, China's leaders broadcast their need for world knowledge and technology.

George's sentimental journey took him to Buffalo, the headline in the *Buffalo News* read: "Ex-Buffalonian became hero of Chinese Medicine." He had left the city when he was thirteen, but "Ex-Buffalonian" he was to remain in the annals of Buffalo. George was quoted by the

Buffalo News as saying,. "I would say I was a friend of Mao, not his physician; I treated him only in passing. I've attended to Mao, but he was usually a very healthy man."

When asked if he thought China was the best of all worlds, George replied, "China is best for China. Each country will have its own problems and things they need to work out, and the people have to work them out the way they feel is necessary." Asked how he became involved in a movement which led to the overthrow of the Chinese Nationalists, George commented that it came naturally: "The social upheaval taking place, the need for doctors, the poverty, the epidemics we saw were impressive to young people interested in the help-your-fellow-man idea."

In 1978 the Hatems summered in good American style with an old friend from Shanghai days, Manny Granich, the founder of Voice of China in Shanghai in 1937. Granich, who was one of George's mentors in his early understanding of Marxism, had a cottage at Truro, Cape Cod, where George was busy with guests, including Barbara Walters and Walter Cronkite. George's appetite for America was superb, and he reported with authority that the hot dog had not changed with his fifty-year absence.

Lloyd Shearer of *Parade Magazine* had met George in Beijing in 1973 and was a warm host in Los Angeles. When Shearer had returned from his own trip to Beijing, a full cover story about George was carried by *Parade Magazine* on August 12, 1973. Shearer, in both words and photographs, caught the essentials of the same man I knew. The cover photograph, in color, was taken in Beijing. George is seated in an armchair, complete with antimacassars. His strong hands, with their fingers laced, rest on his abdomen. The photo also reveals a full head of white hair, black eyebrows, and large, innocent eyes. Those large, bassethound eyes moved Ann Landers to tell me after her Beijing exposure to the ubiquitous George that he was the "most sexy man she had ever met." I offer no opinion on the merits of Ann Landers's judgment, but quickly point out that this was a volunteered opinion and not one resulting from a "Dear Ann" letter from me.

Lloyd Shearer describes George as "a short, stocky, charming and informed man, profound, philosophical and well-read, this brown-eyed, white-haired son of Lebanese immigrants . . ." Shearer learned from George the circumstances of his initial contact with the Communist

Chinese, "through the late Agnes Smedley . . . who was then a corre-spondent for the *Frankfurter Zeitung* . . ., Hatem met Liu Ting, an ardent young communist engineer who graphically explained to him how desperately the forbidden communists of the northwest needed trained and honest doctors. Liu pleaded with Hatem to go north. Altruistic and adventuresome, Hatem, then 26, agreed to give it a try. He made contacts with the Red underground and along with Edgar Snow was subsequently smuggled into Red China."

The Hatems continued on to San Francisco where George spoke before the United States-China People's Friendship Association, and then to Berkeley to visit John Service. Service was one of those Americans who had an early, important contact with the Communist Chinese at Yanan in the nineteen forties.[1]

From there the Hatems went on to Tucson, where George acquired an addition to his wardrobe—a leather-thonged, silver, turquoise, thun-derbird neckpiece and a Mexican shirt. This was followed by a week in Kansas City which they spent with us and Mildred Mackey, Edgar Snow's sister. By the time of his arrival in Kansas City, George had put on a good deal of weight. This gave him temporary encouragement that the X-ray therapy had at least slowed down his basic disease. Sufei not only had adjusted to our food, but also developed a taste for the fast food variety: hamburgers, French fries, Coke, pizza, and tacos.

With George in our home there was much good conversation. He reported his pleasure with endorsement of the new Chinese administra-tion. He volunteered that the senior general, Ye Jianying, could have succeeded Mao and was urged to do so by the party. However, Ye's response was that it was better to have an orderly transition now rather than again be faced with that task in the near future, which would have been inevitable due to his own advanced age. It was Ye who ordered the seizure of Mao's widow and her three colleagues. George con-sidered Ye the glue that had held the administration together and had given it a chance to gain consensus again.

Among other interesting comments and general conversation was the reminder that Mao was actually not in control of the government in part of the 1950s. For example, George said that the reason Edgar Snow did not return to China for many years was not for lack of trying, but simply because Mao did not have real power for a considerable period. At about this time the Russian author Aleksandr Solzhenitsyn gave an address to Harvard University's graduating class (early June 1978).[2] In that address, Solzhenitsyn wove a line of reasoning in which he was able to deal with his objections to Russia with these words: "I have spent all my life under a communist regime, and I will tell you that a society without any objective legal scale is a terrible one indeed."

To me this would seem adequate reasoning by which to recognize the merits and demerits of life in the western democracies—and in essence declare them to have problems—but also to conclude that they are a far preferable place to live. The fact that Solzhenitsyn is in full residence, in safe sanctuary, able to write and speak as he wishes here in the West, would seem to warrant his endorsement of the attributes of our form of government.

Instead, Sozhenitsyn defined our problem as too much legalism. He said, for example, "If one is right from a legal point of view, nothing more is required; nobody may mention that one could still not be entirely right, and urge self-constraint, a willingness to renounce such legal rights, sacrifice in selfless risk . . . Everybody operates at the extreme limits of these legal frames."

He then went on to say, "Destructive and irresponsible freedom has been granted boundless space. Society appears to have little defense against the abyss of human decadence, such as, for example, misuse of liberty for moral violence against young people, motion pictures full of pornography, crime, horror . . . Life organized legalistically has thus shown its inability to defend itself against the corrosion of evil."

He continued his analysis, "A decline in courage may be the most striking feature which an outside observer notices in the west in our days. The western world has lost its civil courage . . ."

He then gave as an example of our debilitation, "Your short-sighted politicans who signed the hasty Vietnam capitulation . . . if a full-fledged America suffered a real defeat from a small communist half-country, how can the west hope to stand firm in the future?" In one sentence he thoroughly summarizes his opinion of our western weaknesses, "The next war (which does not have to be an atomic one, and I do not believe it will) may well bury western civilization."

I felt this was a sufficient indictment of all western civilization, but he had one final blow. He weighed the western world that he had experienced against the eastern world that he found so painful, including prison, in which he had earlier acknowledged, " . . . that a society without any objective legal scale is a terrible one indeed." He said, "Should someone ask me whether I would indicate the west such as it is today as a model to my country (Russia), frankly I would have to answer negatively. No, I could not recommend your society under its present state as an ideal for the transformation of ours."

This commencement address of Sozhenitsyn took courage and received wide coverage. I asked George what he thought of this. George's reply was pragmatic. "He is looking for some kind of Utopia he will never find. He lists all the problems and seems unable to recognize that there are no perfect solutions. I find in his writings a willingness to slide into the security of being somewhat of a mystic. I did not think much of his talk, but then I only saw parts of it in the newspaper. Perhaps he said more in the original presentation."

I interjected, "He certainly reached a significant audience. The Harvard Commencement is an important forum."

George rebutted me, "I know nothing about that, but I do wonder why if Sozhenitsyn was supposed to be such a profound thinker he could write a paper such as this, full of pieces of emotionalism, instead of one that withstands real debate. He impresses me as a Pollyanna who will not recognize the real world and will continue to impress those who do not have objective responsibilities."

At about this time, the policies of the new government permitted Chinese reporters to carry personal news stories. The *Peking Review* carried a two-part story about Snow and George, written by Chiang Shan, and it opened with the following. "One afternoon in June 1936, with the scorching sun bearing down on the loess plateau in northern Shensi and a hot wind whipping clusters of dust, a small group of people trudged along a mountain road leading to Paoan, then the seat of the Central Committee of the Communist Party of China. The peasant in front, leading two donkeys packed with luggage, cameras and medical supplies, were followed by two young foreigners—Edgar Snow, an American correspondent, and George Hatem, an American doctor."[3]

George told me what the facts were in terms of his meeting Edgar Snow: that Edgar had come down from the north by train from Beijing, while at the same time George was coming in from the east on the train from Shanghai to Nanking, and that the two of them met at a guest house where they were separately lodged. George had already pledged himself to be a member of the Communist party, and he was bearing the torn five-pound note which he was to present when he met the agent from Mao's Communist government who would have the matching half. Edgar himself was not a Communist and had no such means of identification. The two men met and Edgar thus came under George's protection, as George was the individual who had the legitimate passport into the Chinese area. This fact does not appear in Snow's writings, and Ed speaks of his own letter written in invisible ink. George said to me, "Ed occasionally upgraded a story in order to make it better, and this is one of those examples. Ed was not always accurate, but we always forgave him because he meant well." I knew Ed well, and took this appraisal with a grain of salt. I later checked with Ed's first wife as to their side of the story, and was adamantly advised that Ed had made his own arrangements for getting through to Paoan, and George had had nothing to do with it.

When I next saw Rewi Alley, I asked his opinion on this comment by George on Ed's accuracy. Rewi's response not only was thoroughly reassuring, but it made one smile at the dimensions of the criticism. Ed came out of the analysis with his reputation intact. Rewi agreed that "Ed sometimes dressed up the truth to make a better story." For example, Ed had written that Rewi had red hair and a cockney accent. Rewi resented this. "I never had red hair. I used to have brown hair, and I certainly never had a cockney accent. I never dropped my aiches nor added them as do people from Yorkshire. I have a New Zealander accent, not a cockney."

He went on to say that Ed was a tenacious reporter who kept trying to get the truth and would go after it time after time, but "sometimes would dress little parts of the story to give it more character, but never altered the accuracy of the reporting."

George acknowledged that Rewi Alley had persuaded him to cast his lot with the Chinese Communist party and was also the person who had helped him understand why it was the logical means of aiding the Chinese people. Rewi had placed it in the context of being the only way to carry out a social revolution for all the Chinese people. The effort had to be something as large and violent and as organized as communism.

George had brought along to Kansas City the article written by him in 1936, *Chromium Toxicity in Factories in Shanghai*,[4] which he told me he wrote at the instigation of Rewi. It described the awful conditions of Shanghai workers that had influenced his political thinking and which had brought him and Edgar to Paoan. In a sense, then, this article was the reason that Edgar became famous, so, in a way, George could claim that it indirectly set in motion the ultimate publication of *Red Star over China*. He said this half-jokingly but with pride as well.[5]

When I heard George laying some claim to Ed Snow's experiences of 1936, I reminded myself that the Chinese government invariably tried to claim more of Ed as one of their own than Ed or his family would have accepted. Ed had gone to Paoan as a reporter getting a story, not as one ready to convert to that cause. This remained true through the years, regardless of accusations by McCarthyites or embracements by the Chinese government.

I also enjoyed learning that at the time of the liberation of Beijing, George had his German shepherd dog which had been liberated from a Japanese general. Giving it the Japanese general's name made him feel that when he whistled for the dog, he was calling the Japanese general to heel.

I asked what had happened to him at the very beginning of the Cultural Revolution. George said he was on a train trip, escorting a foreign doctor to the border. The Red Guards seized the train, and this was George's first knowledge of the Cultural Revolution. As the days passed, it was announced that all Chinese people would have to have passes to proceed to the border even if they were carrying out official functions, and that he was no exception. George said, "So many people were trying to get across the border."

George expressed concern about the future of China's demand for material things. He had learned, while on his American trip, that his son now had a motorcycle. He remembered the transition from bicycles to motorbikes to automobiles in Europe after the Second World War. He hoped that the government of China could avoid this individual ownership of cars and motorcycles which had become an economic base and dilemma for the western world.

He also expressed the hope that as the peasants were given machines, that the factories be placed in the countryside in order not to have congregations of unneeded farmers in the cities. George was pleased with the new changes in China, but it was rather apparent that even facile George was somewhat amazed at the about-face of policy in China since the Cultural Revolution. The loyal years of promoting Mao Zedong Thought required gear-shifting time. George's trip home to America helped in his adaptation.

Because we are both physicians, I asked him what Mao's death and the changing policies would do to the Chinese medical care system. What would be kept and what would be lost?

He gave both a personal and a political response. He believed that emphasis on serving the people was incompatible with such things as a fee-for-service and having prestige or status, values which he believes characterize western medicine. He said that there were many dedicated people in medicine in China, but he attributes the success of the approach in the People's Republic of China to the dedication to the concept of serving the people. I asked him if the new direction of China, rewarding intellectual and productive ability, would not rapidly wipe away the essence of Mao's message. Even if the sloganeering continued, would not the reality be lost? George said that he believed that the real merits of the Cultural Revolution should not be overlooked. In his travels he had quickly realized that many Americans were assuming that the ending of the Cultural Revolution by the new government was evidence that the whole ten-year experience was a great mistake. He said the Chinese leaders were reasonably accurate in identifying seventy percent of the Cultural Revolution as having a lasting, successful value, and thirty percent as having been misguided or destructive. Some felt the figure should be eighty percent and twenty percent.

I interrupted and said that some senior spokesmen were calling the Cultural Revolution a lost and wasted decade. George shrugged and said that obviously it would depend upon one's personal experience, but overall, the lasting benefits were major: the establishment of medical care for everyone, the bringing together of traditional and western medicine, the new awareness that city people and the intellectuals had for the problems of the peasants, and above all, the penetration of the moral precept that one must serve the people into every walk of Chinese life. He felt that this moral indoctrination was Mao's contribution to China and perhaps to the world.[6]

Even later as the Chinese government more thoroughly criticized Mao and the Cultural Revolution, George, Rewi, and Hans were far more positive about his great contributions and continued to have a concern that the good gained from Mao's last great effort should not be totally lost.

13

"DIGGING TUNNELS DEEP"

W HEN Ed Snow returned to China in 1960 he noted a complete absence of underground bomb shelters. Later, with Russian friendship turning to hostility and American air-power pouring on Vietnam and Cambodia, the Chinese saw logic in underground protection. By 1972 there was evidence of substantial tunneling at schools, factories, and in the cities. How extensive this actually was I don't know. I was told that all cities had completed their underground security system which included final access to the suburbs at the periphery of the tunnels, making it possible to empty the cities in a matter of minutes.

I saw many evidences of this construction, but was down in the system only once, in Beijing, below the area near the Beijing Duck Restaurant. I gather from what others have written that this particular site, entered through an opening to the left of the door in a store where the floor slid back, was shown frequently to foreign visitors. What I saw was impressive. But whether this was just a model or was a part of a completed network, I do not know. The Chinese certainly wanted to convey the message that the system was complete and an integral part of their national defense system. Chairman Mao's admonition was quoted frequently: "Dig tunnels deep, store grain, resist all hegemony." Most of us understood about the tunnels and grain, but had to head for the dictionary for the meaning and pronunciation of hegemony. It is a perfectly good word, but is not in the daily American vocabulary.

When learned economists define the gross national product of a nation, I wonder where the remarkable effort involved in building such tunnels would appear in the equation. If one assumes the underground system of China for the 100 to 200 million city dwellers is complete, it is impressive (even if one is wrong by half) to reflect on the man-hours of digging, shoring up, hauling away of dirt, making and pouring concrete, making and laying bricks, stringing electric wires, digging wells . . . all of this done after work hours by the general public. Where does this subterranean, massive effort appear in terms of GNP? Product it is, and in its own way it is as much a part of a national defense effort as building bombers. It is this reservoir of China's national energy which will have a major effect on the world's economy when it is given machines. Equally, it will have an effect on international science and technology as this talent is retrieved from tunnel digging and put into laboratories and sports as their youths enter international competition for the first time.

When George came to Kansas City we surprised him by *our* underground system; in fact, most people are challenged by the thought that Kansas City has the dimensions of several hundred football fields of underground excavation. These areas are so large that whole trains can enter them. Semi-trucks load and unload, winter or summer, in dry, cool, limestone caves. The caves are all man-made and represent a century of carving out limestone for cement and rock. There are no wood or steel supports to hold the sides and roof; instead, huge columns of limestone, forty feet on a side, are saved during the excavation. The ceiling, floors, walls, and columns are of undisturbed stone. With lighting, there is a natural glow from the hewn, white walls, and the black space quickly becomes livable.

We took George to one of these all-weather bomb shelters, and he was almost speechless. I told him that Kansas City was digging deep, storing grain, and resisting hegemony. Our escort was Professor Truman Stauffer, a geologist who has made these underground spaces his special interest. He led us from our home to the entrance of one caved area. The entrance is so large, so well lighted, and fitted out with carpets, lamps, walls, and drapes, that one has no awareness that all this is a building within a cave. George said he was impressed, but there was no evidence of stored supplies and the area would therefore be useless as a sanctuary for the people in case of a bombing. I assured him the wants of man could be met; we then walked through a small part of the huge area. Importers store their inventory here, and the products are international: Italian wines, Scotch whiskey, Japanese sake, German beer. Not exactly stored grain, but a beginning.

We walked on and passed rattan furniture from the Philippines, canned hams from Denmark, dishes, clothing, tableware, furniture. In the adjacent caves were at least 1,000 automobiles and thousands of boxes of canned food, including catsup and dog food. Separate caves have been refrigerated below freezing, and several hundred boxcar loads of produce stored.

George was impressed. The caves were one of the utilitarian, unexpected experiences of his trip. We drove back to our home and on the way I asked the logical question, "What do you think of your native country? You have been away fifty years, you left in the Depression, what are your impressions?" I was asking this question because I had found the George of Beijing always ready to find fault with the social system in the United States and his anticipation of an incipient revolution in the United States a little unrealistic. Now that he had had a good tour of his old country, what did he think? I wanted to ask if he were not amazed, even proud of his roots, but I held back and waited for his response.

He acknowledged the question and first commented that he was astonished at the airports and the amount of air travel. He continued and identified Washington as a beautiful city, the advantages of the multitude of places to eat, and the number of automobiles. He thought we were wasteful in our use of automobiles, and that we had given away too much land to parking lots. He admired the highways. He found it very encouraging to see the number of blacks who were well-employed. He had not realized how much had changed in their integration. He enjoyed our supermarkets, as did Sufei. He said it was obvious that Americans were very rich and should be, in view of their use of energy. He thought the United States had too many expensive gadgets. Just at this point in his remarks we arrived home in our air-conditioned car, ran up the automatic garage door, turned off the electronic security system, stepped into our air-conditioned home . . . I wondered what parts of industrial America he was referring to as unnecessary?

I asked him if the modernization of China would make many of these things happen there. He shook his head and hoped yes and hoped no. So much of what we had was not necessary for China, yet equally so much was essential. How could China choose the right balance? He felt that industrialization of China would be accomplished, but it would be done Chinese-style and the industrial revolution of the West would be softened by Chinese custom.

He and Sufei went to their apartment across our courtyard and came back at once with a gift. This was a wood-block print, recently done, picturing George at his clinic desk, writing a prescription for a mother and child. The artist had exactly captured the man: heavy eyebrows, dark eyes, silver hair, a kind, big smile. The gift could not have been more appropriate.

This reminded my wife that an Independence, Missouri doctor had called and identified himself as having know Hatem at Yanan. The doctor had some wood-block prints from the Yanan days. Would George want to see them? The physician, Dr. Dillard M. Eubank, had been with the American medical teams sent to Yanan to care for American aviators who might be forced to land in the Communist area after a bomb run against the Japanese. George and Dr. Eubank met and the wood-cuts, rare souvenirs of the Yanan experience, were offered as a gift to George.

Dr. Eubank was but one of a series of persons who had been in the Chinese soviet in the 1940s and who wanted to renew their contact with George. Margaret Stanley, a nurse with the American Friends' medical team, sent color pictures of George, a lean, handsome man in a makeshift uniform, taken with the team in 1945.

Later that day we went out to the University of Missouri-Kansas City Library to browse through the substantial Edgar Snow Memorial Collection. This is a collection of Snow's literary production, not only his books in their various editions and languages, but also his magazine articles for the *Saturday Evening Post*. George immediately spied the famous picture of Mao as a man of forty-two, wearing a military cap with the red star. George described the setting of the picture and told us that Ed had to persuade Mao to put on a cap, could not find one, and therefore gave Mao his own to wear for the picture. Ed had forgotten this completely, and George had to remind him of it when they met in 1960. George commented that Mao did not like to wear a hat, and in fact, in those days, was a little famous for his shaggy hair and casual attention to dress. The cap was needed to give him a touch of command style. (Lois Snow gave this now-famous hat to the Chinese National Museum in Beijing.)

That night we were the guests of Dr. William and Frankie Wu at a Chinese restaurant in Kansas City. The Wus, with us, had been hosts when the first delegation of Chinese physicians had come to the United States in 1972. At that time, many American-Chinese were unsure where to stand in the issues dividing mainland China and Taiwan. The Wus had felt no indecision, realizing that one China was best, but two Chinas were not impossible.

On this evening seven years later, the members of our dinner party were now at ease with the fact that Taiwan was a Chinese problem and the solution must be Chinese. There was one Chinese woman at the dinner whose story I wanted to hear in detail. She had lived in Beijing her entire life and had now just arrived with a permanent visa to live in the United States. The lady was pleasant, spoke excellent English, and very readily told me that when she had asked the Chinese authorities permission to leave China, it was given, and here she was. That was the story. All of my questions died before her calm discretion. I will never know her opinion on the Cultural Revolution and Lin Biao. I felt that I was back in Beijing, asking questions and getting no answers. The ultimate example for me of this inscrutable ability to avoid a direct answer occurred when I asked a Chinese physician in early 1976 what would happen to the leadership in China when Chairman Mao died. After several minor evasions, his answer came: "Well, perhaps the Chairman will never die." Such a response stops an interrogation.

Although George could not show his full enthusiasm for the United States, it was apparent that the whole adventure had been impressive, not only because of the wealth and happiness of the people, but because of the genuine goodwill expressed to him. The long years in which Ed Snow had "protected George's family" by not identifying his affiliation with red China were over and George found himself an honored and respected man, a prophet with honor in his native land.

From our home the Hatems went on to Washington, back to North Carolina to his brother Joe's home, and then in October home to China, stopping to see friends in Europe. It had been a full half-year return to his roots and a happy, exhausting journey with no unpleasant "anti" movements or demonstrations. His continued feeling strong, had a good appetite, gained weight, all of which suggested that the X-ray therapy had caused a temporary remission. The whole tour had been an adventure of considerable personal magnitude. An absence of fifty years from one's family is sufficient cause for an emotional moment or two. To compound the event by fifty years as a Communist, returning from a nation not yet recognized by your native country, and adding to it the first visit of your foreign-born wife is adequate material for a film scenario. The story becomes almost improbable when the haunting issue of an unremoved tumor must also be borne.

George carried off the entire event with enthusiasm and spirit. He was easily recognized as a fully mature, intelligent, adjusted man. George Hatem, Shag, Ma Haide, Catholic, atheist, Communist, American, Lebanese, Chinese, all added up to a very complete human being.

In one conversation I told him of a letter I had received recently from certain persons signing themselves as the American Communist party. It was a piece of propaganda in which this group of people announced that they were sure that a group of capitalists and reactionaries had now seized China and had thrown out the real Communists. They, on the other hand, were going to begin actions in support of Mao's widow and the others, and were going to denounce the present new government of Hua Guofeng and Deng Xiaoping. I told George that this group were going to be active in San Francisco at the meeting of the United States-China People's Friendship Association. George, who had just come from the San Francisco meeting, denied to me any knowledge of such activity; he said it was news to him and he would appreciate it if I would give to him the letter I had received. But I had tossed it and apologized that I had no copy.

Two days later I learned that at the San Francisco meeting the American Communist group had attempted to seize the organization by manipulating parliamentary procedure, and that George was entirely aware of this activity. I bear no ill will about this, but it again reminds me that he is a committed man, which is another way of saying that much of what he does and thinks operates at a level that is undercover and not fully exposed to an acquaintance such as myself.

This active, leftist wing of ''progessives'' as they speak of themselves, is still very much alive in the United States as I write this in 1983. There is a considerable contact between them and "progessives" in China, both Chinese and foreign-born. One would call them Maoists. Hatem, Alley, and Müller are not of this group and make it clear that they have no interest in this agitation.

14

A SECOND BEGINNING

GEORGE returned to Beijing, and for a few weeks his condition remained stable. Hans got a supply of oral enzymes from Europe to replace those lost from George's sick pancreas. But nausea, weight loss, and finally, a series of stomach hemorrhages. brought George down. The doctors, his friends, family, and George himself realized that he was in the last stages of his pancreatic cancer. Finally, the hemorrhaging became uncontrollable and he hovered near unconsciousness. As a last gasp he told the surgeons to take him back to the operating room and make at least a temporary repair, if possible. His condition deteriorated to where it was necessary and right for Sufei, Rewi, and Hans to come to his bed and have a farewell moment.

Surgery was done almost as an anti-climax, for it was logical that previously identified cancer was out of control. During surgery, a large hemorrhagic area was found in the stomach. The surgeon removed two-thirds of the stomach and made a new connection to the intestine. The gall bladder was packed with gallstones. Distended and scarred, it was removed. The pancreas was examined thoroughly. The previous mass, identified as a cancer, was no longer present. The pancreas was small, shrunken by scar and by the X-ray therapy.

In the world of surgery, there are areas of complexity which should be reserved for surgeons of unusual experience and skill. George's surgeon was such a man. Wu Wei-jan had first been met by Americans as the surgeon designated for the emergency operation on James Reston's appendix in 1971. In 1972, Wu was the chairman of the delegation of physicians, the first in twenty-five years, who visited the United States.

In 1978, he was again in the United States as the personal surgeon to Deng Xiaoping.

Wu Wei-jan is surgeon of the Beijing Hospital, the German Hospital of the past, now the special, unmentioned hospital for very high-ranking members. It is often referred to as the hospital for the Central Committee. Zhou Enlai was hospitalized there. It is in the old international settlement area, south and east of the Beijing Hotel but close to the center of Beijing.

George's emergency surgery was done at this hospital by Wu Wei-jan. The operation was extremely difficult and required twelve continuous, tedious, precarious, complicated hours. There was no cancer anywhere, the hemorrhaging stomach was due to an irradiation burn from the intensive X-ray treatment. The previous mass in the pancreas was now recognized to have been inflammatory due to the obstruction from gallstones. His original problem had been pancreatitis, not cancer.

Therefore, George had been up to and half through the door of death. No cancer is more lethal than that of the pancreas. His entire experience had seemed to be terminal cancer. From the last-minute, last-ditch surgery, he gained essentially a total reprieve; at least as much as any of us ever do. Now his problem was not cancer but the damage from X-ray therapy. His stomach had to be removed for that reason and his digestion was permanently damaged, with the stomach gone and the pancreas function decreased. No longer was he the stout, filled-out, two-hundred-pounder. Never having been a really large-framed man; he again became a small man, about five feet seven inches, weighing 135 pounds, just about what he did when he went to Yanan in 1936. As Hans Müller said to me, "Even when he was heavy, George had spindly arms and legs." Now sick, he was a small, frail man.

His recovery was slow and his energy markedly lessened. His spirit was intact, and his humor in full force. Finally by November 1979, he was not only strong enough, but eager enough to renounce his fatalistic statement of a year earlier when he had said he would never again leave China. In mid-November he was in Canada at McGill University as a member of a Chinese delegation to participate in a Norman Bethune memorial seminar. He brought Sufei with him and they came on back to the United States to see his family in Buffalo, to New York City to see Sam and Helen Rosen, and back to Roanoke Falls to reverse roles.

A year before his brother Joe had come with a wheel chair to meet George at Dulles Airport; and now George, back from the Shades, was in Roanoke Falls to visit his brother who was now gravely ill with myocarditis.

George's official position in the Ministry of Health was the initial reason for his second trip to North America. Aside from this primary purpose, he was able to include a trip to see his ailing brother in North Carolina. In preparation for the McGill symposium to honor Norman Bethune's memory, he had traveled to Tan Xian in Hobei Province where Bethune had served the Chinese as a surgeon and where he had died. George gathered material there, then returned to Beijing to a Bethune ceremony at The Great Hall of the People. Later at McGill, he stepped to the podium to deliver a prepared manuscript, carefully adjusted very new, never before used glasses and found he could not see the manuscript. In his words, "My twenty-minute assigned time deteriorated as I rambled on, unable to read my paper, for fifty-six minutes. They will never invite me back."

This second journey took them home by way of Hong Kong. There George spoke before a medical group and was asked his appraisal of the status of Chinese medicine. His answer was, "In scientific medicine and medical technology we are about fifteen years behind. However, we have succeeded in establishing the best system of primary medical care in the world. I believe that is a major accomplishment. We are now moving rapidly to bring ourselves up to date in all areas."

15

ZHOU SUFEI

THE trips to the United States gave George's wife her first sustained immersion in the English language. During their marriage, George had been the one to learn Chinese so they could communicate. Bright, curious, and sensitive, she now found herself almost totally dependent upon George's availability as the link to their American friends. She needed to know English if she was not to be but a Chinese puppet doll, and she quickly learned a considerable amount. Her voice was pleasing, well-modulated, and that of a trained actress. An impressive woman: Zhou Sufei.

She of course saw the variety of color and style in the American woman's dress. Her return home coincided with the increased freedom in dress there, and when I saw her in Beijing in October 1979 she had on a handsome, well-cut pantsuit with full lapels, which was certainly not Chinese. Also the garnet pin on her blouse at her throat was almost the first jewelry I had seen in China. I may be wrong, but I believe her nails were manicured and painted with clear polish. Her hair was waved, she was a few pounds lighter, and definitely a handsome woman.

Her return to a full, personal, professional career had begun in 1977, but George's illness and near death had taken her time and energy. For months she had been in attendance at his bedside. Now in the fall of 1979, she was back full-time as a deputy director at the Beijing Film Studio. Sufei's renaissance was apparent in early October 1979, when we were guests at this film studio, which was a huge, State-owned movie-making facility in the northwest sector of Beijing. Movie-making is obviously a major device for propaganda, and was a special enthusiasm of Jiang Qing, Mao's wife.

Now there was a bit more latitude in themes, and creative talent could again be excited by the possibility of movie-making. Zhou had arranged for us to be greeted by a colleague who was introduced as "the famous movie actor, Yu Yang." Yu Yang had wide recognition in China, and later when I told Chinese friends I had met him, I found the same twitter one hears in the United States by claiming contact with a star.

Now when we met Yu Yang, he was making the transition from actor to director. His projection was warm, cordial, hardy, complete with a full smile and a considerable head of hair, an authoritative voice, and a ready wit. He was definitely a movie star, anyplace. He spoke at length about the size and scope of the Beijing Film Studio and acknowledged that he and Sufei were longtime colleagues. Then with a wry smile he said, "We were classmates in the countryside for several years." This last remark was acknowledged by Sufei with a head bow, and I suppose was another answer to my wondering as to how the Cultural Revolution had touched the Hatem life.

We spent a half-day at the Studio and at one point came on a set which was in rehearsal. A senior man was directing, and he called the entire young cast together, and with some eloquence introduced them to "China's famous actress and director, Zhou Sufei." Their faces brightened and they applauded her with a burst of enthusiasm. It was a pleasure to see Sufei recognized in her own element. All of my previous contact had stranded her in a secondary role as George's Chinese wife who could not speak English. During this entire studio visit George stayed in the background and acknowledged that he had never been there before.

One other example of the creeping capitalism that is inevitably altering Marx's theory as it is Sinified occurred when we asked the actor how his pay was determined. His first laughing response was to say "not adequately." He then surprised me by adding that the actors and directors were now having discussions with management over the question of royalties and the possibility of a percentage of the "box office." Nothing had yet been determined, but conversations were going on. A far change from the purest days of the old chairman's ambition.

George and Sufei live well. They each bring in a salary, and Yu Ma, the son, adds his income. A comfortable home, steam heat, at least two television sets, household help, a car with driver, August at the sea . . . with my own version of capitalism I have difficulty living as well as Dr. Horse's family commune.

The furnishings of George's home are western, as are Rewi's and Hans's. Each has been assimilated into China to a different degree. George, however, has married into the country, and although he remains a foreigner his children and grandchildren are Chinese. His heavy eyebrows and full nose may surface downstream from time to time, but in two generations it will be hard to find the genetic evidence of the "horse with foreign virtue." China cherishes its foreign friends, however, and just as Norman Bethune is a public hero known to all the schoolchildren, and as Edgar Snow is a "permanent friend," so will George, Rewi, and Hans have their spot in the Red sun. These very recent years have seen them all honored and made quite visible in China, perhaps as evidence of the new administration's openness to foreign experience, a major change from the years of Mao. All of them, including George's and Hans's wives, have traveled abroad extensively since Mao's death.

These trips were not Sufei's first experience outside China. In the mid-seventies she and George had been in Lebanon on an official trip for China, where they visited George's relatives. In an earlier conversation, George told me that he had not heard from his father for more than thirty years since he had left for China. In 1962 his father, then in his eighties, returned to his native land, now Lebanon. There he contacted what he thought to be the Chinese Embassy to ask for help in locating his son and learned that he had contacted the Taiwanese branch. The old man evidently was indomitable and managed to get across Syria where he did reach the People's Republic of China Embassy. There after a great deal of confusion, he attempted to describe his son, and the Chinese were highly suspicious that there was a strange attempt being made to gain false information. The old man had no idea that his son had become Ma Haide, and the Chinese Embassy in Syria didn't know him by the name George Hatem. Finally appropriate telegrams were sent to Beijing, and George was able to come to Syria in 1962 for a month-long vacation, with his wife and son, to see his father and other relatives. The Chinese put him up in a wing of the Chinese Embassy and supplied him with his own chef, servants, automobile, and chauffeur. All this led his father to be both impressed and at the same time confused at this sign of wealth in a communist. Finally, he one day whispered to George, "How much money have you got hidden away in China?!"

Later, after China had established an embassy in Lebanon in the seventies, George and Sufei returned for another visit and found that he had hundreds of relatives in Lebanon. He and the Chinese ambassador finally came to an agreement that George would invite only one-fifth of them to a banquet at the embassy, and even then there were 300 of them.

Although George has a pragmatic, nonreligious attitude toward life, he certainly never propagates this thought. His benign expression and serene attitude even suggests the well-arrived monsignor. This fatherly mien is enlivened by his natural "breeziness," as Rewi Alley defines it. But George's childhood was spent in parish schools in Buffalo, an experience which he refers to as the Father's Reform School.

At some distant point in the past, his Semitic-Arabic ancestors took on the Maronite faith. Although located in the natural arena of power of Eastern Orthodox Catholicism, this hardy group of martial mountaineers took allegiance to the Roman Catholic church and are now the most numerous religious group in modern Lebanon.

George's pride in his "Oriental" origins was epitomized when, in my home, he pulled the *Rubaiyat* of Omar Khayyam from the shelf, quickly opened to the verse which reads, "Let Zal and Rustum bluster as they will, or Hatim call to Supper—heed not you." He said he was of that Hatim family, perhaps a far reach, but nevertheless a point of pride.

Sufei was born on an island archipelago, of fisherman people, just southeast of Shanghai. She had come to Shanghai at an early age, and had become a prominent actress, definitely a national figure, before the Japanese invasion. In 1939 she came through Haiphong, Hanoi, by truck to Kunming, as did Hans Müller, on to Yanan. Rewi had volunteered that in 1966 Sufei had been arrested. The Red Guards had scaled the wall at George's house, had ransacked it, and had thrown their belongings into the street. Sufei's release from prison was accomplished by Zhou Enlai's personal intervention. One can well imagine the cautious but urgent message going out to Soong Chingling, asking for her help.

I asked Rewi if now, with different circumstances in the Chinese government, George would reconsider writing his memoirs. Rewi said he did not feel George was quite yet ready to tell his story, but believed he was getting more interested. At Beidaihe, in the summer of 1979, two women journalists who had been "rehabilitated" tried to interview him, but they were unsuccessful. They had followed him to Beijing and had some success getting a story out of him; George had sat down and put together 1,000 words for them. In 1981, CBS was in Beijing, interviewing George. Also, in 1981, several articles appeared in the Chinese press, about and by George. In one of these, a eulogy to Soong Chingling, Hatem made direct reference to how he had first become involved in what was to become his life's commitment. "In the spring of 1936, I received a letter from Soong Chingling asking me to go over to her home. The moment I stepped into her sitting room she greeted me with the following words: 'Good news for you. Your wishes will soon be fulfilled. The Party Central Committee has invited an American journalist and an American doctor to northern Shaanxi to inspect the situation and to learn about the Communist Party's advocation for resisting Japan. You are to take Edgar Snow with you.' I was very glad for I had applied to go to the Chinese communist area."[1]

This would seem to be the clear, definitive statement which expressly describes Hatem as taking Edgar Snow with him. As in many things in life, two observers see the same event differently. Snow wrote his version of who did what on that clandestine mission. ". . . I went to Sian and put up at the Guest House, where I was told to expect a call from a certain 'Pastor Wang' . . . Soon after my arrival George Hatem introduced himself and told me that he was aware of my mission; he was also waiting for a call from Pastor Wang."[2]

There is also a nuance of disagreement as to whether George had a British five-pound torn-in-half note given him by Soong Chingling that acted as their identification, or whether Ed did have a cryptogram written in invisible ink prepared for him by the Peking underground. I turned to Helen Foster Snow, Ed's first wife, as a reliable witness and she was adamant, "Possibly Hatem never told Ed about the torn bank-note, nor would Ed have even mentioned to him his secret letter. This would have been idiotic. All such things would be secret; it was dangerous to talk at all. Each one had his own arrangement to be made. It was entirely

Ed's idea . . . to get the facts because the time was so desperate and dangerous for the Chinese.''

Rewi added that a lost part of George's career, one which George never identified, had taken place when he was assigned by the Communists to the Marshall Mission. In those early years at the end of the Second World War, the American government attempted a variety of diplomatic moves in an effort to resolve the conflict between the Chiang K'ai-shek government and the Communists. Involved in these missions were General George Marshall and Ambassador Patrick Hurley. At the same time the United Nations Relief and Rehabilitation Administration was formed (UNRRA), along with the Chinese Liberated Areas Relief Administration (CLARA). George was sent to Peking to be the spokesman for the Communists and for the first time resurfaced as "George Hatem" since he had entered the Communist areas in 1936. Now George moved into the first floor of the Peking Hotel in order to be near his task. Rewi also said that George went to Shanghai at that time when the message got out that Chiang K'ai-shek was about to authorize the breaking of the levees of the Yellow River to slow the Japanese. George felt there was insufficient warning of the Chinese peasants as to their risks from the flooding, and he went to Shanghai to persuade the newspapers to spread the message.

One evening we were guests at a small informal dinner at the apartment of Professor Wu Yingkai. His apartment is in the original living quarters of the Peking Union Medical College. George was there and I told him I had written a book about him and wanted him to know about it, but that I was not asking his opinion or endorsement. He saw the logic in this approach, raised his hands, palms up, and said, "I guess you are not open to persuasion.'' That was his only comment.

Later in the evening at Wu Ying-k'ai's he volunteered that in the summer of 1939 he had treated Zhou Enlai for a compound and comminuted fracture of the right arm, suffered when Zhou had fallen from his horse in a riverbed. At that time and in those circumstances, they had not been able to get a perfect repair, and Zhou had a permanent limitation to the movement of his right elbow. In all the formal group pictures taken in the Great Hall of the People, one notes Zhou's angled, wrongly-bent, right arm.

George asked if I had ever heard about the time he was sent to Xiling

(Hsiling) to examine the Panchen Lama, who was ill with an unexplained fever and skin problem. George said it stymied everyone until he used a tongue blade and flashlight, and on the inside of the Panchen Lama's cheeks were small telltale spots, called Koplik spots, diagnostic of the measles. The Panchen Lama, saint or not, was a young boy with the measles.

During that same dinner, Professor Wu Yingkai served, with some pride, a port wine he had had for some years. I would like to know where it waited out the Cultural Revolution. It was quite good, but poor George had to deny himself a sip. He has no tolerance for alcohol since gastric surgery and rearrangement of his digestive tract. Helen Rosen was at the dinner also, and she asked George if he had ever liked alcohol. He looked at her with some sadness. "Oh my, and how! When I was younger, I would drink anything. I loved to drink. Even the Kumass, the fermented mare's milk of the Mongols. When we were at Yanan we used to make some awful stuff, but it was alcohol. Miss it! And how!" George spoke with enthusiasm and his wife lowered her eyes, demurely, and with discretion.

Zhou Sufei and Shafik George Hatem are partners in a considerable love story. Yanan, the war against the Japanese, Liberation, the rehabilitation of China, the Cultural Revolution, acting, directing, doctoring, raising a family, an earthquake, the cancer, the return to the United States and through it all sustaining love and respect sufficient to bridge two cultures. The House of Ma has strong foundations.

In February 1982 Sufei wrote an article, "I Took up My Challenge," which was published in the February issue of *Women of China*. In this article she tells that she was born into an intellectual family, that her father studied civil engineering abroad, how she had refused to live under the Japanese when they invaded China, and had, therefore, at the age of seventeen gone to the interior and joined the resistance activities organized by the Communist party.

In this brief article she also tells of her love affair with the young American, how she was advised to avoid romance with a foreigner, and how she "took up my challenge and decided to ignore the well-intentioned advice from my comrades." Of their romance she writes: "Under a star-studded sky, we walked along the bank of the Yanhe River. He expressed his love for me, then told me about his family background as was the custom. He told me he had failed twice in love and it was all because he was a foreigner. I told him about the debate that went through my mind and came out with 'I love you, too.' "

With the approval of the Political Department of the Eighth Route Army, they were married on March 3, 1940. Sufei concludes: "All that was forty years ago. Ma Haide and I have all along remained in China. Over the years, we have kept the companionship of the Yanan days alive."

16

TRUE SCHOLARSHIP

THE American scientist-physician, Arnold Katz,[1] was with me in one of our talk sessions with George in 1973. The influence of the Cultural Revolution and Mao's full power were still the message. We asked George to meet with us and discuss the future of science in China. Arnold Katz led off with this remark to George: "One of the things that worries me about China, now . . . in the present context, what is the place of the true scholarship? Academic, intellectual scholarship? I speak of the true basic sciences, the non-goal oriented work. The man who is left alone to work because he enjoys working on a problem in the hopes that some benefit will come of it. The nonpractical endeavor even, let us say."

George replied with a nod, and said: "I think the closest thing to an official policy is the way it is stated for the medical services. The problems we face are outlined . . . the most prevalent diseases, the infectious diseases, parasitic diseases and so forth . . . we must handle first. Your research must be oriented towards these most immediate problems—and a few people must carry on research on the borders of these immediate problems."

Arnie Katz then asked, "Are these few people given the tranquility, the freedom from pressure, to carry out creative research? This is the chief ingredient of creative research. Technological research is easy. The principles have been worked out. Like the Manhattan Project in the Second World War—the Einsteins, the Fermis worked out the fact that it could be done, and then it was a matter of making enough P-235 or whatever, P-238, to make the bombs blow up. That's done by groups.

But it is the really creative stuff. . . . the guy sitting there doing nothing useful for twenty years, maybe for his whole lifetime, but every now and then somebody comes out with something vital to all mankind . . . Is this kind of research being supported at all now?''

George replied, ''There are two aspects to that question. One is how do you 'organize' research and still make room for the oddball. This is a problem that must be worked out in a more adequate way in China. The priorities are so imperative at present, and the scale of our research people in the amounts needed is so small, that we can't afford to have many people sit there for twenty years doing nothing. There is no philosophical, practical, legal or regulatory reason to prevent people from doing this, but there is no encouragement at all at the present. It is incorrect for me to say that there is 'no encouragement at all', because all of our sections of the Academia Sinica, all of the mathematicians as far as I understand . . . they sit around and play with all the stuff without immediate practicality, in relation to our problems. I would like to have your ideas on how to find these people. How much of the population can you afford to tell to take twenty years and go ahead and do your own thing? What are the factors to use to pick out these jewels? China will definitely have, in the not very distant future, a great body of that kind of work and talent. I know I've said this, perhaps too often, but the first order of business when we took over China was to solve the question of the survival of the people. We went about solving these problems with definitive programs, and I described what we did in what were relatively small areas compared to the whole . . . venereal disease, prostitution, drugs. The very large issues in health, however, are the fundamental ones in all of the world's poor, underdeveloped countries. I do not criticize our lack of basic research in medical science or our lack of elegant equipment in our hospitals. It is a matter of priorities.

''Not to be unkind but to keep you on your toes,'' George said with a gentle, understanding smile, ''I understand that the real health problems in the United States now are related to highway deaths, murder, narcotics, alcohol, and, perhaps, pollution. I've even heard that child abuse is a recurrent cause of death. I have of course wondered why you continued only to build your great medical centers, rather than solve your problems.

"Also, as I have read of the American efforts in medical educatiion overseas, I know you continue to plan programs that create specialists which the overseas country cannot use. I read someplace that there are thousands of Philippine doctors settling in the States, yet I know that the rural health problems of the Philippines are immense.

"Here in China, as in all poor countries, the true beginning of good health is with the basics: nutrition, pure water, sanitation, vaccinations. We made those our targets and essentially we have solved those problems. Perhaps we have neglected coronary bypass surgery, you would say?'' One of the listeners was Don Effler, an American surgeon of bypass fame, but with enough judgment to listen and not debate.

"Well, perhaps we have, but our policy has been one of not only totally mobilizing all physicians, but also curbing our expenses in those areas with marginal yield. Even our own medical facilities and large city hospitals did not fully appreciate the significance of the word 'priority'. In fact, because of their desire to concentrate on their specialities, the physicians were made a special target for reeducation at the beginning of the Cultural Revolution. And it was drastic reeducation. The government closed all the medical schools and directed that they be reopened only when new curricula were worked out that would decrease the time in school. Our schools were following the full eight-year plan, just as if we had all the time in the world. With practically no physicians settling down in the rural areas where ninety percent of the people lived, the government simply could not wait for medical help. You know the details of how we now rotate hospital staffs to the countryside, and how we have encouraged the full use of the traditional doctor. The traditional doctor had been declared taboo by our western-styled facilities and our overseas advisors prior to the revolution. You know that we have made a major effort to get medical-aid workers available everywhere. You are now discovering them in the United States, and with enthusiasm creating physicians' assistants. What you call them is not too important. Our term here is barefoot doctor, but the same kind of first-line medical help is in the factories and in the neighborhoods of cities. I think they are called something that translates like 'factory-worker doctor' and 'health lane doctor', but regardless of the label the real idea is that most things that happen to people: colds, itch, cough, can be solved by very simple remedies and not much skill. The 'heavy' training of real doctors to do plain old general practice is not our intent.

"When I was listing the health problems of developing countries, perhaps I should have mentioned birth control. I realize that that can be a touchy subject. But one does not solve mankind's health problems if one does not think of the fixed size of the earth and the resources on it. We have used the same mass-line, mass-education, mass-discussion approach, and we have endorsement from most of our people that two children make an ideal family. Now don't translate that into my claiming that we have totally achieved that goal," George cautioned, with a raised hand.

"In rural areas progess is slower. Also, among minority groups who are very limited in numbers, we have never tried to persuade them about the merits of birth control. We have tried to make it a national policy to strengthen the internal pride of the minority populations. If at the same time that you are extolling their merits you tell them that they must not increase in numbers, and you, the Han people, are very, very numerous, then you are not likely to gain any level of confidence with minority people.

"To get back to basic research. China will very soon make major moves in those areas now that we have achieved our intial goals, and now that we believe we have an effective health care system.

"Frankly, I see no fault nor criticism if all poor nations solve their basic health problems *first*. What is wrong with recognizing basic science knowledge as 'world property'? Why should not the rich, developed nations carry on most of the basic research? In a sense they owe it to the rest of the world—because the only reason they are rich, or at least one of the reasons, is that they have grown rich by using a larger percentage of world resources. A developed nation is simply a nation that got ahead more quickly. It should carry the cost of basic research.

"China has no mental block or edict against 'creative thinking'. The records, not only the historical records of China but the achievements of Chinese workers overseas, certainly indicate the ability is present in the Chinese. Now that our initial obligations to the people, to the peasants, and to the factory-workers, are essentially solved, I can assure you there will be intense concentration on basic research. Never underestimate the pride of the Chinese. They are very patient, but they are also anxious to take their historical place as an able people.

"One last comment: Many of my American friends come here and assume that the real answer is for us to send our young talent to Harvard or some other such place. That is very unlikely to happen. The Chinese will certainly send delegations to observe and to exchange information. We will send our mature workers. But China is not likely again to send considerable numbers of college-age students to the West. Intellectual barriers won't be created; however, don't forget that phrase about 'standing on your own two feet'. I can predict that that will be a very tenacious concept here in New China.''

By 1983, there were Chinese scholars at Harvard, Yale, Massachusetts Institute of Technology, University of California-Berkeley, Stanford, and even the University of Missouri-Kansas City. They are of all ages and number in the hundreds. The speed of change after the end of the Cultural Revolution impressed even old-timers George and Hans Müller. Hans wrote me, "Everybody is trying to get to the States to study!''

One of the major reasons for optimism regarding United States-China relationships is the freedom with which Chinese citizens are coming and going from the United States. Scholars of all ages, delegations, actors, athletes, and musicians have not only been well-received by Americans but there is a remarkable degree of free egress from China. This can only be considered as a positive benefit for the future and one regrets that the United States and Russia have never been able to find a similar intellectual good fellowship.

Many of my medical colleagues both here and in China would be surprised to know that Mao had, indirectly, been associated with Yale. At their Yale-in-China campus in Changsha, Mao had an active, though brief chapter. A collector's item, at least in terms of the editor's later career, is the *New Hunan Yale-in-China Medical School Newspaper of 1919*. The last seven of its ten issues were *edited* by Mao Zedong.[2] I wonder how many good Yalies know that such a successful editor was in their ranks in China.

One can enjoy such a wide range of conversation with George that it is easy to forget that he is a very informed dermatologist, backed by a life-experience with the skin problems of the world's largest population.

His huge knowledge about venereal disease and associated social problems is an additional facet, as well as his knowledge acquired in the national program to suppress leprosy. George is not only an experienced skin doctor, but has a warmth, sincerity, and honesty that makes him an outstanding physician, unconfined to problems of the skin. He is a true and dedicated healer in the finest sense of the word.

Others have noted this steady essence of physicianhood. "In Peking, George worked in the Skin and Venereal Disease Research Institute and seemed to spend the rest of his time solving other people's problems. He was everybody's friend, everybody came to him with their troubles. If there hadn't been the phrase 'Let George do it', we would have had to invent it. He would listen carefully, thoughtfully, to what you had to say, then offer some suggestion that suddenly made the whole thing obvious and simple, and usually with a quip that tickled you into a grin . . . He's the world's greatest calmer-downer."[3]

I have never practiced medicine with George, but have repeatedly been aware of his wide range of knowledge of medical literature and his sound, calm judgment. I judge him to be an exceptional physician. In 1972 he and I saw acupuncture as practiced in a commune. I asked him what he thought about it and he said frankly he knew nothing about it, but felt it deserved study. This was not a guarded reply, but the honest answer of a western-trained physician.

17

THE RETURN OF DENG XIAOPING

I HAD just returned to China the night before. In the United States, I had followed the series of events of the past year, 1976. In a nine-month period, the three leaders of China's revolution had died: Zhou Enlai, Zhu De, Mao Zedong. An earthquake of massive devastation had occurred in the midst of this loss in leaders. And now, there suddenly was a Gang of Four upon whom to blame everything.

George was away at the seashore on vacation, with Rewi. I was to join them later, but now I was in Beijing visiting hospitals, and filled with curiosity and questions. I had been awakened early by firecrackers. Something was happening, and yet there was no change in my schedule. My colleague came to the hotel for me at 8:30 A.M. We were in the familiar Chinese-made, gray color, four-door sedan, with silk curtains on the rear windows and the driver wearing gloves and pushing too hard as we headed out into the morning traffic. Our horn was never quiet; I would dearly have loved to tell the driver to take it easy and ease up on the horn. However, this would have accomplished little, as all other sedans were clearing a path by the same heavy-handed noise.

This main avenue of Beijing was overwhelmingly crowded, in part by the streaming of bicycles, trams, trucks, buses, and chauffered cars which makes even the ten lanes of Chang An Jie congested, but the animation of the usual traffic was compounded by organized groups walking four and eight abreast, each group led by a great eight-feet-in-diameter, red lacquered Chinese drum. The drums were usually on a wheeled chassis and pulled by men; some were on truck beds. With each drum stood two men with large wooden mallets or felt-wrapped pieces the size of baseball bats, beating a deep, resonant throb. One's feet sensed the vibration thrust into the earth from the massive instruments. The war drums of Genghis Khan must have been their direct ancestors. The groups walked in an orderly fashion, but not in military cadence. The first rank of each group, and the groups varied from a hundred to a thousand, carried large painted banners tied between two bamboo poles. The banners identified the groups: school teachers from a certain district, workers from a cotton factory, representatives of a union, of the firemen, of an institute. My host told me we were watching the beginning of a three-day celebration to honor the accomplishments of the Eleventh National Congress of the Communist party.

Suddenly our Chinese friend turned to me and with a huge smile exclaimed, "Look at my face! You have never seen me smile like this. Listen to me laugh!" He then gave a resounding, "Ho, Ho, Ho!" and said, "All of us in our hearts feel free. I can truly laugh and the people are parading because they are happy. The real reason we are all happy is Deng Xiaoping is back! We now know we are safe."

I was not prepared for this unusual effusion from a Chinese man. A constant reserve is usually present, although wit, retorts, and joking are certainly a steady, daily pleasure. My own experience with the steady Chinese "reserve" has been during the years of the Cultural Revolution, compounded by the long years of nonrecognition of China by the United States. However, I have had a multitude of other contacts, socially and professionally, with Chinese physicians and collegues over a thirty-year period in the United States and in Taiwan, and the qualities of dignity and reserve persist. The influence of the Cultural Revolution produced another kind of reserve, however. There had been a constant guardedness and carefulness of remarks and actions. My friend with his sudden revelation of happiness was trying to break out of this sadness and depression that I had seen from 1971 through 1976.

A few days later I was received at a major hospital and we gathered for the usual briefing and tea. The hospital was again under the control of its physician-director. The party indoctrinator and the army man, constant factors in 1971, 1972, 1973, were now gone. I began to enjoy myself because I anticipated a good, open, give-and-take conversation. The senior clinician present leaned forward across the table, slowly ground out his cigarette, and in a quite animated voice, with gestures, began a fifteen-minute speech. Speech it was. There was not one spontaneous word. He gave a well-rehearsed presentation extolling Mao Zedong Thought: the rich treasure house of traditional medicine, the need to serve the people, the obligation of the hospital to the proletariat. He concluded with scathing remarks about the awfulness of the Gang of Four and how they had undermined the efforts of Chairman Mao. He smothered me with generalities, dogma, and "gang of fourisms."

In the automobile, upon leaving the hospital, I said to an English-speaking physician that I had initially been very disappointed that this distinguished physician was unable to take off his coat of caution and could not feel able to speak with his own mind, and not parrot the party line. "But," I went on and suggested, "if I had been through the Let One Hundred Flowers Bloom experience[1], the Great Leap Forward, and the attacks that were made repeatedly against physicians in this ten-year Cultural Revolution, I think I would know that it is better to play it safe and not rise to this new bait. I would keep my veil on, hide behind the right words, and wait until it was clear who was running the country."

My Chinese friend rested his hand on my knee and almost whispered, "Dr. Dimond, you are not a cardiologist. You are a psychiatrist . . . you have actually begun to understand the Chinese mind. Yes, you are right. We all hope that the new announced policies will be the new course, but any wise person simply hides his own feelings and speaks publicly only through phrases we have read in the paper, or heard on the radio as the authorized words."

This seemed too good a conversation to allow to end and I pushed my luck a step further. "Doctor, I must admit that I find the method of blaming all problems of the past ten years on the Gang of Four a little hard to accept. In the beginning of the Cultural Revolution there was certainly a Gang of One, Chairman Mao. If we agree that he became old and lost some degree of control, don't all of you, in your own mind, know he was a fundamental member of the Gang of Four? How can you all, nationwide, so enthusiastically separate the chairman himself from the problems of the Cultural Revolution? How can you do that surgery?"

My colleague hesitated, cleared his throat, and replied, "You see, the Chairman is truly respected by all of us. We know that he was the leader that pulled China back together and made us again strong. We all want him to be protected, we want him separated from the others. It may require microsurgery, but it will be done; very, very delicate microsurgery!''

This was a considerable bit of progress in our conversation and I took another charge. ''So perhaps most people knew it was a Gang of Five?''

My colleague looked at me, very innocently, and replied, ''Could we say a Gang of Four and a half?''

He went on. ''You see, in spite of the bad experiences most university people have been through, we all do know that for China, the chairman and communism have been a good thing. We above all are held together by patriotism for China and for the Chinese people. The Communist party could not remain in power if the people did not want it. We have suffered from some of the excesses of the party, but even at the worst point we have been held together in our loyalty to our families and to the rebuilding of China. If the party had not sensed the need to turn away from the Cultural Revolution, gang of fourisms, I believe the people would have turned away from the party.''

I thanked him and said I liked the term ''microsurgery;'' it answered my question. This conversation was in the summer of 1977 and a year later when I was again in China I found the caution of a year earlier markedly lessened. This was apparent in several ways. For example, in Guangzhou a large medical audience voluntarily separated itself into two groups: those who would need translation of our English—and a group of thirty physicians who not only spoke English quite well, but more significantly, had no hesitation in demonstrating it. This may seem a very small degree of change, but in my four previous visits to Guangzhou it had been practically impossible to find a physician who professed an English-language ability.

Again, a professor, speaking beautiful English, acknowledged readily how pleasant had been his years of training in the United States. In fact he asked me if I remembered a song, ''Oh, I'm Pop-Eye the Sailor Man. I eats my spinach from a can.'' He had the tune exactly right, and when I assured him that his memory was working well, he next asked if Olive Oyl was still Pop-Eye's girl friend. This exchange is trivial, I know, but in the setting that it happened and with the memory of previous barriers, it was a clear, brilliant moment of the best of human communication.

In my visit in the fall of 1978, the new message of the government was being not only heard, but believed. Acquaintances I had known since 1971 were shedding their protective reserve. Constantly I heard of the individual's anticipation of an opportunity to study abroad. Reprints were requested. Informal, personal conversations were enjoyed. I could not keep from reflecting on the night of my first arrival in Beijing with Dr. Paul D. White, in September 1971. We had all gathered in a receiving room at the Beijing Airport and after a pause for manners and tea, Dr. White spoke out to say how delighted he was to be in China, and how he was looking forward to having graduate students from China once more at Massachusetts General Hospital. This heartfelt invitation was received by a long, cold pause. Finally, the military-clad member murmured that such was not possible. Now in 1978, the cordial original objective of Dr. White is the national message of the Chinese: "We are looking for places to send our scholars. We welcome advice and help." Paul White was not premature; it simply took seven years for the message to reach the right ears.

However, such an about-face in policy leaves one insecure. Is this a solid policy, backed by the necessary power, or is there still an undercurrent of hidden contesting? How can a creation as overwhelming as the Cultural Revolution be turned-off and set aside? There must be millions of people who thoroughly believed and fought for this great effort led by the chairman. My second insecurity is for those teachers, doctors, professors, and administrators whom I now find almost intoxicated with their new stature. Will they go too far? Will their enthusiasm for their new opportunities, raised from the "stinking ninth," carry them so far that the peasant roots of the Communist party demand a rectification? Will there be a clipping of their flowering, as followed another effort of the chairman: "Let a Hundred Flowers Bloom"?

I asked a Chinese professor these questions and the quickness and assuredness of his answers were impressive. He did not hesitate to speak out. I initially asked if the provinces had remained steady during the turnabout period when the Chairman's wife had been eliminated from the contest. He replied, "One heard that Sichuan was unpredictable, but I am convinced it is now stable, totally. Recently Xinjiang had a replacement of its top leader because he was not considered reliable by the new government. In Shanghai, the home base of those supporting Jiang Qing [Mao's wife], the change in leadership had been immediate and total at the top level. This was one reason there had been no uprisings in Shanghai, but the real reason was the people were totally behind the change. The public was fed up with the program of the government and Mao's wife was beginning to be the primary target of complaints even before the Gang of Four was officially designated.

"There is real risk in our new schooling system because we are putting an overemphasis on grades. We professors are going to be very vulnerable as we get caught in our self-congratulatory elitism. There is strong risk of hostility from the peasants.

"The problem is still one of transition. Deng Xiaoping gives us that security now, and he is trusted by the people because they loved and trusted Zhou Enlai. The effectiveness of the Chinese Communist government in the beginning was due to Zhou Enlai. It was Zhou who had the faith of the people and not Mao. Hua Guofeng now has an opportunity to prove himself, but the time is critical in which he must do it. Sending him overseas was an excellent way of making him aware of the world. This was one of the flaws in Mao as head of China. He had no idea what the rest of the world was really like."

The fact that the central government only means to allow this second flowering to go so far was spelled out in an article by Huang Zhen. Huang Zhen had been the initial ambassador from China sent to the PRC Liaison Office in Wahington, D.C. He is a man of major world experience and a painter of considerable and honored skill. Upon returning to China from Washington, he became minister of culture. In the late spring of 1978 he published an article relating to the role of the creative and liberal arts under the new government policy. Following is an excerpt from that article.

". . . Our literature and art should depict the revolutionary struggles led by our Party over the past decades. They should portray Chairman Mao, Premier Chou, Chairman Chu Teh of the N.P.C. Standing Committee, and other proletarian revolutionaries of the older generation. There should be works reflecting China's socialist revolution and construction, especially the fight for socialist modernization; there should also be works which portray worker-peasant-soldier heroes and outstanding people of today in the fields of science, culture, and education, and works depicting the people's heroic struggles to transform nature and society in past history . . .

"Writers and artists, the same as intellectuals on other fronts, are mental labourers serving socialism. The overwhelming majority of them constitute a force to be relied upon in developing a new socialist culture. Their work should be respected, their achievements commended. Going deep among workers, peasants and soldiers, studying Marxism-Leninism-Mao Tse-Tung Thought and remoulding one's world outlook are all fundamental for building a force of proletarian workers in literature and art. In the meantime, writers and artists must study hard so as to constantly improve their professional skills for the revolution . . .[2]

If one were a writer or film-maker in today's China, it would be difficult to allow one's full talent to flow. A hidden, heavy hand would help one steer into safe shoals.

The tension within Chinese society must be great, however, and Mao's (or the Gang of Four's) spartan communism is giving ground. Whether this is a definitive change or a temporary release valve is hard to judge. The clues are interesting.

A news release describing a fashion show presented by Pierre Cardin in the Great Hall of the Nationalities in Beijing (*Kansas City Star,* March 20, 1979), may be evidence of a new openness in China's policy. It also undoubtedly made quite sick those many American travelers who have admired the spartan, no-nonsense attributes of life in China.

Hair styling has come to China and this rationale for its appearance was given.

HAIR STYLE DEBATE

"Chinese women in the cities are curling their hair again, and this has led to some uplifting of eyebrows. 'Another manifestation of a bourgeois life-style', some charged. Others do not think so.

"The 'hair-do' debate is a minor one, but one of many subjects of lively discussion in Chinese cities today.

"For instance, when a woman model worker in Beijing handed in a half-length photo of herself to put up on the factory's honor roll, it sparked off quite a stir. She had permed her hair! One of her workmates said: 'We can't stick up a photo like that on our honor board. It is a sign of decadent bourgeois ideology.' Someone decided to write and ask the workers' daily, *Gongren Ribao,* what it had to say about this: *Gongren Ribao* replied in length that a comrade was judged by his or her attitude towards revolution and work, not by hair-styles or clothing. The daily further declared that the ideological consciousness of a worker was manifested mainly in the way one worked. That woman worker had been a model worker for many years, thus, a fine member of the working class. She should not be accused of being ideologically influenced by the bourgeoisie just because she permed her hair.

"The ideological confusion is a hangover from the days when Lin Biao and the 'Gang of Four' stood everything upside down. Those political tricksters had proclaimed that the poorer the country and the lower the living standard, the 'purer' was the socialism. They wanted people to live in bare austerity, like religious recluses of a bygone age. It was hypocritical, because the life-styles of Lin Biao and the Gang were anything but proletarian, to say the least.

"The goal of socialist revolution and construction is to raise standards of living, both materially and culturally. As production and income rise, people naturally wish to have a richer and more varied life, and this expresses itself in the way they like to do their hair and so on. What is there to reproach anyone?

"Of course, people should do a good job in their work and study, not spend all their time and energy preening and primping. But people are living better under socialism," the national workers' daily concluded.[3]

When I was in China in 1979, the Chinese academic world was feeling very secure. Freedom was a heady wine, and I was surprised by the frankness of remarks. I found myself in the strange position of defending Mao and the Cultural Revolution. To one highly placed professional in Beijing I said, "Chairman Mao was one of the great men of this century. I think everyone accepts that." My friend dropped the title chairman and replied, "Mao lived fifteen years too long. If he had died in 1956, his work would be respected." I was not prepared for this direct attack on the previously revered chairman, but found him, in different Chinese cities and by a variety of people, still the respected leader of the early years. But for the moment at least, he was reduced to human size and the frequent subject of direct citicism and even gossip.

18

REHABILITATION—CHINA STYLE

ALL of the gleanings of historical experience and diplomatic finesse must have come into play among the very inner-team of Chinese leadership upon the death of Chairman Mao. How to handle a dowager queen, a dead hero, and his unwanted program!

The new leadership was essentially in place by October 1976. The Political Bureau membership of 1977 and 1978 affirmed a return to old policies. The significant addition of Zhou Enlai's widow, Deng Yingchao in 1978, stated clearly the continued respect for Zhou. A rapid rehabilitation of senior members brought the Political Bureau back to its 1966 make-up, allowing for natural deaths. The very old guard from even before the Long March were back in charge. Hua Guofeng as chairman was the evident commitment to a younger line of succession, but the power base remained with those whose allegiances went back to 1927. Mao told Snow in 1960 that about 800 comrades were still alive who had survived the massacre of 1927, and that these 800 would run China for the foreseeable future.[1] In 1976, the 800 were only a handful but still in charge.

No time was wasted in inventing a Gang of Four and giving the Gang a remarkable list of condemnations. Many of the charges were very specific, such as interference with university-level education, but there was also a large mélange of faults including railroads not running on time, slackness in the patriotic physical fitness program, and bad manners of children toward parents.

Fortunately, Chairman Mao had recorded a useful comment concerning his own impression of the Cultural Revolution. He had appraised his results as seventy percent good, and thirty percent bad. This equation provided the new inner-team with their opening wedge, and with every evidence of external calm and reverence they extricated the chairman from the morass of the Cultural Revolution, credited him with the meritorious seventy percent, blasted the other Four during a two-year period of continuous criticism, identified his Thought as their ideal resource and embalmed and placed him in a marble hall to dwell in splendor.

No crude Russian tactic of eliminating the one cohesive force, the banner under which they could unite: Mao Zedong Thought. No overt "de-Stalinization." No shooting; instead, a secure house arrest. It is better to have alive someone who may still have usefulness. The shot opponent, although eliminated, is still testimony to the crudeness of the judges. Who knows at what point, in ten years or so, young Wang Hongwen, the single product of the Cultural Revolution to have moved from factory laborer to Political Bureau, might be found to have redeemable qualities. There may then be a very sound reason for showing the possibility of Wang's rehabilitation through study of Mao Zedong Thought.

As I meet Chinese friends, in China and in the United States, I try the good American technique of talking politics. This is essentially nonproductive. I am a foreigner and Chinese Political Bureau membership is not something to review with me. At the upper levels of contacts, with those closer to the power arena, there is an absolute silence. One cannot move into this range of conversation. Direct questions receive deft responses, but the response is not related to the question. Friends whose English has been perfect develop a sudden inability to comprehend my question.

I have a notebook in which I list the Political Bureau membership, just as one would record the roster of an athletic team. I have found it useful to produce my list and ask direct questions about the background of the individuals. This produces some information, but if one really has great curiosity, Chinese-American gossip exchanges are an unrewarding monologue. George is equally unable to understand English when it comes to this subject. He is a fountain of remarks about our American political scene and personalities, but voiceless when the conversation turns to China.

By the end of 1978 the new leadership was secure enough to tell the Chinese people that it was time to stop the attack on the Gang of Four and Lin Biao, to put aside the analysis of the Cultural Revolution, and to work on the immense task of bringing China up to a world-level power. The Central Committee's statement of December 22, 1978, is straightforward, no-nonsense advice. One enjoys its nonlegal, pragmatic style:

Communiqué of the Third Plenary Session of the Eleventh Central
Committee
of the Communist Party of China
(Adopted December 22, 1978)

"This session holds that the great cultural revolution should also be viewed historically, scientifically and in a down-to-earth way. Comrade Mao Tse-tung initiated this great revolution primarily in the light of the fact that the Soviet Union has turned revisionist, and for the purpose of opposing revisionism and preventing its occurrence. As for the short-comings and mistakes in the actual course of the revolution, they should be summed up at the appropriate time as experience and lessons so as to unify the views of the whole Party and the people of the whole country. However, there should be no haste about this. Shelving this problem will not prevent us from solving all other problems left over from past history in a down-to-earth manner, nor will it affect our concentration on efforts to speed up the four modernizations, the greatest historic task of the time."

The Russians, upon Stalin's death, had faced up to the truth about the tyranny of Stalin and, finally, Khrushchev's Secret Speech[2] had laid directly on their shoulders the awful facts done by Stalin and Beria. Stalin was dead and his punishment was to be certain that the historical record thoroughly indicted him. The punishment for Beria was final; he was shot.

Shot is forever. Russia's technique of "posthumous rehabilitation" leaves a considerable value not rehabilitated: the talent and potential of the dead. China's Cultural Revolution did bring death and imprisonment to some of its targets. Some of those dead are now having a "posthumous rehabilitation." However, the major Chinese tactic, the Chinese solution, identifies an individual, places every blame on him, drives the party message through with a tedious consistency, and offers not only a means of survival, but ultimately, a useful return to the system.

The Chinese solution also made possible the double rehabilitation of Deng Xiaoping. Zhou Enlai, in his last months of life, rehabilitated Deng, knowing that his own time was short and knowing that Deng was not only able, but devoted to the modernization of China. Shortly after Zhou Enlai's death, at Chairman Mao's direction, Deng was again put down. On this last go-round, one realizes the chairman was very old and failing, and perhaps misled by an aggressive wife. However, what about the drumming out of Deng ten years earlier?

The January 1979 *Beijing Review* listed thirteen posthumous rehabilitations of individuals who had been removed from office between 1967 and 1972. Other rehabilitations, alive and posthumous, announced and unannounced, continue to confuse the American visitor whose orientation is limited by the dogma of the Cultural Revolution.

Lin Biao has a very slender candidacy for rehabilitation in view of the official statement made by Premier Zhou Enlai condemning Lin. Lin Biao died September 12, 1971 in an aircraft crash near Undur Khan, a town in Outer Mongolia, part of Greater Russia, about 250 miles outside the Chinese border. Dying with him or in a related helicopter crash were a considerable number of powerful military figures. All were fellow-plotters of Lin's, yet they can be assumed to have been supporters of Mao Zedong in the early stages of the Cultural Revolution. The date of their attempted coup, fatal to them, was just five years after the beginning of the Cultural Revolution.

The strength of this threat to Mao Zedong and his leadership is indicated by the makeup of the plotters. First was Lin Biao, minister of defense, and the designated heir of the government. Also present and dead in the fleeing plane were the chief of the general staff of the army, the commander of the air force, the political commissar of the navy, the general-in-charge of logistics of the army, the commander of the Beijing Garrison, a general from the same garrison, the director of the Political Department of the navy, Lin Biao's wife, and his son, an air force commander.

It is safe to say that this group has little chance of posthumous rehabilitation, but then, who knows?

In addition to the possibility of "rehabilitation," there is the remarkable process, perhaps best described as "de-habilitation." I refer to the Chinese technique of total removal of individuals from official photographs by skilled adjustment of the negative. In official pictures of the assembled Political Bureau there are some "removed" examples. Pictures taken in September 1976 when all was superficially serene, within the Political Bureau, were not published until late 1976 after the Gang of Four downfall. Airbrushing, graying away the existence of the four downcasted members, was done, and the official photographs show the usual solid phalanx of members interrupted by unexplained spaces. De-habilitation.[3]

Another example has been the prompt release of a postage stamp offering the likeness of Yang Kaihui, Chairman Mao's earlier wife. This quick elimination of Jiang Qing from her wifely role has been furthered by a new play with Mao Zedong and Yang Kaihui as lead parts, and a rash of paintings and artworks featuring this wife, now the wife of official history.

Undoubtedly the best example of full rehabilitation is Deng Xiaoping. His visit to the United States in January-February 1979, with the attendant full media coverage, made him an instantly recognizable world figure. Ten years earlier he was a sixty-four-year old nonperson with every evidence that his career was as low in promise as that of our resigned president.

Those few Communist members who were in the small group that survived the Long March of forty-five years ago are an aristocracy fully as rank-conscious as those who came with William the Conqueror. A second tier of rank, very high in status and still full, contains those who shared the Paoan-Yanan years and the anti-Japanese War. When that twelve-year period of isolation, spartan preparation, and fighting ended, the real knighthood of China's social order was identified. These are the trusted men and women who are first among equals. Deng Xiaoping's power comes from that group.

Deng Xiaoping's rehabilitation represents this group's endorsement, and changes now in the Central Committee represent his. At age seventy-eight he can probably count on the group to remain intact long enough to see him to the end of his days' concerns. The steady attrition by death is now rapidly taking its toll of the first rank of power, those who were on the March and at Yanan. With Defense Minister Ye Jianying rests the balance of power which made it possible for subordinate-in-theory, Deng Xiaoping, to coexist under the leadership of an unknown, nonmilitary newcomer, Hua Guofeng. Hua Guofeng's titles all indicated that he was the man in charge: chairman of the party, chairman of the military commission, and premier; yet one assumes that the Mandate of Heaven is a coalition. Hua's short term as the head of government suggests he was but a transitional compromise.

Does the coalition of power now existing which has permitted Deng his "rehabilitation" have stability sufficient to hold after the passing of Ye Jianying? Equally, who would be a candidate of sufficient political strength to gain the needed power coalition upon the passing of Deng Xiaoping? Can Hua Guofeng build a power base in these intervening years and regain power, although he is now overshadowed by the pent-up energies of Deng Xiaoping, and Deng's ability to "stack" the Political Bureau?

China still has not faced the inevitable question: what will be the acceptable antecedents of power and prestige when death removes those who came with the army prior to victory in 1949? Whether the Central Committee and the Political Bureau represent a consensus or not, it is not as important as how power will transfer when the original military connections are gone. Will military power always be the inevitable answer?

Mao's Cultural Revolution was to have been the means which would define and test the next generation of trial-by-fire leadership. Sixteen years after the initiation of his training program, no product of it has surfaced who is permitted a position on the Political Bureau. Deng Xiaoping and his Political Bureau represent a continuity of concepts and intents of 1956, 1957, and 1958. Swings and deviations of vast proportions have occurred, but the economic and development policies of today's Deng are in harmony with those carefully developed by Liu Xaoqi and Deng from 1956 to 1958 before Chairman Mao's demand for a new revolution.

At a small dinner party at the Sichuan Restaurant in Beijing in 1978, my hosts were being reflective, and they agreed quite assuredly that ". . . the best years were 1956 to 1958. The streets were cleaner, the people committed, the children obedient, the trains better. . . ." This was in October 1978, and they were all enthusiastic about the rehabilitation of Deng Xiaoping. By indicating their endorsement of 1956–1958 and now of Deng's return, they were speaking positively, but in so doing, of course, they were also exempting quite clearly the years of Mao's return to power. One of the hosts murmured, "We respect Chairman Mao; we loved Premier Zhou." By 1980 this opinion has became even more pronounced and I was told, "Premier Zhou remained quiet when he should have contested Mao. He cannot be considered free of guilt. The truly honorable man was Peng Dehuai." This surprising evaluation makes me hurry to my reference book. Who was Peng Dehuai? He was the senior general who directly and personally contested with Mao at the Lushan meeting of August 1959. This was the critical meeting at which Mao made his major effort to recapture power. He succeeded, and Peng, regardless of his record on the Long March and as a leader of the Chinese forces against MacArthur in Korea, was put out of office and finally arrested in 1966 by the Red Guards. Now, as the post-Mao dust settles, Peng's good name has been restored and he is honored as the first among the leaders who tried to block that movement which evolved into the cultural revolution.[4]

George also enjoyed a considerable political rehabilitation. Although he came through the Cultural Revolution without overt evidence at least to his foreign friends, of personal attack, I gradually learned that all had not been serene. His role as advisor to the minister of health and his position as deputy director at the Institute of Venereology and Skin Diseases ceased. He was returned to practice dermatology in an outpatient clinic. Attacks were made on his foreign origins and his level of living was criticized for its bourgeois elegance. Protection by the highest levels of leadership was necessary to protect him and his family. However, the complete endorsement, or final rehabilitation, took place on February 12, 1980 when 1,200 ranking Communist leaders and friends gave a reception to honor the three "international physicians": George Hatem from the United States, Hans Müller from Germany, and Richard Frey of Austria. Extensive newspaper, radio, and television coverage told all Chinese that these three men were Chinese citizens, old, trusted revolutionaries who made their commitment in the lean, dangerous years of combat. Smiling, cordial photographs of George with Deng Xiaoping, Hua Guofeng, Ye Jianying, and Li Xiannian made clear the absolute benison of the Political Bureau. George was once again identified as advisor to the minister of health.

A Chinese physician read the article to me, slowly, dramatically, interrupting himself to say: "Oh, this is a very important action! This is a total rehabilitation and endorsement of not only George, but an endorsement of foreign contacts. Oh, this is very significant!"

Even though the February 12 reception can be interpreted as the official, ultimate, absolute endorsement of Doctor Horse of China by his party, one must note that even during the bitter years of the ubiquitous Gang of Four, George was able to reach a sensitive ear in the upper reaches of power and gain permission in 1972 to take an entire medical team to Ed Snow in Eysins, Switzerland. Even shadowed years had moments that suggested the young American from Buffalo was a trusted friend of those who control power in China.

Rehabilitation is not only for the leadership or for the individual. In Chinese-Marxist language, the social classes are noted carefully. In the last class, the lowest class, the "stinking ninth" was reserved for the intellectual group. The removal of the intellectuals from their stinking ninth category was a group rehabilitation. Here too, some of the action required posthumous effort, evidence of the severity of the initial assault of the Cultural Revolution.

Even ping-pong coaches had been accused of false communism and have now been "rehabilitated." In January 1979 the momentum of the new leadership and its confidence was clearly expressed by its removal of any stigma from the children of the wealthy landowners, bankers, businessmen, factory owners, i.e., all of those who had employed the labor of others. These reversals in policy are the more remarkable because they alter a policy covering the full thirty years of the People's Republic of China. Forced labor and denial of political rights that transferred to their descendants have been lifted from those designated as "landlords," "rich peasants," "counterrevolutionaries," or "bad elements." All have been cleared of being "enemies of the people."

Artists, writers, generals, party members numbering thousands, athletes, musicians, professors, businessmen, scientists, physicians, children, all have been given clearance, charges in the records have been ordered destroyed, and they are now rehabilitated. The malleability of Mao Zedong Thought is impressive. It served as the reference text for the Cultural Revolution and now for their industrial revolution. Bamboo, bending in the wind, surviving all storms . . .

The calling out for the youth of China to form Red Guards and attack the system, and thirteen years later the calling out for the youth of China to prove their worth in a competitive, technological world, has been equally validated by this subtle strength of Mao Zedong Thought.

The changes in China's leadership following Mao's death took time to become fully seen. The public announcement of "rehabilitation" was slower than the act itself. I was visiting a friend, just beyond the northern edge of the Forbidden City. My host pointed to a substantial modern building and commented casually, "That's Deng Xiaoping's home." I nodded and asked, "Is that where he is under house arrest?" My friend's response was quick and unguarded, an answer given by someone who knew the inner circle. "Oh, he's been back at work full time for several months. They will announce it one of these days. He will be back on the Political Bureau." Four months later, the public announcement was made.

I saw another example of this disparity between reality and public awareness during my visit in late 1979. We had been to a luncheon hosted by a member of the foreign office. Afterwards my wife and I rode back to the Foreign Ministry with a woman "cadre," someone who had joined the Communists at Yanan in the 1930s and therefore is one of the very knowledgeable (and powerful) females often overlooked by foreign experts. We passed a flock of bicycle riders heading back to their offices after the usual long noon break. My friend exclaimed, "Oh there is Wang Kuangmei!" It took me several moments to sort this rapidly-spoken name out of my inaccurate memory for Chinese, but finally my haze cleared. I asked hesitantly, "Do you mean Liu Xaoqi's widow?" I was indeed hesitant because Wang Kuangmei had been put through one of the major public harassments and disgraces of the Cultural Revolution. It was generally acknowledged by the Chinese that she was not only in prison but had been prohibited from seeing her husband and children. Now suddenly she passes by on her bicycle, on her way to work? My hostess went on to say that Wang Kuangmei was in an executive position with a new social science organization. Not until the spring of 1980 did public statements hail her rehabilitation. *China Reconstructs* carried her photo on the cover and a detailed article described the awful things done to her by the Gang of Four and how she now was fully vindicated . . . and this recovery was "due to Mao Zedong Thought!" And now, in 1982, her daughter is in college in Boston.

Even these dramatic events at the high levels of power did not quite tell the story of the "rehabilitation" of the educated professionals (intellectuals). Formal acknowledgements by the Chinese government carried no hint of what was really happening. One suspects that the leadership found it wisest and unnecessary to tell the Chinese nation at large about the new life of the intellectuals. The huge peasant base of Mao's strength could not be ignored; hence, the government increased the peasant's income slightly, permitting private ownership of small plots and the right to sell the produce from this land on the open market. They hoped this would satisfy any major restlessness of the essential agrarian power base. But for now the leadership needed the urban professionals who could provide the brainpower necessary for modernization. The ancient division of China into peasants and mandarins was back, with a different vocabulary.

The rate of the intellectuals' "liberation" could be judged in part by their trips, and their children's visits, to the United States. Being buried deeply in the United States, in Missouri, I am not exactly on the usual tourist's circuit.[5] My exposure to Chinese travelers, therefore, is but a small sample of what is happening in San Francisco, Boston, New York, and Washington. The total number of delegations and solo visitors has gotten beyond even the control of the American State Department. In late 1979, my phone rang in Kansas City and a male voice identified itself as calling from the State Department. Then, slightly embarrassed, he said that he was calling to see if I knew of a Chinese reimplantation surgical team that was said to be in this country. He said he had no records of this delegation. He believed that in addition to the various delegations in the United States and the students officially supported by the Chinese government, there were 600 other students here in various schools, supported by private means. Most of them were funded by Chinese-American families, but he really didn't know where most of them were. I assured him that the lost delegation was in San Francisco. He thanked me and added that many American organizations were inviting Chinese professors and scholars as their guests; his office tried to keep up but it was impossible. He sounded somewhat frazzled.

My own experience suggested he did indeed have a problem. Here in Kansas City, we had a visiting professor from Shanghai for seven months in 1979. He was a great professional and social success. His calendar of engagements became so complex that he needed to have his personal stationery printed, and one of the senior staff took on the almost full-time task of engagements, handling transportation, and airline scheduling. The professor returned to Shanghai in November and five months later was in the United States again at the invitation of a new international center. On the program with him was Mr. Kissinger. My Shanghai friend, in gray slacks and blue blazer, had become a member of the jet set. The American State Department could no more catalogue his itinerary than they could chart bumble bees in a field of clover.

In the fall of 1980, my university was host to a second visiting professor, here for a full semester. A pianist from the Beijing Conservatory, her repetoire featured Mozart, Chopin, and Lizst. She spoke Chinese, German, and English, and was immediately launched on extensive tours of the United States. In 1981, we had still another visiting professor, this time a lawyer . . . and lawyers were considered nonexistent in China in 1976.

In addition to these lengthy visits, we had in this same time a gay procession of one and two-day visitors, each armed with a complicated itinerary for covering this country. Almost all were here as guests of some enthusiastic American host group and almost all were earnestly discussing what arrangements might be made for future advanced study for their children. In 1981, official and unofficial Chinese students and scholars in the United States probably number 10,000. I must say "probably" because the latitude for travel is so great that neither country actually knows. But another evidence of the great enthusiasms between the two countries is that 75,000 Americans were in China in 1981 and 100,000 Americans there in 1982.

Even though the resurrection of China has been accomplished under a Communist government, Chinese abroad have not hesitated to tell me of their satisfaction in the return of China to a world-power position. Perhaps my antennae are oversensitive, but I believe there is a latent continuation among my Chinese friends of the age-old feeling of cultural superiority. As China prospers and gains in economic and political significance, one suspects that a certain hauteur or subtle attitude of superiority will quietly but surely return to the Chinese. The wording will be different, but the concept of the central place of China in the world, The Middle Kingdom, will return.

The significance of being Chinese and all of the historical facts meant by that—and of the unremitting influence this must have upon the Chinese Communist party, is captured in the message sent by the People's Republic of China to the Chinese Taiwanese: "Every Chinese, in Taiwan or on the mainland, has a compelling responsibility for the survival, growth, and prosperity of the Chinese nation. The important task of reunifying our motherland, on which hinges the future of the whole nation, now lies before us all; it is an issue no one can evade or should try to. If we do not quickly set about ending this disunity so that our motherland is reunified at an early date, how can we answer our ancestors and explain to our descendants? This sentiment is shared by all. Who among the descendants of the Yellow Emperor[6] wishes to go down in history as a traitor?"[7]

To be Chinese today, whether on the Mainland, in Taiwan, Hong Kong, or the United States, must mean a sharing of pride. The last sentence of the above quotation was written by someone within the Chinese government who is sensitive to this shared satisfaction of those who are Chinese and is skillfully playing upon the strings of this emotion.

19

A VISIT WITH MADAME ZHOU ENLAI

ALTHOUGH George knew "everyone" in the top hierarchy of Communist China, he never volunteered to gain me an introduction to inner-sanctum power. I never asked, either. But it would have been nice to have had a cup of tea with Mao Zedong and to have asked him how he felt his Cultural Revolution was succeeding. There are few figures of history who had the evidences of success that came to Mao. The tapering down of his image still leaves secure his essential role. It would have been exciting to meet Madame Sun Yat-sen (Soong Chingling) and, although she was George's special security source through the troubled years of the Cultural Revolution, he did not volunteer to introduce us.

The Chinese, as we westerners slowly learn, have been in the business of government for a long time. Although dynasties change and revolutions occur, the same language, same customs, same names, same canals, same walls have endured through the rising and falling of much of what we know as our western civilizations. It seems reasonable to believe that effective management and diplomatic skills have become refined attributes, and if not codified, at least reflex actions. How to handle a difficult issue with quiet dignity, poise and composure—how to turn a problem into a success. How to have and use patience. How to stage the correct level of recognition of a foreign mission. How to negotiate, contract, bargain. How to maintain a security blanket of smaller, adequately friendly nations around their borders. How to move away from the unwanted social demands of the dead chairman and toward practical economic solutions. How to not shadow his image, but instead place him in permanence, to be honored and when needed, to direct his blessings toward his successors.

Many of my friends upon their return from China, as well as many reporters, will write sour comments about the difficulty in getting a yes or no answer to a difficult, penetrating question. A useful Chinese lesson is that many penetrating questions do not have yes or no answers. In fact, the guest perhaps should understand that guests do not have to ask the difficult question directly. A circuitous route, perhaps requiring days and gradual steps *toward* the difficult question, will often give the needed answer, but never with a direct yes or no confrontation.

Much of what one experiences in China under communism is remarkably similar to experiences in noncommunist Japan. The Orient and the Occident are different. The issues may be practical and large: money, factories, arms, oil, treaties, exchanges, but the Far East has a slow, mannerly tempo in moving the negotiations along to the yes-no point. And if the ultimate answer is no, that fact may be finessed so skillfully that the westerner can be back home before it dawns on him that the final happy banquet complete with toasts of friendship had omitted totally a yes or no response.

China has already proved to be an effective participant in the United Nations debates, offering sound analysis of problems and demonstrating conciliatory solutions. Now with its economic engagement with the world, it will be interesting to see what influence Chinese diplomacy will have upon the industrialized nations.

Beijing will become a focus for the world's salesmen, bankers, politicians, and educators. All of these visitors will hope that they or their delegation receive the summons to "be received at the Great Hall of the People." This honor is titrated as finely as the steady hand of a chemist adds acid to base, waiting for the exact color change. An invitation to the Great Hall of the People is always unpredictable, but one can be certain that his delegation was of no official worthiness if an invitation does not come. The importance of one's group is the major factor in this decision, but equally there is the factor of what national message the Chinese wish to disseminate at the moment.

For example, in 1971 all Americans traveling in China, no matter at what remote spot or for what purpose, were informed suddenly that they were wanted in Beijing "to be received." As often, the Chinese do not give all of the information in one statement. All of the Americans were gathered back into Beijing, placed in expectant positions in various hotels, and finally came the critical message: They were to go to the Great Hall of the People and to be received by Premier Zhou Enlai. Thus did the premier clearly indicate China's willingness to espouse American friendship.

Such staging and performance is centuries old in China, and throughout history foreign guests have awaited their audience. Some, in days past, have waited a year, two, or three. Such receptions must become extremely tedious for their top leadership just as they are for the American president in his rose garden. Therefore, a large corps of ranking individuals are consumed in this essentially ceremonial task. Depending upon the level of the delegation to be received, all levels of top leadership of China handle this official activity.

In order to assure a constancy of message and to be certain that all officials are holding to the party's current message, there is evidently a standard briefing utilized. Lesser members of the Central Committee, older members, and as I have said, members carefully matched to the merit of the delegation, are used. Twice I have had my "audience" with Dr. Guo Moruo, the senior in-house intellectual and author, poet, physician, and, although very old and feeble, a charming personality.[1] These receptions were well-staged and exact attention given to protocol, rank, seniority, position . . . regardless of China's basic claim to be a classless society.

On my 1977 visit, at the peak of the rise of Deng Xiaoping and the abuse of the Gang of Four, my wife and I went through all of the whispers, excitement, and scurrying of our third reception. We were asked to remain in our room. At 9:50 the phone rang and we were asked if we could come again to the lobby, for we were being received by Madame Zhou Enlai (Deng Yingchao). Our hosts were very animated and could not hide their excitement. We too were a bit excited, unprepared, and without an agenda. A limousine was waiting for us in front of the hotel; with us was only our interpreter.

We drove quickly down the main ceremonial avenue of Beijing, past the entrance to the Forbidden City, and turned left on the west side of the Great Hall of the People. This is a great, modern architectural effort, fully 300 yards by 300 yards square and perhaps five stories high, with giant columns. We came to the center of the west side and armed sentries, alerted to our coming, swung open the steel gates. Our car turned right and came to a broad esplanade of steps, two flights of five each, and fifty feet across. Waiting for us on the steps was the minister of health and he came forward, followed by the heads of the Chinese Medical Association, the International Division of the Chinese Medical Association, and of the National Heart Hospital. They each shook hands with us and inquired about our health.

We were then quickly escorted up the steps, and standing just outside the door was Madame Zhou Enlai. Remembering that Premier Zhou Enlai died at age seventy-eight the year before, and that they had sixty years of marriage, she is obviously a very senior woman. She proved to be a diminutive lady of perhaps four feet eleven inches, agile and alert. She was wearing a gray, lightweight Chinese suit, with a three-button tunic and trousers. The tunic buttons were mother-of-pearl color, approximately an inch in diameter. The tunic had no breast pockets, but had two pockets at waist level. Beneath it she had a white cotton blouse, and peeking through the cuff of her jacket you could see the cuffs had been unbuttoned and the sleeves turned back a notch. She had on brown suede and cloth low shoes with a half-inch heel. Cutting diagonnally across the instep of the shoe was an insert of leather, simply a slanting bit of leather as decoration. She had on a white leather strapped, stainless steel wristwatch, and no jewelry.

She had a quite round face and wore her hair in a straight bob, cut at a level just below the earlobes, and parted just to the left of the midline. A single bobby pin on each side held back the hair from her brow. She did not have glasses. Her eyes were alert and bright, her hands tiny, her nails not manicured but well-filed. There were brown spots on the backs of her hands. Her lower left incisor tooth was stained and darkened. There were no nicotine stains on her fingers. This was Madame Zhou Enlai, or more exactly, Deng Yingchao. Snow gives her biography in *Red Star over China:*[2] born 1903, educated through college in Tianjin, helped through Japanese lines by Snow in 1937, disguised as an amah, and one of the few women on the Long March.

Immediately upon entering the large foyer we were surrounded by photographers, perhaps eight. Two had motion picture cameras, one a television camera, and the others were taking still pictures. The room was floodlighted and informal photographs were being snapped steadily as we exchanged greetings. She immediately escorted me to a platform which was in the center of the room, directly in front of a large Chinese screen as decoration. Our hostess grasped my elbow and with the firmness of a dance-master placed me on the left, my wife in the center, and after carefully reviewing everyone's position, nodded her head and stepped into her own chosen spot. The photographer snapped the two official photographs. From the moment I had left the car until I had met Madame Zhou Enlai and the official photograph of our visit had been taken, was not more than one minute. Lyndon Baines Johnson could have taken lessons.

We were then escorted by her into a huge reception room, perhaps sixty feet by forty feet, with ceilings thirty feet high. The Great Hall of the People has one of these rooms decorated by each of the provinces, and this room I believe was decorated by the province of Kiangsi.

The madame had me firmly by my right elbow and with small, steady steps took me across the room and firmly pointed to the chair she wanted me in, turned and got Mrs. Dimond by the elbow and did the same thing. There was no doubt who was in charge. The three of us, seated, were arrayed facing the entrance door; the medical officials were in sequence in a straight line on our left in order of their rank, minister of health, head of the Chinese Medical Association, head of the International Division of the Chinese Medical Association. An equal number of chairs on the right had been set aside and in the first chair sat Professor Wu Yingkai, with the other seats empty. There were nine of us for our conversation in this huge room, including interpreters.

Behind me sat my own interpreter, Mr. Gu, and behind madame was her interpreter, a slender young woman who I soon realized had been the official interpreter for the Chinese Ambassador to the United Nations, and a woman who had helped me previously in New York City over a four-year period. This lady is Madame Shih Yenhua. She is a slender, quite handsome woman. She was wearing an attractive, figured blouse, cotton slacks, and no jewelry.

When we were all seated, the madame opened with comments that she knew we were old friends of Edgar Snow's and old friends of China, and that we had been here four times before. Any old friend of Edgar's was a friend of hers.

She then promptly went into a detailed discussion, describing in full the events of recent years in the inner circles of the Politburo of China . . . the contesting for power that had occurred. This went on for not a half hour nor an hour, but for two hours and forty-five minutes. It was a detailed, elaborate scenario with careful attention paid to developing each of the individual personalities and each point of the conflict. She began her review with the beginnings of the Cultural Revolution and carried through a detailed analysis of Hua Guofeng, Deng Xiaoping, Mao's widow Jiang Qing, the other three ousted members of the Political Bureau from Shanghai, Wang, Yao, and Qiang. She leisurely and thoroughly, as if we were sitting on the porch swing gossiping, took each of the Gang of Four apart and gave me chapter and verse of their faulty pedigree and bad points of character.

She reviewed the calamities of the last year and discussed the illness and death of Mao, of her husband, of Zhu De; she discussed the earthquake, how severe it had been and what a demand it had made on the national economy.

She described in detail the attempts to manipulate power and the Communist leadership by Jiang Qing, and for the first time I was told that Lin Biao had been conspiring with the four from Shanghai and that there had been a total conspiracy in 1971, involving Lin Biao, his military colleagues, and the foursome. She referred to Wang as an "unknown upstart," and she referred to Yao as "the son of a renegade." She said that Mao had for the past four years been warning his wife that she was on a bad course and had issued an order that under no circumstances was anything to be taken as official unless he himself signed it, and that nothing was to be carried out "in his name" when that term was used by his wife. He warned her to dissociate herself from her Shanghai colleagues and not to try to contest with the rest of the Political Bureau. He warned that her downfall would come from her overwhelming ambition. She further said that when Mao was dying and Jiang Qing was sent for, that Jiang Qing insisted upon finishing her bridge game before going to him, and then in his last days "badgered and disturbed him." Madame Zhou Enlai went on for one straight hour without interruption and then stopped, looked directly at me, and said, "You want to hear all this?" I had the sudden sensation that she realized she was enjoying herself exchanging backyard gossip, and was for a moment concerned that she might be an old lady boring me with her chatter. I assured her that we wanted her to continue, and she did.

The visit had begun at perhaps five minutes after ten, and I do need to place in this note that at 11:17 and 12:47 the old lady thoroughly cleared her throat, leaned forward, and spat into her cuspidor. It was between us and I quietly began moving my feet closer to my chair.

Among the interesting remarks was this bit of inside, thoughtful comment: "If the Gang of Four had won, you would not be here [pointing at me], and for some of us our heads would be rolling on the floor." With the last remark, she swept her hands to include all of the Chinese present and they thoughtfully nodded.

She said that the *Journal of Academia Sinica* had been used to push the line of "Down With Deng" by having writers from Yenching University write negative things. She commented that the *Chinese Medical Journal* had not been allowed to publish some scientific reports and had been used as a political tool.

She commented that my visit last year had been indeed at a bad time, and that the last year had been the saddest year in the current history of China. She said that when the good news of the decision by Chairman Hua to throw down the Gang of Four was received by the people, there was so much excitement and celebration in China that a Japanese newspaper reported that one could not buy wine anyplace, that 50,000 kilos of wine had been sold in Beijing, and all stores were sold out.

She said to me, "You are a heart specialist and you know all about these things, but let me tell you that not only were our hearts all happy at that time, but we also had our very sad time, and with the death of Mao there were many heart attacks; and I have been told that the hospital emergency rooms were crowded with people who were suffering from the grief and bereavement and had their heart attacks brought on by this bad news."

Early in the meeting she offered me a cigarette. I thanked her and told her that although I did not smoke, I would take it to remember the occasion. She laughed and handed me the entire pack and said, "Here, take the pack and share your memory."

I replied, "I would show them to people, but I won't share them. I want to keep them.'' She turned to the interpreter and said, "Give him plenty of cigarettes so he can share them with his friends,'' and again chuckled.

She then recited for an hour the new chairman's record and how much he had done successfully, and how he had been recognized as a talent by Mao and brought forth and made a first deputy, and had been the only first deputy. Her story was essentially as I had heard it, but she sought to stress the fact that Mao had without a doubt personally chosen Hua to succeed him.

She also recited Deng Xiaoping's record as a general and the numerous victorious battles that he personally had led, and how he was respected by the army. She said that the tremendous celebration that we had witnessed in China during the last three days was because the public was pleased to have Deng back in power, and because the people felt that ten years of disruption had ended. They knew that many good things had been caused by the Cultural Revolution, but they also knew that the Gang of Four had allowed it to become dangerous, and had actually allowed the army to distribute arms, and that people had died in it. This had been contrary to the wishes of Chairman Mao, who had specifically said that no one should be harmed, that everyone should be given a chance to discuss and think his way through to correct solutions.

In the past year, madame commented, there had been armed interference with government, and in Hangchow for example, there had been killings. She said that when Hua Guofeng was the interim chairman after Mao's death, he discovered the Gang of Four had organized a deliberate conspiracy to disrupt production throughout the rest of the country, while keeping Shanghai operating extremely effectively. With Shanghai as the principal industrial center of China, and with Qiang as the head of the Communist party of Shanghai, the Gang of Four would have a strong base to operate from if they needed it. In fact, they had organized the militia there to come out if needed and give them the armed help.

The madame continued to relate that two days prior to their planned coup, Hua Guofeng learned of it and immediately had them placed under house arrest. As two examples of their activity, she said there were "no firecrackers and no red crepe paper available in all of Shanghai,'' because of the Gang of Four had so carefully prepared with their colleagues the celebration they were going to launch. Just two days before their planned coup they were put down. This strong, decisive action by the interim chairman was "good evidence of his judgment."

She also indicated as an example of their attempts at sabotage, that they had through their connections in the railroad union disrupted railroad service so that a contract with Japan to deliver coal for Japan could not be met, and that the coal could not be taken away from the mine and was stacked there, and "finally had to be burned in order to get rid of it."

She stated that Mao in the last year of his life ordered his wife to quit issuing documents and to stop making preparations for seizing power. But in the end when he was ill and isolated, she tormented him and alternately would distress him and later gain his approbation for something that he really was not healthy enough to have considered.

Madame Zhou Enlai had a good, healthy laugh, and was witty. There was a steady twinkle in her eye. I would like to know her better.

I should add that an excellent green tea was served, as well as a glass of cold orange pop; and she reached over and tapped me on the hand, pointed to the tea and said, "hot," pointed to the orange pop and said, "cold," and then grunted—a hostess at work.

She also went on to say that the Politburo does have the final document which Mao wrote: "With you in charge I am content." This was his message he handed to Hua, and I gather, at the point of his dying. There was evidently some forgery and manipulation of documents at the very end, which was attributed to Mao's wife.

Marshal Ye and Deng now are strongly behind Hua and are helping him, and Hua has pledged that in one year he will straighten out the production and transport difficulties, and in three years China will be truly in motion toward its goal of world-level industrialization, volunteered the madame.

"He had pledged himself that we must now concentrate on science and basic research. He has made the statement that 'a nation can still have satellites in the sky and still hold high the Red banner'. He is saying that 'we can still be a socialist-communistic nation and worry about the common man, at the same time not be against scientific thought'."

The madame continued, "For example, the Gang of Four thought that all that was necessary was to 'have revolution', and then everything else would work out. This is obviously foolish and such talk had disrupted schooling and caused disobedience among the youth. Too many of the young people fell for this talk and felt that if they loudly proclaimed they were revolutionaries, they would not have to work.''

The madame moves with deliberate motion and would slowly lift her left leg and cross it over the right. She would equally deliberately reach the lower edge of her tunic and give it a firm slow tug to straighten it, just as women do all over the world.

During her prolonged monologue, she toyed with three packs of Panda brand cigarettes that were beside her. I commented that her husband had given two pandas to the United States. Her cryptic reply was, ''I hope they are happy.''

Each of us had a washcloth folded beside our chair for cooling our face and hands. This is usual and almost expected. What I did note though, was that the hand towel for the madame was very carefully folded, and two red wires came out of the back of it. She had a buzzer hidden in the towel, and when she felt we needed tea or attention or perhaps when the interview would end, she would casually dip her hands against the towel as if cooling them, but was actually pressing the buzzer.

She repeated the new phrase, ''We must be concerned about the peasants, workers, and intellectuals.'' This new slogan is an operational party line. The madame said, ''We must use our most intelligent people well, and we must give them the equipment they need.''

At the end of two hours and forty-five minutes madame said, ''There is much more for me to tell you, but I'll have to let your friends tell you as you travel about China. Only the Chinese people can tell you; I cannot tell all of it myself.'' As she made this statement she leaned forward, looked straight ahead, and smiled. I smiled at her and a flashbulb went off. Through her hidden buzzer she had prepared the photographer and he was ready. This was the point at which she would sit forward, a smile would come, and that was to be the official photograph terminating the interview, and so it happened.

We all proceeded ceremoniously back to the entrance hall and my Chinese friends lined up in order of descending importance and shook hands; the madame saw us through the door and out to the steps; we were placed in our limousine and turned to wave at them. There they were, Madame Zhou Enlai, the minister of Health, the head of the

Chinese Medical Association, the head of the International Office of the Chinese Medical Association, the head of the National Heart Hospital, all standing on the steps of the Great Hall of the People while two people from the United States were slowly driven around the circle and out the steel gates. It was quite an experience.

Later, I shared my experience with Hans Müller. He said he was impressed and what I had heard was either exactly true or was what was going to be true in Chinese history. He predicted that in twelve months there would be no evidence in China that Jiang Qing had been Mao's wife, and that the "wife of record" would be the young woman who died in the 1930s.

Others visited with me at the time, a good mixture of Chinese and foreign friends. All were stalwart in their endorsement of Madame Zhou Enlai and shared a respect for her. They all slowly nodded their heads and stated that it was a considerable honor to have been rewarded with a reception "at this level."

I recognized that my rank had risen slightly among my Chinese friends, and that in an unwritten, quantified sense their own self-esteem had come up along with mine simply because they knew me. Meeting Zhou Enlai's wife was an honor, I agreed.

George cautioned me, however, not to place any credence in the possibility that through this long conversation with the widow of Zhou Enlai and with all the discussion of personalities there was any probability that I had been given even a slender iota of new information. He deflated me further by saying that all delegations being received that day, and for days preceding and following, regardless of their host, were getting the exact same facts, paragraphs, witticisms, and messages.

I recalled this remark several months later when I read the report of the American Cancer Society, telling of their day at the Great Hall of the People. Their visit there was within a few weeks of mine. In their report, *American Cancer Society Delegation Report, Trip to the People's Republic of China, 20 April to 12 May, 1977,* one finds a transcript of complete remarks made by Ulanfu, the Central Committee member who had the duty of receiving them.

Any similarity of their experience to my own is purely factual. Here is what the Cancer Society wrote:

"A most unexpected event took place on return to Peking . . . on arrival we were informed that we were to be accorded a special honor. Ulanfu, a Vice-Chairman of the Standing Committee of the National People's Congress, had invited our delegation to meet with him at the Great Hall of the People at 10:00 A.M. the next morning.

"Our program for the next morning was cancelled and we were told how to prepare for this signal event. Ulanfu is an old friend of Mao's. He is an ex-Mongolian cavalry general who, as we were told, "left the saddle" in 1969. He was at the time of our visit one of ten vice-chairmen of the National People's Congress. Since we were in China, Ulanfu has been elevated to membership in the Chinese Communist Party Bureau, the highest policy and decision-making body in China. There are only 23 members in this group.

"What we had expected to be a thirty-minute 'audience' with picutre taking and gratuitous dialogue, turned out to be an eighty-minute session with him advising us in very clear terms the conditions on which relationships between our two countries could be normalized!"

There then follows a full transcript of Ulanfu's remarks. Here is one of the tidbits of information Ulanfu gave them: "At that time many families bought wine to drink and to celebrate the occasion—at that time all of the wine was sold out. There had been such disastrous things done to the country and the people hated the Gang of Four." The American Cancer Society and I had the same scenario.

I continued to ask the same question that I had been asking, usually obliquely, but with the same objective. "How can everything be blamed on the Gang of Four? How can they be sold as the sole purveyors of all things bad?" Hans Müller gave me an answer, one I felt tempered by a substantial historical perspective.

"The system of government in China has changed from the imperial dynastic custom to a new communist plan. Those in charge would have you believe that the education of the mass of the peasant people is now complete and that they have thrown out old ways, dropped old superstitions, and now understand that they 'run the country'. You know our term: 'dictatorship of the proletariat'? Well, such is certainly more true than it was when we came into power, and each generation is better prepared to live within this new plan of government. But the old ways of thousands of years do not die out nor are forgotten. Especially in times of trouble, the value of the old ways will be recalled and questions raised as to whether something is amiss with the gods-that-be.

"Here, in the years of the drought, there were many farmers who went along with the government's policies of assurance about the adequacy of dams, electrical pumps, scientific irrigation—but just the same made certain that the appropriate offerings were made to those whom traditional superstitions believed were truly in charge of rain.

"But the largest piece of what still remains at the heart of the peasantry of this country is the belief that all things run well and there will be good crops and dependable conditions, provided that the person at the top has been doing his job well and has the full approval of whatever celestial authority controls these things. You know what I mean: I speak of the Mandate From Heaven."

I interjected, "Do you mean the peasants have transferred the old imperial concept of all is well in heaven, to now, the Political Bureau?"

My friend went on, "Yes, much more than anyone will remotely discuss. However, I can tell you that at the very peak of the troubles of these past few years: the death of Zhou Enlai, of Zhu De, of Mao Zedong, the huge earthquake—you know that 800,000 people died—think that over—that within the innermost circles there are enough very old party members who know this country well, who made it clear that a decisive plan of action had to be made that would purify the evidence of this group's Mandate From Heaven. A Communist party is certainly in power in China, but one is ignorant if he believes that a small superimposed group of leaders can truly control 800 million, 850 million, or 900 million people. The power that rests in Peking rests there because of the willingness of the people, and because a coalition of powers exist in the provinces and the army.

"The strength of Chairman Mao's own personality had been the power that held the loyal core together at that time. In a true sense the Mandate of Heaven had rested with Mao Zedong. With his passing and with the overwhelming cluster of disasters in a twelve-month period, it was essential that the party scourge itself—and the Gang of Four was used for that purpose."

20

MI LI DAIFU (DR. MÜLLER)

AMONG those visiting my home in 1980 was George Hatem's longtime friend, the third member of Rewi Alley's tea party, Dr. Hans Kurt Müller. Hans is vice-chancellor of Beijing Medical College. He had been included in the festivity in February in Beijing, at which time George, Dr. Richard Frey, and Hans were publicly endorsed as foreign physicians who were appreciated in China. Hans and his wife toured the United States as guests of a Portland, Oregon group identified as the Friends of Evans Carlson. Carlson was the American soldier who was assigned as an observer to the Communists in Yanan and later applied their guerilla concepts in the organization of the Second World War combat unit, Carlson's Raiders. Hans is a very open, free-speaking man and makes no attempt to cloak his remarks in dialectical materialism or Hatemisms.

Hans is Teutonic, direct, a bit satirical, and very skeptical. These qualities hide, or perhaps are the result of, a considerable bit of living. He was born in the Rhine region in 1915; at eighteen, he was arrested, imprisoned, and ruthlessly interrogated by Hitler's storm troopers. He fled to Switzerland and earned a medical degree at Basel. In 1939, he determined to somehow oppose fascism and what he saw it doing to Germany. By this time, Japan and Hitler had formed the Axis, and Japan had invaded China. Hans, without the slightest orientation towards communism but determined to help those fighting the fascists, sailed from Marseilles to Hong Kong. There he quickly learned that Chiang K'ai-shek was, in his own way, a cruel dictator. Müller met Sun Yat-sen's widow, Soong Chingling, and she told him of the resistance group at Yanan. He also met Ed Snow who was trying, as a reporter, to get to Chongqing (Chungking). Müller probably would have joined them, but could not get on the same plane. Instead, he took a ship from Hong Kong to Haiphong, and then to Hanoi. Then by truck, bus, and stealth, he worked his way the entire width of China to Yanan, where he was expected and needed.

A small group of physicians from other countries, including Dr. B. K. Basu from India, and Hans, finally got through and went to work at the International Peace Hospital at Yanan. Dr. D. Kotnis, also from India, sent personally by Prime Minister Nehru, died while helping the Chinese Communists. I asked Hans if Sufei had been a part of their travel party. He said no, but they had arrived at Yanan at the same time.

For Hans, this relatively safe base quickly ended and he joined the guerrilla forces behind the Japanese lines in the northeast territories, in the Taihang Mountains. His original training was not in surgery, but under these war conditions he quickly became a surgeon. For these years, in the Jehol area and east of Tianjin (Tientsin), he was in constant guerrilla combat. One of his experiences had a lasting influence. At one point, north of Tianjin, a major Japanese force was wiped out. A Japanese hospital came into Chinese hands and became a medical base for Hans. War and romance are not incompatible, and Hans met a young Japanese nurse who became his wife, Kyoko.

Hans was in the northeast territories with Lin Biao's 4th Army group, and at one time was with the 194th Force with Deng Xiaoping as the political commissar. Again, while back at Yanan he had been the roommate of General Peng Dehuai. Obviously, his connections were of a considerable magnitude.

A Chinese artist, the same man who caught the essence of George in the portrait in Hatem's living room, has also done a strong, dynamic one of Hans, placing him in rough clothes, a physician's coat, high on a mountain trail during combat on the Shandong Peninsula.

Hans freely admits his spoken Chinese is poor and his written Chinese worse. Thirty-one years in China with almost ten of it in combat has preserved a very dignified German. In his work as vice president of Beijing Medical College, he uses his Chinese name, Mi, and is Mi Daifu, Doctor Mi (daifu for doctor). This is a fortuitous derivation: Müller to Miller, and Mi is a Chinese word for grain, thus he has the satisfaction of a similar meaning (miller-grain) and spelling (Miller-Mi). This latter approximation is made even better by combination with his Chinese given name: Mi Li.

Hans did not return to Europe for thirty-eight years. When he did return in 1977, he found he was legally dead. He could find no relatives who had survived Hitler. Hans's father was Jewish; his mother was not. He had been born in Düsseldorf and all of his father's family were killed by the Nazis. His mother's sister's children survived and, finally, Hans successfully reestablished his legal reality and found a cousin in Hanover and another in Spain. The German government made a restitutional settlement for the lost family estate and Hans suddenly had a modest inheritance. After his visit to the United States he stayed several months with these relatives and with his daughter who had married a Swiss. Hans is an international organization: wife Japanese, cousin in Spain, cousin in Germany, son in United States, daughter in Switzerland, American daughter-in-law, and Swiss son-in-law. He is a sincere, forthright, cosmopolitan man.

His son is now an American citizen and has returned to Beijing as a representative of American and British trading companies. His son married Frank Coe's daughter (Frank Coe was an American economist who came to Beijing in the McCarthy era and served as an advisor to the Chinese government).

Hans's daughter is working in computer programming in Switzerland and her husband is editor of *Friends of Nature,* a magazine of a social-democratic labor organization. They are building a new home and Hans and Kyoko are moving steadily into a retirement pattern, with a half-year in Beijing with their grandchild as their responsibility and pleasure—and a half-year in Switzerland with the grandchild's parents. Kyoko's mother still lives in Japan and wants to remain there. Kyoko, now fifty-two years old, left Japan at age fifteen and has been in China for thirty-seven years.

Hans has sampled the variations of Chinese wines, and has found a dry white wine, which, well-chilled, is a good facsimile of the dry wines of his memory. We had a little before lunch and chatted, randomly. He introduced me to his new dog, named without imagination, "Doggie." This is a very small, part-Pekinese dog, which Hans explains "was a dropout from a Chinese circus because she was too shy." Doggie has mastered the trick of ''rollover,'' but then immediately scoots for shelter, in embarrassment.

His granddaughter's name is Julia, pronounced Hulia. She has brown hair with a red glint, blue eyes and, to me, looks just like a Swiss baby. A Swiss citizen, she completes the great circle for her grandfather who went to China in 1939 to fight the fascists and now has a German-Japanese-Swiss root in Europe. Of the three old comrades, Hans could most readily return to his roots.

21

MAO AND HIS THOUGHT

THE Chinese "intellectuals" indeed recovered. They recovered so well that I found myself wanting to restrain them. They made comments that seemed unnecessary. A senior professor of language stunned me with a choice gossip item, "We need to carefully study Mao's sex relationships. There is considerable evidence that he forcibly took another man's wife and had children by her. This fellow, Wang Dongxing, who is now on the Political Bureau, was Mao's bodyguard and in charge of getting women for Mao. He has all kinds of records telling about this and about the private life of other high-ranking members. They would throw him off the Political Bureau, but they are afraid of him and his files." As a modest China-watcher of the days when Mao was referred to several times each hour as the Great Helmsman, I was not prepared for this style of besmirchment. Most intellectuals I talked to were more circumspect and used the logical approach of saying that the chairman had been old and ill, and was manipulated by his wife. I usually let this pass as a logical means for the Chinese to protect the image of Mao, but on occasion I would say, "His health was evidently quite good at the beginning of the Cultural Revolution and he had enthusiastically welcomed the students, the Red Guards, in Beijing. How can you claim he was not responsible for the Cultural Revolution?" This effort at reverse dialectical materialism usually brought a reluctant agreement and the usual response was, "We will have to study that period very carefully. We must go into that fully."

The diminution in Mao's public image coincided with an increased enthusiasm for Zhou Enlai. In professors' homes, one saw Zhou's picture and only rarely Mao's. Even on the occasion of the thirtieth anniversary of Mao's official launching of the People's Republic of China, October 1, 1979, the changing role of Mao was expressed by closing to the public Mao's mausoleum in Beijing, although there were hundreds of thousands of visitors in the capital for the great celebration.

There was another level of criticism now apparent in China, and that was frank criticism of the Communist government itself. The enthusiasm of the public to criticize the Communists is either a very healthy sign, suggesting the whole situation is as normal as that in any country or, it is a real warning to the leadership that the people are losing confidence that communism as a method can successfully provide the leadership to govern.

These criticisms about the Communists were at all levels and from all regions in which I traveled:

"The bureaucracy in Peking is unbelievable. You have to go out into the provinces to find out the truth. In Peking everyone stalls and covers up."

"There is too much corruption among the middle-level Communists. The real old-timers are excellent, but the new ones are bad."

"The Communist management in the countryside is as bad as the old landlords. They are not only dumb, but they are dishonest."

"Socialism says all people are equal, and what we have to show for this are lazy employees. The Communists are supposed to teach us by their example, but they have become lazy, too. They are even corrupt."

"They have had thirty years to show what they can do. Now they are saying they are not responsible for the last ten years. Well, who is then? How do we know we would not have been better off with capitalism? Why do they always have to blame it on someone else?"

"I think the very top leaders mean well, but why can't they get younger people into leaders' places? Most of them are too old. Something must be wrong when a whole country can't produce new leaders after thirty years."

"When the movie was over last night, I was amazed at the big Red Flag limousines taking away the children of the local leaders. I stood at the curb and cried 'Elitist!' at them!"

My access to this type of comment did not include the major population base, the peasants. The criticism I was hearing came from the university-trained population. How happy or unhappy the peasants might be, I don't know. They have been the origin of the Communist power and the source of the army manpower. As the new push for modernization and college education has stimulated the urban population, so has new government policy appealed to the farmers. Some land has been turned back into private plots and as much as ten percent of the farm produce can be sold privately. The price paid for grain has been increased, also. These measures may satisfy the peasants' present expectations.

However, the range of criticisms, open and sharp, from the urban professional was a keen reminder that China is undergoing a major change.

In one conversation I asked a thirty-four-year old professional: "If Lin Biao had been successful in his attempt to take over the government in 1971, would he have been a hero?" This was a strong question and my Chinese friend tried to evade, "That is conjecture and impossible to analyze."

I tried another route, "I ask that question for two reasons. First, Lin Biao had almost all of the military leadership on his side. Evidently they also were willing to dispose of Mao. And six years later when Mao did die, all of those he had put down are back in power, and the first thing they have done is eliminate the majority of programs backed by Mao in his last ten years. Lin Biao was already designated to succeed Mao. Don't you think the majority of the leadership would have preferred to have never experienced Mao's Cultural Revolution? A friend said to me that Mao lived fifteen years too long. Wasn't his end what Lin Biao was attempting to bring about?"

The Chinese man nodded his head and agreed, "Mao's mistakes need public discussion. That we must do. Right now, however, there is concern for the present. We are beginning to wonder if Deng Xiaoping can provide the leadership for the four modernizations. He is respected, but now there are some doubts; he must show some success soon or there will be criticism. The young are confused. They cannot see evidence of leadership and the present leadership is not clearly stating policies. One of the slogans now is that we must have the four modernizations, but also a fifth one: a modernization of the thinking of the Communist leaders!

"The Communist party is showing bad judgment in not being able to find forty and fifty-year old members who can replace the ancient power group. When I meet with my friends who are the same age as myself and have professional jobs, all of them have considerable criticism of the government. We see too much inefficiency and even corruption. It would surprise you to know how many of my friends have applied for permission to leave this country and move to the United States."

I shook my head and continued, "I can't believe there are many who want to go and in fact, I hope not. If there is too large an exodus, your government will inevitably become hostile and clamp down again. I hope you don't go too far."

He nodded his head and said that the party really could not stop the expectations of the people now. At the universities the talk openly criticized the inefficiency and corruption of leadership. Beijing University had been the first place to lead the attack on the Cultural Revolution. Criticisms are not yet up to the level of making a public protest, but the time could come rapidly if the government made a major mistake and tried to return to its old ways. "The biggest risk is because the leadership is so old and so removed from real contact with the people. Too many of them think in terms of the Yanan days and not how it is now."

"Where do you get your outside world news from? How do you get around the control of your newspapers?" I asked.

"All of us listen to the Voice of America. That is no secret, everyone does. It is legal to do. We listen and we talk it over among ourselves."

I asked, "Is it good? Do you think you can trust the Voice of America?" He said, "Yes, it is excellent, especially the panels where you have several people from different places and levels discussing a topic. We don't have anything like that in this country."

I asked him, "What do you think about our form of government? We have our difficulties but we certainly are able to say what we think, go where we want to go, work where we want to."

He shook his head, "I don't think we are ready for that yet. We are too poor to allow anyone to not work. We couldn't afford your welfare system. We have too many uneducated people to really have a democratic vote. Our real problem is to find out if socialism can truly work. Is it possible to have efficient, productive people under socialism? How to reward individuals for good work and how to discharge the incompetent if they are all to be rewarded equally? Can a Marxist philosophy developed in Europe and under their social conditions of more than a century ago be adjusted to China's reality today? The present need is for intellectual and technical competence, and the country is too poor to do two things at the same time. It cannot solve the problems of the peasant and at the same time get on immediately with the massive industrial and scientific needs. Modernization must begin with able, modern leadership. The peasants should be given all the help possible to keep them able to provide the food, but otherwise they will have to be left alone for the time being and the major effort spent on technical, scientific, and economic management personnel.''

From George Hatem, I found none of this criticism. He is perhaps too much ''of the system.'' He is one of the old guard and close enough to those in power to see their problems and understand the limits of leadership. The ''four modernizations'' is not a policy that when launched today produces results tomorrow. The public hears of great activity in terms of plans and contracts, but sees no results. From the beginning of the intent to build a vast steel plant until that plant results in an end-product, a refrigerator, for example, could well be ten or more years. Those at the top, including George, understand this, but some of the criticisms stem from the promises made in 1977 by the central government in pledging far more than could be delivered in the short range.

I tried to draw George into direct comments on Mao's status and the government's current policy. He spoke enthusiastically of the performance of Deng Xiaoping, and how awful the Gang of Four had been. I saw him immediately after he had attended a National Day Rally on September 29, 1979 in Peking. This was a large affair held in the Great Hall of the People and was essentially a gathering of the powerful to receive the new, official party policy: the party line. Those present were the Central Committee of the Communist party of China, the Standing Committee of the National People's Congress, and the State Council. Hua Guofeng, as chairman of the party and premier of the State Counci, presided. George was there as a full-fledged delegate to the National People's Congress. Those present were the ''who's who'' of China power. I was delighted to hear that Mao's benevolent portrait was the center backdrop. At least he was still among those present.

George said with emphasis, ''It was a very important meeting and the major speech was extremely important. You must study it. It clarifies everything.''

I hesitantly asked, ''Did they get around to agreeing that the Cultural Revolution was led by Mao, or do they still claim it was all due to the Gang of Four?''

George raised his hands for emphasis, ''One must understand that today's statement was not the opinion of one man nor a trial balloon. This was the unanimously adopted policy of the entire State Council, the entire Political Bureau, the entire Central Committee. You must study it. Every word of it is carefully weighed. Read it and you will have your questions answered.''

I suggested, ''Perhaps I won't have my questions answered, but I will have a clue as to what questions will be accepted. Tell me how was the speech delivered? Did Hua or Deng Xiaoping deliver it? Was it well done?''

I asked these questions as a victim of my own society. In the United States a politician is made or sinks on the basis of his vaudeville performance on television. We don't even care who wrote the speech as long as the president or candidate speaks well, dresses just right, and gestures effectively. Even a lack of message is made up for by a stylish presentation.

George's description of how this critical document was delivered, summarizing the official stand of the party at the end of thirty years of power, helps one understand how differently the two forms of government, ours and theirs, function. The speaker was not Premier Hua nor Vice-Premier Deng. Instead, it was the senior-by-age member of the Political Bureau, Ye Jianying. Chinese logic brought the eighty-five-year old marshal of the armies, comrade of the Long March, close friend of Zhou Enlai, source of the decision to arrest the Gang of Four, forward, to give this significant document. But the style of presentation was the surprise. George explained: ''Marshal Ye addressed us by reading the introductory paragraph and greetings. He then turned the manuscript over to a well-known radio announcer, who stepped up to the microphone and read the entire paper. It took two hours.''[1]

I asked further about this Chinese method of speechmaking, and it obviously had its merits. First, the intent was that the document itself was the message, not the performance ability of the speaker. The elderly warrior had done the mannerly thing of reading the words of greeting and acknowledgments, but then he sat down on the rostrum, had tea, relaxed, and spared himself the ordeal of a two-hour presentation. The audience had the benefit of a trained voice, with clear enunciation, and could concentrate on the message. In the United States, the trained actor is the politician, and the trained politician is the actor.

The next day I had a copy of this speech. George reminded me three times of its importance. It was a mixture of information. Throughout there were the typical phrases and clichés which, at least in the English translation, obfuscate the message. For example, "Whereas under Lin Biao and the Gang of Four there were people who had been unjustly charged throughout the country, and the rights and wrongs of many historical issues confused, today most cases have been redressed and most questions of right and wrong clarified. . . . there must be a correct understanding of the interrelations among masses, classes, political parties, and leaders. Leaders play an important role in the development of history. Leaders who play a progressive role are representatives of the interests of the masses and executors of their will. Leadership doesn't consist of a single person, but a group of persons known as leaders. It is impermissible to belittle the collective or the masses or to exaggerate the role of the individual leaders."

A reading of this does not clarify much for me. By underlining positive statements in the entire document, one can find the party line, which George considered helpful. At least at his level he knew what had been agreed upon. For example, Mao was given a clear endorsement, and it was evident the party intended to hold him in an officially honored position. The public may gossip, but the Chinese history books have their instructions. The document said: "Without Mao Zedong Thought there would be no new China today. This is in complete conformity with historical reality. The Chinese people will always remember the immortal contributions of Mao Zedong, and resolutely define and develop the scientific system of Mao Zedong Thought."

For those who feel this adequately protects the role of Mao, the next paragraph provides a reminder of the skill of nuance. Mao the man is separated from his Thought. "Mao Zedong Thought is not the product of his personal wisdom alone, it is also the product of the wisdom of comrades-in-arms, the party and the revolutionary people . . . [the]

Thought was . . . the crystallization and the collective wisdom of the Chinese Communist party.

Thus they have indelibly thanked Mao, set him aside so he may be analyzed separately, but claimed the Thought as a collective effort.

There are useful clues in the document and a listing of factual accomplishments and a listing of errors. For example, there is a justification of the origins of the Cultural Revolution and an explanation of what went wrong. Lin Biao and the Gang of Four are designated ''counter-revolutionary swindlers.'' ''The havoc which the counterrevolutionary gang wrought for ten long years spelt calamity for our people and contributed the most severe reversal to our socialist cause since the founding of the People's Republic.'' Chairman Mao and Premier Zhou are fully protected from responsibility simply by not being mentioned.

Deep in the document was a commitment which will be the major test of the viability of their governing authority: ''Both party discipline and the socialist legal system must be improved, democratic rights ensured to all party members and citizens, and inner-party democracy and socialist democracy institutionalized and guaranteed by law. All are equal before party discipline and before the law of the land. It is absolutely impermissible to have privileged party members or special citizens not subject to party discipline or law; there must be no prerogatives transcending party discipline and the laws of the state.''

The truth of those words is obvious. The application in reality will be the challenge, a challenge not yet met by communism in any country. Can the Chinese modify nineteenth-century Marxism and a revolution won by guns into a governing authority restrained by law? Can a single-party government, which considers the party as above even the people, develop an orderly, coup-free, means of transferring power? The ability to survive Mao's Cultural Revolution and thwart his widow's bid for power indicates an inherent stability which is reassuring.

However, one continues to wonder if a totalitarian government can give the people a degree of freedom, or will the taste of freedom make the restrictions of the government unacceptable. The experience of Poland is a prime example of this dilemma of communism. The post-Mao government has promised much and the people are testing that promise.

By 1982, the new international trade agreements and opening of the economy of China were beginning to reach into the lives of almost all Chinese. In a trip over a mountain route, from south to north on Hainan Island, one was never free of evidence that, even on this remote island, the outside world was touching the average Chinese citizen. At lunch, in a commune town we were offered our choice: Chinese Qingdao, Japanese Asahi, or American Millers High Life beer. In the "free-market" stalls along the streets of Sanya, certainly a very isolated community on the southern tip of Hainan Island, peasant women were covertly, but not very covertly, huckstering new Seiko digital wristwatches. In a small, 100-person Meio minority village, high at a mountain pass, I was shown a washbasin for washing up before lunch. While drying my hands, I peered over a folding partition, and looked immediately into a tiny bedroom, packed with three mosquito-netted beds. But filling the center of the bedroom was a large, bright red, very new Kawasaki motorcycle.

All of these are but examples of what one saw everyday. When I was back in Guangzhou, I asked a Chinese friend about these experiences. He acknowledged them and shrugged, "There is no way to control all the smuggling and of course all of it is not smuggling. There is so much new money in Guangdong Province that almost every family has plenty of money."

The next day I went to the Guangzhou Friendship Store and learned that it is now open to the Chinese, not just foreigners, for buying. The reason is that the entire area has been declared a free-trade zone, and industry from all over the world has already poured in. Factories, built with Chinese labor, are filled with foreign equipment and are now in production, selling their products all over Asia. From Ford trucks to Pepsi Cola, Chinese labor is the grist, and foreign currency is changing life in this huge province, with its population of two and one-half times that of California.

The *Wall Street Journal* (June 24, 1982) in a brief report on one "joint venture" captures this new entrepreneurial excitement: "Pepsico invested $5.5 million in its first bottling plant in China. The plant is part of a U.S.-Chinese joint venture in China's Shenzhen special economic zone, about 20 miles north of Hong Kong. The zone let Pepsico export machinery for the plant tax-free. Only 20 percent of the plant's production is to be sold in the zone, under a February 1981 agreement establishing the venture. Pepsi said it doesn't plan to sell the plant's soft drinks elsewhere in China. The rest of the million-case-a-year capacity will be exported to Hong Kong for sale there and elsewhere in the Far East. The 5-year agreement gives Pepsico 45 percent of the profit for the first five years and 40 percent thereafter, the company said. The soft drink and food company said the 31,000 square-foot facility started bottling in February and canning in April, although its official opening won't be until August. Coca-Cola Co., Pepsi's major competitor, last year opened its second Chinese plant. Coca-Cola has been selling products there for about three years.''

The Chinese workers at these joint-venture factories are paid in the same specially identified currency which all foreigners receive when they convert money in China. This special currency serves to regulate the black market and, in theory, keeps foreign money in foreign hands, readily identifiable, for it is money not to be in Chinese hands. Of course, this does not hold in Guangzhou where a free market has been officially recognized. Nor does it hold in Shanghai or Guilin. In both cities I was approached by the classic black-market operator wanting to exchange money.

Foreigners are a minority at the Friendship Store and the Chinese are there with money to spend. The Chinese system is cash and carry. All around me husband, wife, and children staggered out, with all hands beneath their new color TV set; men were teaming together to move each other's new refrigerator to the street. Hi-fi sets were strapped precariously on the back fender of the new owner's new bicycle. The cosmetics counter was busy and fountain pens were selling fast. But the largest action was in sewing machines. Happy couples were hurrying out with their new possessions and it was obvious that as new money flows into China from industrialization, there is going to be one continuous, enthusiastic acquisition of material things.

Eleven years ago I had stayed at the Tung Fang Hotel in Guangzhou, and I have been there several times in the intervening years. It was always a bleak experience. In 1982 I got a taxi (impossible in 1971), was driven in it (Toyota), passed huge Parker Pen, Coca-Cola, Pfizer pharmaceuticals, Norelco razor, Beechum toothpaste billboards, paid my fare, was given a receipt printed by the taxi meter, and strolled into the Tung Fang Hotel. I wanted a haircut and was heading for the one facility of the Tung Fang that I had thought was just about right from my previous visits: a white tile, no-nonsense barber shop, circa the 1930s in the States. It was gone. Instead there was a French salon in muted pastel colors, automatic sliding glass doors, and carpeted, cooled, hushed elegance topped off by a chic Chinese receptionist, also in muted pastels, presiding behind a French, *directoire*-period desk. I was the only American in the reception room. The others were Chinese, some sleek and from overseas, some local young men with full heads of hair, in for their razor cut and styling, and wearing high fashion blue jeans.

This new China is not confined to Guangzhou, but obviously it is more reality there than elsewhere because the free-trade zone is a definite experiment by the Chinese and the contiguous setting to Hong Kong made this the logical place for the trial. But in Shanghai a week earlier, the changing China was also readily seen. Friends whom I have followed through the Cultural Revolution and whose life-style I have been able to watch for more than a decade, invited me to be their guests for dinner at a *French restaurant*. From onion soup, to French bread, to delicate chicken, to a chilled dry white wine, it was a French restaurant. My host, relaxed and happy, sat at the head of the table, placing us in proper seating, western-style. His wife and daughter, very handsomely dressed and wearing lipstick, were sophisticated, proud hosts. And this was the Shanghai which was cited as the Gang of Four's power base.

The next night I was again taken to dinner by a very happy, relaxed family, well dressed with lipstick, perfume, a touch of jewelry—this time at a well-known Chinese restaurant, The Sparrow Cloud. These also are people I have known for several years and have followed the change and rate of change in their living standards. From clothes, to television, to refrigerators, to extra pocket money, they are all moving upward. But more than that they have convinced themselves that they can afford to expose themselves as having these material possessions and, equally important, openly having foreign friends. All discretion has not been tossed away, and I am sure that my friends are looking very carefully over their shoulder to watch for any change in signals from the Communist party. No matter how much the change, I am still well aware that it is a "regulated" friendship, a friendship that can blossom or very rapidly wither, depending upon the central signal.

However, as we left the restaurant that evening, we watched a small drama which reminds one that when restrictions are removed, the new generation, the one that never knew the Cultural Revolution, will explore the limits of their freedom to the outer reaches. As we waited for a taxi, a group of young Chinese men came down the sidewalk, arms locked together, singing and swaying along the way, dressed in tight blue jeans, T-shirts with a variety of legends, including Beethoven's portrait on one. They were happy, noisy, aggressive—they were drunk. This diagnosis was immediately confirmed by one of the young men, who wobbled to the curb, sat, feet in gutter, and gave himself to a dreadful bout of retching and vomiting. I thought of similar scenes in Stockholm, Tokyo, Utrecht, and of course, certain parts of my own growing up in the United States. The new government has, to a degree, liberated China and with it must come all the bad, with the good. There will be drunks in Shanghai, smugglers in Hainan, gays in Guangzhou, and murder, rape, and thievery, for civil liberty automatically releases civil conduct to find its own level. The price a people must pay to have the kind of individual freedom we have in the United States is the misbehavior of a small percentage who cannot handle their liberty. It is always a contest, everywhere, between too much permissiveness and too much restriction.

The inherent control of behavior which flows from the respect for family and for one's elders should not be underestimated. Critics of the Communists castigate them for having broken the traditional family structure. This is too simple a charge. The family complex with extended family housed in a single living compound, with all levels of in-laws, cousins, aunts, (and all levels of pecking order) has stopped (even this is not a complete truth in some rural areas)—but life in China today is still family structured. Mother and father, children, and grandparents are a three-generation structure of daily life, very often housed together. Closeness to brothers, sisters, aunts, uncles, and cousins is very much a reality, far beyond what most Americans can visualize. The influence of this social system upon one's conduct is a major resource which helps sustain and regulate the individual's behavior. Personal liberty is not the issue that it is in our western society, and the individual in China automatically regulates his or her conduct with consideration for the family. Chastity is not regulated by a government decree, but by appreciation of what the family expects. Of course, one billion people do not all conduct themselves well, family or no family, and premarital affairs, rape, drunkenness, and murder, are happening, have happened, and will happen. The calming, guiding, restraining influence of family is still a major strength of Chinese society. And it will be, with or without communism.

From Mao's death in 1976 to now, there has been a phenomenal change in China's policies. I asked one of my dependable contacts if he thought all this change had been good for China. By my question, I was suggesting that some of Mao's efforts should not be discarded. My friend responded, "Oh, things are much better! All we need now are a few more deaths at high level!"

22

THE TEMPLE OF HEAVEN—AND RELIGION

It is interesting to note that both George Hatem and Ed Snow were raised Catholics. Both men left the faith in their adult years. George does not discuss religion other than to reject it for himself. He has a scholar's considerable interest in China's religions and has an objective, not emotional, interest in the role of Buddhism, Muslim, Christianity, etc. in China's history. I do as well, and have tried to trace the strength of religion in today's China. By now I have traveled over most of China and in my travels have looked for evidences of religion. One September day, I asked a friend to take me to the Temple of Heaven.

A late September day in Beijing means ideal weather, a beginning of lovely autumn, and the end of a scorching summer. Beijing spring and fall are perfect months; Beijing in February is a burden of penetrating chill, wind, and dust. Beijing in mid-July is hovering dust, smog, and Kansas City heat. But on this particular morning it was a day fit for an emperor, and we were following imperial footsteps.

We were walking, two of us, a Chinese man and an American man, through the lovely grounds of the Temple of Heaven, relishing the day. For both of us it was a complete holiday. We had no duties; we were free of formality and protocol.

About us were Chinese parents, children, grandparents. A young soldier, his wife, and their little boy, walked three abreast, holding hands, the boy between. A covey of preschoolers paired off, encouraged along by three teachers. Vividly colored prints, tiny dresses and skirts, saucy hairbows, and that most vulnerable of sights: small, plump buttocks peeking through little boys' split trousers. Gardeners pruning, shaping,

215

tying, creating the seemingly natural, twisting silhouette of trees in the Orient. Sweepers with their strangely efficient cluster of twigs, scratching equally across sidewalks and grassless earth, gathering every leaf, twig, paper, and popsicle stick.

It was early enough in the day so that the procession of foreign visitors had not begun. Later there would be parties of travelers from all over the world arriving by bus and automobile. This land of proletarian equality never misses a nuance of rank or status. The first level of guests flows through the crowded streets, hidden deep in lovely, black Red Flag limousines, tan crêpe de Chine silk curtains pulled across the rear windows, fluttering in the breeze. The next level of recognition is conveyed by a smaller, Chinese-made, four-door sedan, usually gray or green. If your party requires more than one such car, then meticulous consideration has been given to the rank and age's of your members: a large placard bearing the numeral identifying the sequence in the procession for your car: #1, #2, #3, etc., is placed in the right front window. Many a pained moment has been experienced by the foreign guest who learned only on the hotel steps that he had been weighed, appraised by the Chinese, and assigned to car #2, #3, etc., not #1. No matter how many cities are visited, how many different convoys of automobiles are used, or your own rejection of your status, once your car assignment has been made, you will remain in #3 automobile for the twenty-one-day experience. This delicate bruising of the guests' psyche cannot be overcome by rebellion or logic.

One of my colleagues was urged by his wife to "seize car #1." They hurried from the hotel at the earliest moment, scrambled into car #1, securing their new base. There was absolutely no moment of hesitation, no caucusing, or no attempt at persuasion. The automobiles were filled in appropriate sequence, with displaced #1's in abandoned car #2. A very smug smile came from the pirates in car #1. The Chinese solution came about very smoothly. The automobiles moved away from the hotel entrance out into the main street, but the procession assumed the following sequence: car #2, car #1, car #3, car #4, which sequence it maintained through the day. By the end of the first "briefing," the Chinese completed their adjustment. The numbers in the automobiles were switched, the rebellious couple tamed and sullen, secured in their #2 position.

Our September morning at the Temple of Heaven was free of automobiles and status. We were also free of the stifling constrictions of the Cultural Revolution.

We had been sauntering through this remarkable park for fifteen minutes. I learned that through 500 years the emperors of China had come here "to speak with the heavens." It was here the emperor made his sacrifices, gave his report, rendered homage to the heavens and sought to "gain their confidence." In a sense, it was here that the transaction took place, the Mandate from Heaven which justified his absolute imperial authority. Separate from the impact of this historical vestment of power is the beauty of the architecture of the temple. The thoughtful tourist should claim a half-day of illness, avoid the planned schedule, and as soon as all good, sturdy colleagues have hurried off to a factory visit, take a taxi and head for its main entrance. If you are feeling strong, go on foot straight south on the main road leaving Tien An Men Square, first passing around the Mao Zedong Mausoleum and the great Main Gate, and go on for a mile. The entire Temple of Heaven area is east of this main road, and is now a huge park.

My companion and I spent a full two hours viewing the magnificient buildings, and then we agreed to "take a little rest" at one of the little limestone tables. We bought Popsicles from a vendor and I commented that it must have been remarkable to have witnessed the imperial procession from the Forbidden City, out through the Great Gate with all of the pageantry. My companion said, "Oh, I don't think anyone was allowed to look. As I understand it, all the citizens had to close their shutters and remain inside."

I queried, "Is that true? I never knew that. I always thought it was supposed to be a great public ceremony."

My companion held his hand in front of his face and said, "Don't ask me, I was a Christian. And so were my parents. I don't know how it was done."

This was a considerable acknowledgment. I of course know many Chinese who were educated in mission schools, although this was not information volunteered or even hinted during the Cultural Revolution. From 1977 on, however, this began to change, and in a variety of ways one gained an awareness of the considerable influence of the mission schools on university faculty. In fact, one met very few physicians and professors in responsible leadership positions who had not received their degrees prior to 1949. The disruption of the Cultural Revolution had not been helpful to the production of new scholars, scientists, and physicians.

With this ready, cheerful Christian identification by my friend, I recognized that the new administration's encouragement to the educated was accepted and trusted. I asked the logical question, "What were you?" And he said, "My family has been Catholic for years." At one time in his life he had been "David."

He said he had not been emotionally committed to his western religion and had no interest or concern now. I asked if this was a matter of simply showing good judgment in view of the handicap a western religion would be to any possible promotion for him. His reply was an earnest one. He said that among the Chinese there had never been a large Christian element, and that it was a rare Chinese who could really believe the Christian story. He said, "The myths and miracles really do not make practical sense." I asked him if his mother had dropped her religion and he replied, "No, she goes to Mass each week."

He then explained to me that the Communist government had not interfered totally with the religions, and the Muslims especially were very active in many parts of the country.

My friend did not go on to tell me that the Muslims had indeed been "active" at several points in the history of China, and they had often been in revolt. I recalled the considerable discussion in *Red Star over China* over the relationship of the Chinese Communists and the Moslems of northwest China.

"With the autonomy slogan the Moslem population was naturally in sympathy, for this has been their demand for many years. Whether the majority of them believed the Reds were sincere in their promise is quite another matter. I doubted it. Years of maltreatment by the Chinese militarists, and racial hatreds between Han and Hui (Chinese and Moslem), had left among them a deep and justified distrust of the motives of all Chinese, and it was unbelievable that the communists had been able to break down this Moslem skepticism in so short a time."[1]

Although Snow's comments related to 1936, there was later evidence that all was not happy between the Muslims of far west Xinjiang and the preponderant Han people. In 1961 there had been a mass flight of the Uzbeks from the Chinese territory of Xinjiang-Uighur autonomous region to the neighboring Soviet territory, as Jacques Guillermaz has described.

"Worsening Sino-Soviet relations, as much as the Great Leap Forward, encouraged the Chinese to make a great effort toward colonization in Sinkiang. Local nationalist tendencies were consequently intensified. They found further nourishment in the fact that Chinese held posts of responsibility in all sectors, including teaching; while Peking's land policy was not approved of by the Muslim population. In 1961, groups of rebels tried to create a Republic of East Turkestan. In July 1962, part of the population of the Ining (Kuldja) region, and of Tach'eng, possibly threatened with deportation to the interior, emigrated en masse to Soviet Kazakhstan. The Chinese held the Russians responsible for this."[2]

Although an autonomous region, the major movement of Han people as permanent settlers into the area, for the first time in history, probably has had a continuing unsettling effect on the Moslem population.

I asked my friend, "Do the Moslem people resent the atheism of the Communist party?" His reply was skillful, "Our constitution carefully protects religious freedom. The wording, as I recall it, is that we all have freedom to believe in religion or not to believe in it. The Moslems vary in their degree of religious activity. In many areas they have taken Chinese names and intermarried so that they almost disappear."

This of course is essentially a definition of what historians claim has happened to all outside beliefs that come within China's own continuing culture. They are simply absorbed, become sinified, and disappear. I had already learned that the two largest Jewish communities had been at Kaifeng and Ningpo, and that these two Jewish populations, although maintaining some identity into the nineteenth century, had finally been absorbed into the Chinese mainstream.

The fact that China has not recognized Israel is a large political reality which was not altered by the formal recognition between the United States and China. Not of the same political importance, but of continuing social concern, is the question of whether there are any Jewish communities carrying on within China. A 1979 article in *Jewish Digest* offers a synoptic view of the Jewish people in China. In one paragraph, Gross states: "In recent years, American tourists have begun to visit

China, and among them have been American Jews. None of them have been able to date to throw any light on the fate of the ancient Jewish community of Kaifeng.''[3]

One learns nothing about this community by asking questions in China. A reference from more than one hundred years ago, however, is fascinating. In a chapter entitled, ''Visit to a Colony of Jews,'' W. A. P. Martin wrote of his travels of February 1866: ''Kai-fung-fu, the abode of the Jewish colony, being four hundred and fifty miles to the southwest of Peking, I engaged a cart drawn by two mules to carry me there in fifteen days . . . After a full month of this luxurious motion I had to descend to a humbler vehicle because the road became so narrow that it would accommodate only one wheel. My wheelbarrow, the common conveyance in that region, was pushed by one man and drawn by another . . . Some of these barrows were fitted with mast and sail, so that when the wind was fair the driver had nothing to do but hold the helm and 'keep her steady'.''[4]

After this considerable expedition, Martin reached Kai-fung-fu, and found not only a solitary stone inscribed to commemorate the erection of the synagogue, but met six men who represented the seven Jewish families still then existing. These six said they no longer knew the language and no longer followed their rituals. They estimated their number to be three or four hundred, but did not know exactly. They maintained no register nor did they assemble together as a congregation. Martin did obtain a copy of the ''Law'' inscribed on a roll of parchment, a sacred book they could no longer read. He presented the roll to Dr. S. Wells Williams, who presented it to the library of Yale College.[5]

A current interview with Bishop K. H. Ding, head of Nanjing Theological College, is reported by Howard S. Hyman. Bishop Ding, a protestant, studied at the Union Theological Seminary in New York. The Bishop said, ''To my knowledge, there are no believers in Judaism in China . . .''[6]

An adjacent area, beyond the Amur River and in Russia's Siberia, also is of interest to the Jewish people. This region was set aside as a Jewish Soviet in the area of Yevreysk; its capital is Birobidzhan. I understand it is nonfunctioning as a Zionist state.

My friend and I continued our conversation at the Temple of Heaven. He commented that there were still some areas with Buddhist activities, and in fact Buddhists from other countries were coming to China to visit certain important Buddhist shrines. He said there was one such shrine in Hangzhou which is visited often by certain sects of Japanese Buddhists.

He went on to tell me that the present government permitted Catholic worship, but the Chinese Catholic Church was no longer connected to Rome or the Pope; it was a freestanding Chinese Catholic Church. I already knew this and I asked him if it were true that an archbishop of the Roman Catholic Church was still in jail. This question surprised him and he asked where I had heard this. I assured him such an event, although it had occurred more than twenty years ago, had been well covered in our western press.

I told him that at Christmas I received a number of Christmas cards from China, complete with a "Merry Christmas!" message. He said that such cards were coming from Chinese who were still Christians, and that they were completely free to send such greetings. I said that I was surprised because I thought such a sentiment was frowned upon and could get one in trouble. He replied that there certainly had been times in the past thirty years when one would have been foolish to make his religious sentiment an issue, but that the new government was trusted, and the guarantee of the Constitution was being accepted.[7]

He said all Chinese schooled by the missions had been urged to take Christian names or to westernize their names. For example, it had been very popular to simply use the initials of your given name: if you were born Chen Tung-kuang, you would enter the western world as T. K. Chen. He said it would be a rare university professor now teaching in China who had not at one time adjusted his name in such a manner, or had had a western given name. All of this rapidly had been dropped when the war ended in 1949. He went on to say that much of this reversion to the Chinese pattern had been a matter of patriotism and a desire to recapture Chinese ways. He pointed out that the national hero, Sun Yat-sen, had kept the traditional style, as had Chiang K'ai-shek.

I told him that there was a large number of Americans who were very "religious" in the western Christian sense, and who really felt that there were millions of Chinese Christians who were hiding their faith and waiting, hoping for the day they could be liberated and express themselves again. He laughed and said, "Although I am a bad example because my own mother has remained a Catholic, I must tell you that the Chinese people just are not religious in the way you mean. We have never through our history taught such things as original sin and going to hell. Even though I went through years of Mass with wafers and wine, it never in the least was something I believed. My oldest brother told me not to worry, it would not hurt me, and learning English was very important. Later on, he guided me into a medical school run by an American university, and I was called David, took all my classes in English, and never again went to church."

I asked, "Could you be a Communist now with that background? Would they accept you in the party?"

He shrugged, "Oh, they would accept me. Some of our best leaders had early Christian exposure. It was hard to avoid it because the missionaries were everywhere and especially dominated the schools. I have enjoyed my profession and I never felt I wanted to do the hard work necessary to get into the party."

I asked, "Will the new easing of pressure and the open declaration of enthusiasm for western help encourage a new religious movement here?" He shook his head, "No, most Chinese, even those who had a good education because of the missionaries, are willing to agree that the overall intent of the missionary effort was harmful to our society. By that I mean, harmful to the Chinese concept of morals and ethics. We are now eager to learn all that we can of the best in the world in science and technology. But we are pleased with our own way of life. We will surprise you if you think we are going to become 'westernized' by all of this new movement. We won't. We will try our best to not only catch up, but we want to show the world that the Chinese are able to be as good or better than the rest of the world in science. You must understand that we are very aware of our ancestors' leadership in the world. We intend to be that good again."

To complete this small departure into religion—and to convey the remoteness from our culture which completely surrounds the traveler from the western world, it is important to understand that one is totally and completely removed from daily world events while in China. Only in Beijing is one likely to receive a daily English-language news bulletin. Once one leaves Beijing, then all knowledge of what we daily consider "the world" stops. There is no newspaper, no radio, no television, no magazines, or no mail, in the English language. After a day or two, a serenity comes over one, along with a freedom from any knowledge of the latest in world catastrophes, terrorists, or revolts. This peace, or at least an absence of stimulation, must be similar to that of rural life in the Middle Ages.

The absence of world contact is magnified by the essential indifference of the Chinese to the affairs of the western world. The ancient assumption that China was the center of the civilized world is attenuated somewhat, of course, but there is nevertheless a China-oriented central theme to almost all aspects of conversation and action.

The massive effort to modernize may alter this "Middle Kingdom" perspective—but one hundred years of intense western missionary, economic, and military penetration did not really leave a dent much beyond a few coastal cities.

While I was in China in 1978, the entire world followed the drama of the death of a very new pope, the regrouping of cardinals, and the stunning choice of a pope from a communist country. I knew nothing about these events. On the day before leaving China, in Guangzhou, I met a newly-arrived American and learned of all this for the first time. I turned to our interpreter and to a physician-friend who had been with me for the previous three weeks. I chastised them for not telling me of this significant event of world importance. They comfortably advised me that they had not heard about it either. It had not been an item carried by the Chinese news media. A pope died, a new pope was chosen—and eight or nine hundred million of the earth's people went on about their work, not involved, and one suspects, not especially concerned.

23

SHADOWED CHINA

GEORGE's China of course has its critics. The large majority of American visitors, at least among my own contacts, come home excited, exhausted, and just recovering from the upper respiratory infection which had begun on their second day there. Everyone, however does not come away with enthusiasm for what they have seen. Some have been outright, severe critics, quite convinced that they were shielded from the truth and exposed to stage settings, not true Chinese life.

One such commentary, widely distributed, has been written by Edward N. Luttwak, associate director of the Washington Center of Foreign Policy Research at Johns Hopkins University.[1] Dr. Luttwak's article is full of precise criticism. He was a member of a group headed by former Defense Secretary James R. Schlesinger, and perhaps the members of the group were unusually expert, and therefore able to recognize hoax and finagling better than others who have the same "twenty-one-day treatment."

For example, Dr. Luttwak spotted the fact that his own immediate escort ". . . Mr. Ting Yuan-lung, head of the American desk at the Chinese Foreign Office and my assigned escort, employed the car rides to and from in order to flatter and to question. Well-briefed on my background and experience, he would ask his questions in a casual fashion, and it was only after two or three days that a clear pattern emerged, and the intelligence motive came to the surface."

He writes further: "Everywhere we went in China women were part of the reception committees and revolutionary councils of town, province, commune and factory. Hardly ever did we hear one say a word;

they smiled and nodded but did not speak.'' And ''. . . in our walks through Peking on which we were followed only at a distance . . .''

These experiences led Luttwak to bitter suspicions. "It is an intellectual mystery which deserves careful study. After the great warning of the Russian Potemkin tours of the 1930s, how could our intellectuals and our journalists, often explicitly mindful of the precedent, fall into the very same trap? What is the powerful urge to believe against all reason? I asked myself the question after just reading John Kenneth Galbraith's scholarly explanation of why there are no queues in China, and then looking at the very long line of hopeful Peking shoppers waiting to buy vegetables. I asked myself the question remembering James Reston's enthusiastic articles while I was being given a medical examination in the same hospital where he was operated upon, an examination in which ill-calibrated instruments yielded fantastic, impossible readings. I asked myself the question, in beautiful Kweilin, visited by congressional ladies and sundry Senators, none of whom appears to have seen the grinding poverty evident in the thousands of women and old men harnessed like animals to carts loaded down with concrete blocks or heavy tanks of night soil.''[2]

Dr. Luttwak concludes his unhappy experience with his challenge: "How could all of this pass unobserved, when all the signs are in evidence? It is possible that our scholars and our journalists can only recognize repression when it is crude and unsuccessful, and therefore requires the visible presence of armed men in the streets? Is it that they can only recognize inefficiency and weakness in liberal democracy? How could the procession of Chinese scholars who have written our tour books fail to highlight for us the fact that they were denied any contact whatsoever with any Chinese not specifically instructed to speak to them? Was it because of their over-riding professional need to be re-invited?

"Perhaps so. After all, that is how the Chinese press department controls the journalists who have fed us much of what we think we know about China. Resident Peking correspondents do not file stories offensive to the Chinese because they are all specialized Chinese experts whose jobs depend upon their visas. Visiting correspondents are often equally dependent on periodic access. And so it is only the rare newspaperman who makes his own prior decision that he will seek no second visa, who can be counted upon to serve us, and not the Chinese. The matter has long since acquired the full dimensions of a scandal. In the press that investigated Watergate, is there no one ready to investigate?''

I have feelings of both envy and sadness when I read Dr. Luttwak's report. I envy his keen eye in detecting this considerable evidence of falsity in the Chinese scene. I envy his ability to spot the fact that he was being followed, that women did not speak up, that a steady effort was being made to slyly interrogate him. I have walked miles upon miles alone in Chinese cities, and no matter how quickly I turn or how cleverly I look for the secret agent, I never find anyone. No one has ever quizzed me about anything except about the care of a specific patient. I feel sadness because Dr. Luttwak found silent women and that they knew they were but window dressing. I have perhaps not had the honor of being followed or visited by the intelligence service, but I certainly have met and talked with pleasure with Chinese women who were in positions of leadership. Whether this was the vigorous director of a hospital, or a member of the Foreign Office, or a member of the Academy of Medical Sciences, or a member of the Political Bureau, or a leader of a commune in the Taching oil fields, I have found women in powerful positions to be fully as vocal as their male counterparts. They have not reached a fifty-fifty parity in top positions, but of course neither have we. So much of Dr. Luttwak's report was different from any experiences of my own that I can only suggest that we must each have a bias.

Dr. Luttwak saw his own China and reports it in his own style. Other observers have made their negative comments. For example, John Cleverley included this paragraph in his analysis of the effect on the university system, written in May 1977, "A brief euphoria followed the crushing of the Gang of Four in October with every talk of a second liberation."[3] I find the euphoria not brief but continuing.

Cleverley quotes a Chinese: "Students don't know anything. They are too ignorant to be employed. Young people think themselves too important to study." If I did not know the comment referred to China, I would believe I was at a faculty meeting in the United States.

John Cleverley begins his essay with the following words of reprimand: "Too often visitors to China have taken statements of purpose and intent as evidence of successful practice. Now the 'Chinese Way', proposed by some as a model for western and developing societies, is in the process of a major evaluation.'' Cleverley is right and his own repeated visits give him the necessary wide view of the changing process called "social engineering."

One might add that no society remains static. The major expenditures and publicity of the "Great War on Poverty" by the Johnson administration would have led the reporter of that period to describe exciting, innovative adventures, which are now being steadily abandoned.

Perhaps the mature opinion among the reflective, cautioning reports is Simon Leys. This is the pen name of Pierre Ryckmaus, a Belgian whose field is Chinese literature and art history. His book, *Chinese Shadows*,[4] should be read by those who seek a certain comfort from objective reporting which is "negative." I use this term in an encouraging sense, just as I would make the comment that Han Suyin would believe she is an objective observer but her observations are reflected in a "positive" sense. It is the balance of adjectives and adverbs that helps to sway the mood of the report.

Saturday Review, June 25, 1977, presented an excellent essay by Simon Leys. The caption or heading of such a magazine piece is never the author's doing (and in fact, can be his undoing). *Saturday Review* elected to use the subtitle: "Now a vast cultural graveyard, China draws on its Golden Age for set pieces fitted to the 'truth' of the moment."

From that considerable indictment of present day China, Leys, of course, begins with a certain proposition that all is not well in China. He moves rapidly to strengthen this thought in his first sentence: "The death warrant of China's intellectual life was given by Mao Tse-tung in Yenan in 1942 when he delivered his famous 'Talk on Arts and Letters'."

This essay is an excerpt from Leys's book, but one line of his reasoning finds me and perhaps Leys trapped between dilemmas of value judgment. He agrees with what is a universal analysis: The Chinese have reduced the illiteracy rate from ninety percent to now less than forty percent. While this has been accomplished by wider insistence upon schooling, it has undoubtedly been facilitated by simplified characters. Leys reaches an interesting conclusion, that by teaching the new generation through the use of modified characters, the Chinese people will be totally deprived of all antecedent Chinese literature. Using the same information, I would conclude that the previously used, very complex

Chinese characters had served to limit access to the written word to an extremely small number of people. If more intensive efforts at schooling, plus an improved means of written communication, have raised the percentage of those who can read from a previous ten percent to a steadily growing figure of more than sixty percent, then I would find a more optimistic view than does Leys.

First, the problem of the lost ancient literature is, of course, only a problem of translation. This literature survives as has Plato's, but the world has not been deprived as follows from Leys's line of reasoning. Few can read Plato in the original, yet access to Plato's words are readily available.

Far more important, moreover, is the rate of speed at which all Chinese are mastering the written, common language. This universal emancipation will not be stopped by such tactics as indoctrination and prescribed reading. Nationwide ability to read and write is a greater victory than the loss of the ancient characters.

In fields of significance in the modern world: science, technology, and medicine, the western literature is widely available in China. The analytical mind can handle the truth of thesis, research, data, and conclusions, all basic ingredients of the universal scientific method. There is no evidence of censorship or governmental interference in giving the literate Chinese full access to this important scientific aspect of mankind's creative effort. All viewers of the China scene will agree that the academic community was cruelly attacked by the policies of the Cultural Revolution. However, to use that particular quotation of Mao's from 1942 as Leys did is, of course, excessive. Suddenly in 1978 Chinese scholars were alive and well. They have been through difficult times, but to draw sweeping conclusions from a small sample of time is not a creditable use of the western analytical mind.

I have found these words of John K. Fairbank helpful:

"The Chinese language today consists of well over 40,000 characters in the biggest dictionary. But these boil down to about 7,000 necessary for a newspaper font, including about 3,000 that one needs to know in order to be really literate . . . "This was one factor helping to keep China, down to the 20th century, in its archaic Confucian mold. The language inhibited easy contact with alien socieites whose students of Chinese found it even harder then than now.[5]

"Perhaps enough has been said to indicate why written Chinese became a monopoly of the scribes. The Chinese language had the character of an institution, rather than a tool of society. Men worshipped it, and devoted long lives to mastering even parts of its literature, which was a world of its own and to which one might gain admittance only by strenuous effort. The Chinese writing system was not a convenient device lying ready at hand for every school boy to pick up and use as he prepared to meet life's problems. It was itself one of life's problems. Thus the Chinese written language, rather than an open door through which China's peasantry could find truth and light, was a heavy barrier pressing against any upward advance and requiring real effort to overcome— a hindrance, not a help to learning.[6]

"Since the Chinese written language has been one of the tools by which the upper class has enjoyed the fruits of Chinese culture and maintained social dominance, language reform and the class literacy which it might make possible has been a fundamental problem in China's revolution . . . Among the new scholar class, leadership was taken by the noted writer Dr. Hu Shih. While a student at Cornell and Columbia during World War 1, he had advocated the use of the *pai-hua,* or Chinese spoken language as a written medium for scholarship and all purposes of communication . . . The use of pai-hua spread rapidly; the tyranny of the classics had been broken.[7]

John Fraser, a Canadian correspondent assigned to China in recent years, put his experiences into a book. He was painfully harsh in his judgment of Rewi Alley.

". . . Alley cast his lot with Mao Tsetung and for years has contributed sympathetic and usually lugubrious prose and poetry to . . . newspapers and magazines. A fantasist who sees only what he wants to see, he is fixated with a vision of revolutionary China that rarely differs from the propaganda department. In the past when outside observers talked about the foreign experts in China, they usually were referring to Rewi Alley. He gave them all a bad name in precisely the same way that the legendary writer Han Suyin gave all official 'friends of China' a bad name: they seemed to be toadies to whatever faction or party had power in Peking.'"[8]

As I read the remarks of Fraser's (and the rest of his book), I appreciate his frustration in being unable to be an effective newspaperman in

China. It is a closed society and neither Canadian nor American reporters will have the access they enjoy in their own society. Japan is not communistic but it too is a closed society, and western reporters can only hover on the edges, collecting bits of pollen like angry bees. Fraser did not get to know Rewi Alley and this obviously irritated Fraser. To assign Alley the responsibility for the bad reputation of "foreign experts" is doing injustice to the man who devoted years of his life to helping all of China through his founding of the original industrial cooperatives (Indusco), through founding and running a successful boys' school, and, in his early years in China, long before the present agreement, doing all he could to improve the working conditions of the Shanghai factory workers. Fraser sullies Alley without knowing him. Fraser also sweeps all of those who believe they are "friends of China" into a category of "toadies." This quality of emotional writing is probably a useful purge for Fraser, but it leaves no latitude for those who believe that friendship with a country and with its people is a diplomatic maneuver, perhaps more effective than a soldier and rifle. Rather than faulting Alley, one can only regret that there were not a hundred thousand more of him in China all these years, voicing moderation, optimism, and encouragement.

In reflecting upon the criticisms of Leys, Cleverley, and Luttwak, and the latter's call for good, honest Watergate-type of reporting on China, I of course pause to ask where I fit along the spectrum of such reporting. My access to China has been considerable. I have reviewed what I have written. I find that I have held to my original and continuing goal to report what I saw and avoided strong adjectives, adverbs, and conclusions. I have understood that I was a visitor and that the scene I was observing was under rapid change. A truism of 1971, "All Chinese people carry little red books," was no longer true in 1978. The fact of 1973, "All middle school graduates must work for a minimum of two years before consideration for college," is not a fact in 1980.

As I read my own published words, I find that I have been expressive about my own lack of enthusiasm for China's regimented life. I have repeated most carefully that I am an enthusiastic, although not markedly successful capitalist, not a communist. Equally, I have little doubt but what I would have spent, if living in China, most of my time in a May 7 School, correcting my thought. The Cultural Revolution would have been my undoing even if I had lasted from 1949 to 1966. With all of its blemishes, the American system suits me. None of these remarks has seemed to produce a "blackball" for future visas. Professor Luttwak will of course visit China again. I look forward to his second look.

I fully agree that far too many Americans have returned with enthusiastic endorsements often summarized as "I have seen the future, and it worked!" Such positive spirit seems to me as uneducated as the call for the release of investigatory reporters, charged with ferreting out the Chinese Watergate.

China is another man's house. It is one remarkable house. For better or worse, I interpret the evidence to indicate that the rest of the world is likely to have a very large, commercial, economic, cultural, scientific, technological, and medical intercourse with this changing China. Equally, I suggest that world peace, reasonable world peace, is much more likely to be achieved if China has an accepted, recognized role in regional zones of political and military stability.

Upon reading the cries for accuracy in reporting the flaws of the China scene, my feeling is of full sympathy. But such reporting, perhaps, should avoid large conclusions, such as: "The death warrant of Chinese intellectual life was given by Mao . . . in 1942," or Luttwak's declaration: "The matter has long since acquired the full dimensions of a scandal. In the press that investigated Watergate is there no one to investigate [China]?"

Of course an appropriate Chinese response could be that it had not occurred to them that they should send their reporters to Washington, as they had respected that as an area of another man's house.

If we Americans continue to utilize our relatively easy access to China for developing and opening communications that are mutually useful, it seems reasonable to assume that this form of shared experience may have influence in bringing China into open communication with the rest of the world. It would be more beneficial than constantly declaring that all is not well there, that progaganda is rampant, or that all of the public was not sympathetic to the conflicts of the Cultural Revolution.

Those nations which have come through a period of colonial occupation are finding the attitude and hospitality of China comfortable. These nations frequently are the sources of raw material for much of the world. Equally, their impoverished, numerous people represent the world's largest market for sewing machines, bicycles, railroads, tools, and machines. The raw materials of these nations and China's developing industrial production will have a natural affinity for each other. Ross Terrill's comment sharpens this fact.

"Chinese bicycles and clothes and plastics fill Asia's department stores, just as Japan's used to do when Japanese labor costs were still low. In Hong Kong, joint ventures between local companies and the Chinese government are underway in ship building, machine tools, and other fields.

"Some Hong Kong electronic manufacturers are using semiconductors from China instead of from Japan, as formerly.

"The old slogan, 'oil for the lamps of China', has been turned on its head for China produces one hundred million tons of oil each year, and its reserves are enormous—Peking considers them to be as large as those of the entire Middle East. Oil exports to Japan pay for the import of Japanese steel. China's oil helps fuel Thailand and the Philippines. In Hong Kong, trucks of China's state Oil Company make deliveries to gas stations."[9]

The Chinese experience is not occuring in a vacuum. An international dependence upon shared resources, an impossibility to censor world communication and information, and the enduring capacities of the Chinese people regardless of their form of government, will bring them the liberties they want. And their definition of liberty may well not be the same as ours.

24

THE NATIONAL EXAMINATION

For the intellectual Chinese family, the exciting event has been the reestablishment of a national written examination, taken at the same time throughout China. I say "reestablishment," because for centuries the administrative leadership of old imperial China was selected in a remarkably similar manner.

Charles O. Hucker described the structure of Ming Dynasty China (1368–1644), and although there are obvious differences, some of the eternal facts of China call out to us.

". . . There was only one avenue of entry that could lead to a successful career. That was a sequence of public, competitive examinations.

"Students in government schools and privately tutored scholars alike could qualify for these examinations. Provincial education intendants visited all campuses once a year and certified all male citizens of proper scholarly attainment and of good moral character as Bachelors (Hsiu-ts'ai)—titles that had to be renewed at intervals of not less than three years, and they could be revoked at any time for improper conduct. Several privileges were afforded Bachelors, one of which was the right to participate in the examinations conducted under imperial auspices of the various provincial capitals every third year. The provincial examinations were exhausting ones, covering three full days of writing spaced over a week. Those who passed were entitled licentiates (Chu-jen) and given new privileges. Their success qualified them in turn to participate in an empire-wide metropolitan examination conducted at the national capitol several months later, also every third year. This examination was still more difficult, and those who passed received still greater privileges and certification as Doctors (Chin-shih). In all, 24,874 doctorates were conferred in the 90 metropolitan examinations conducted during the Ming period, an average of 267 per examination. The smallest number of degrees granted at any examination was 32; the largest, 472.

"The rosters of all the degree-holders were maintained by the Ministry of Personnel, which was in general charge of assignments in the civil service. Bachelors who obtained no higher degrees could not expect governmental appointments. Persons who got no further than the Licentiate Degree were eligible for assignments, but seldom were able to move into the higher ranks of the service. A Doctor, however, was almost guaranteed an appointment and could expect, if all went well, to progress steadily up the ladder of civil service ranks and perhaps to emerge later in life among the greatest dignitaries of the realm or as a Grand Secretary, a Minister or Vice-Minister, or Censor-in-Chief."[1]

The Communist party version of this ancient single examination taken to decide the career options for the rest of one's life has had a profound effect. For those who care, and in China whole families care about the academic success of their children, the new examination provides a stimulus, a goal, and a future. No longer must one, with patriotic enthusiasm, synthetic or otherwise, wave banners and cheer as sons and daughters march off to an indefinite period of "lao-dung," hard work, in the rural areas.[2] The national goal now matches the traditional goal of the Chinese people. Hard schooling, diligent study, and success based upon hard work and ability are now again legitimate. The national examination has regained for the teacher the recognition and satisfaction destroyed by the Cultural Revolution. "Getting ready for the examination" has become a national family purpose. Tutoring, special classes, full-time preparation for a year, have all become a part of this new Chinese version of an age-old testing for talent.

Can the peasants accept the automatic elitism now set in motion? The cities have more and better schools; their science teaching and equipment is better. The communes are disadvantaged. The availability of good schools, good teachers, and good equipment in the countryside is sparse. What adjustments can be made to prevent a polarization between city and country? Eighty percent of China's people cannot be bypassed or handicapped in their once-in-a-lifetime chance with the national examination.

The examination is in five parts, each worth one hundred points. The student can accumulate his score from all five parts, and thus his determination of success may be based upon strong scores in two or three subjects. The subjects tested are mathematics, science, chemistry, the Chinese language, and "politics": Thus, a score of 500 is possible. The so-called passing score varies throughout the country, depending upon the reputation and the quality of the preparation offered at the middle schools of each region. For example, a score of 350 used to be required in the Beijing area; a score of 270 was acceptable in Tsinan. Fukien has long had a reputation for outstanding middle schools, and the Fukien candidates scored high. A score of 400 was outstanding anywhere in the country.

The upper age for taking the examination is twenty-five. A student may take the examination more than once, but not after age twenty-five. Students who do not feel adequately prepared or who have been out of school in non-learning positions, have the opportunity to take intensive preparatory courses before the examination. The factories and mines in Beijing and the communes on the outskirts permit applicants to take fifteen days off with full pay, to review.

Although a second language such as French, English, Japanese, or Russian is not tested on the examination, the candidate should have a second language. English is the second language of China, with almost eighty percent of the students selecting it. An interesting prospect: it is possible that more people will speak English *there* than *here* in a few years.

In general, the students may compete for the college field of their choice, but where the need is great and there are too many students for specific fields, the authorities may assign a student to a university major.

Taking the examination requires prior selection on the basis of adequacy: moral, intellectual, and physical. All applicants first apply at their factory, mine, commune, office, or school. The names of those considered "qualified" are forwarded with approval from the county or city enrollment committees. Preliminary entrance examinations are then given in most cases and lists drawn up according to grades obtained. At this point the candidates also need approval "politically and physically." One wonders how bias and favoritism affect this level of decision.

Science and liberal arts candidates take separate exams. The science candidates are examined in mathematics, politics, Chinese, physics, and chemistry; the liberal arts candidates in mathematics, politics, Chinese, history, and geography. Those wanting to major in a foreign language take an additional exam in that field.

The "political" requirement for sitting for the examination is obviously how the party maintains control. "The student's political record must be clear, he must profess devotion to the Chinese Communist party and socialism, not be averse to labor, abide by revolutionary discipline and is set on studying for the revolution. . . ." Seventy percent of the students come from workers, poor and lower-middle peasants, and cadres. The children of former small traders, urban poor, professors, scientists, and physicians made up twenty-eight percent. A few come from the bourgeoisie or parents "with grave political records."[3] The evolving debate going on among the Chinese leaders, which suggests that Chinese logic is influencing Communist dogma, was made clear in late January 1979 when all class distinction for children taking the examination was eliminated.

The examination questions are the same throughout the nation. Larger and larger numbers qualify each year: 278,000 in 1977; 290,000 in 1978; in 1979, 270,000, and 350,000 in 1981. A small number of students still in middle (high) school who had exceptional qualifications were allowed to take the examination. For example, of 700 freshmen admitted to the Chinese University of Science and Technology, ninety-two were under sixteen years of age. Several were fourteen years, and one was twelve. This young genius finished primary school at five and a half.

George's children were already into their careers and therefore not involved in the national examination. (His son, Yu Ma, is a professional photographer for one of the major national pictorial magazines.) His grandchildren are young, but already the family conversation refers to the day they will take the examination.

There is little doubt that the city-educated students are out-scoring all others and are now enrolled in the best universities. High-ranking political administrators live in the large cities; their children therefore go to the best middle schools. These children score well on the national examination, and therefore get into the university of their choice. I asked Beijing friends if this is fair. How can a farmer's child compete if his basic schooling is poor? The similarity to the problem in the United States in rural and poor areas is obvious. The Chinese had no answer. They agreed it was unfair, but gave no suggestion that a quota of places should be held for the less well-prepared peasant's son. The answer was that China now needed its best talent; talent was in the cities, and therefore it was logical that high-ranking government officials, physicians, and university-educated parents would have the majority of university prospects among their children.

An interesting result of this form of bias is that many of these parents were educated by the Christian missionary effort. Although this had a negative value during the Cultural Revolution, since Mao's death the missionary influence is again acknowledged. This missionary effort is having a second and third generation effect, resulting in a new generation of university-educated Chinese who speak English. The majority of these Chinese families have several relatives living abroad, usually in the United States or Canada. These overseas Chinese are often well established in academic or business careers, and offer a strong family and financial prospects for future graduate study in the United States to this new generation of Chinese scholars. This United States-China tie is perhaps China's most significant overseas connection. One learns on every hand that there is a cousin, brother, sister-in-law in Boston, Philadelphia, or San Francisco. The Chinese place great reliance on family connections, and this North American academic and professional network is rigorously at work, with books, calculators, cameras, and tape recorders flowing to China and graduate students coming to the United States. By the summer of 1980, 1,200 advanced scholars were studying in American institutions; these are official, government-supported scholars. By 1982, 12,000, official and unofficial, had been here.

In addition to these government-sponsored scholars, there are several thousand students here under private sponsorship. Usually this means funding has been worked out within the Chinese family, with the help of family members who live in the United States. Often, however, the sponsor is an American school or college, interested in helping Chinese

students, or an American who through travel in China has met some young Chinese person and invited him to come under their personal guarantee of support.

China's willingness to send scholars to the United States is worth analysis. Why this willingness to ignore the very antagonistic American national policy toward China, which from 1949 to 1972 prevented any contact? Why not France, the United Kingdom, the Netherlands, Sweden, West Germany, Canada—all scientifically advanced countries and all with an early acceptance of the reality of the People's Republic of China? Why not use these countries for the Chinese scholars and preempt the United States?

The willingness is one of the messages of this book: the goodwill stemming from the early friendships at Yanan, from Snow's writings, from Hatem's continued presence, from Soong Chingling's American education, from the American exposure through the missionaries, and from the advanced education many Chinese received in the United States prior to 1949. But, even more important, the large number of Chinese relatives already living in the United States offered the strong bridge of family connection. With no other western nation does China have this special relationship.

Instead of a hesitancy in sending scholars to the United States, the problem now, in the second half of 1982, is one of excess. Too many families have made private arrangements for too many children. The unofficial movement of Chinese intellectuals' children, coming to the United States through private arrangement has had to be regulated. These intellectuals are often in the very highest of Chinese leadership circles, and the criticism of their willingness to send their offspring abroad for education has been considerable. This has placed these particular highly-positioned Communists in a difficult position. First, if their children get official scholarships to the United States, there is the question of selection through nepotism. Second, if their child gets support from a private American source, there is the challenge made, "Would a good party member accept capitalistic backing?"

There is an additional problem now surfacing. Those scholars coming under official Chinese endorsement have stayed one or two years and returned home. The privately-sponsored children are slow to return to China. Many seem to be taking permanent root in the United States.

So many young people came between 1979 and 1982, that in early 1982 an unwritten but definitive bloackade by China was imposed. No more privately-supported offspring may come, until they have graduated in China and have given two years of work in China in their special field. The term "brain drain" quickly became a part of the Chinese vocabulary. This caught a large number of the young, literally with tickets in hand, and not allowed to leave China. Their anguish has been considerable. It will now be interesting to see what happens. Will these young people be allowed to come, after they have given their two years of required work? In other words, is this but a two-year slowdown? And, a more sensitive concern, will those Chinese (several thousand) who are in the United States through private support, *ever* return home? Will the majority, already with family in both China and in the United States, elect to become permanent members of the family's American branch? My guess is that this will often happen, and it is an early sensitivity to this reality which has caused this two-year embargo on privately arranged scholarship to the United States.

All of this first became apparent to me when a good-hearted American family noted the homesickness of a young Chinese college student, and offered a gift trip home during the summer vacation. An urgent response came from the father, a highly placed person in government: "No, thank you! Not now. The time is not right to come home. Matters are not yet clear. It may not be possible to return to the United States." A few weeks later, the Central Committee's new requirement of two years of employment in China before overseas study closed down all private arrangements.

But all of this is but temporizing, maneuvering, dancing, by the political leadership. They will not be able to resist the massive momentum of the Chinese people. The party's problem now is how to de-Marx their message, launder their Leninisms, and release their hold on the country, before the country takes hold of them. The Communist leadership is very much in the role of having a tiger by the tail, and hoping the tiger interprets the holder's intent as supportive.

25

THE INFLUENCE OF THE OLD CHINA HANDS

THROUGH Edgar Snow's writings, the large numbers of Americans visiting China, and his own United States tours, George has become the most famous American now living in China. There are others there, some who have been employed in China as journalists, interpreters, and editors, and a few others who remained, married and settled in China after their capture as enlisted men in the Korean War.

This group of "leftist" westerners living in Beijing at the beginning of the Cultural Revolution became very enthusiastic about the Revolution's goals. They earned the label "The 300 percenters." They made direct attacks on the foreigners, such as Rewi, who maintained their foreign ways and lived in a definite degree of comfort. They successfully isolated him, shunned him, and for a period a security policeman was detailed to watch him for any evidence of espionage. For three years he was forbidden his summer stay at Beidaihe. Some of the "300 percenters" became such activists that the Chinese government jailed them. George and Rewi carefully separate their own moderate position from these "leftists."

As one visits now with the three old friends, it is not difficult to detect a certain moderation in the conviction that Marxism is the answer to the world's problems. They still can subscribe to dialectical materialism and offer it as a rational, factual analysis of conditions. At the same time, they express pleasure in seeing private enterprise return to China, and the opening of family-owned restaurants, cleaning shops, tailoring stores, and markets. George and Rewi comment that such enterprises add to the quality and pleasure of life.

Not only from George and Rewi, but from others as well, one hears the comment of how innocent and enthusiastic almost all of China was at the beginning of liberation. All things seemed possible, and party doctrines were followed with the fervor of genuine goodwill and belief. The Cultural Revolution was a hardening experience for many and left some with no great confidence in communism.

George seems to have mellowed in 1982 and at times not even certain what the future holds for the governing policies of China. His fervor for Marxist communism is muted and there is a willingness to settle for a Chinese brand of social democracy. George and Rewi quietly voice the feeling that it is China that will survive, with the form of government to be evolved by the Chinese people. They are agreed that some dependable means of legal protection of the people from government is needed. At the same time they comment on how deep are the imperial traditions and customs and how difficult it is to truly liberate the minds of peasants who have been subjected to thousands of years of feudal indoctrination. They both identify the continuing flaw at the very pinnacle of the present system: the lack of a dependable, safe means for the transition of power.

One finds the two men quieted in their "party line" acceptance, and in a sense, almost where they began: devoted to the cause of the Chinese people, willing to commit their careers and lives to the survival of China and not party men who came to China to create a revolution. At one time and under a given set of circumstances, revolution under the banner of communism, imbued with the honesty of young Mao, Zhou, and Zhu De, seemed to them the right way to fight for China's survival. China was their end, communism a means to that end.

The decades have passed and now they can see that China did survive; the famines, plagues, servitude, and foreign domination have ended. But they have also seen that the decade of the Cultural Revolution showed the risk and foolishness of a total, all-out effort to thoroughly communize a people. In a real sense, the Cultural Revolution, stripped of its Gang of Fourisms and anti-Lin Biaoisms, was a fatal social experiment for those who proclaimed that the ultimate goal for a peaceful mankind is complete communization. The Cultural Revolution took this long-cherished credo of ultimate Marxism, field-tested it, and destroyed it. The "promised land" where there would be one class of citizen, with common equality, all beginning with the propertyless and poor, was explored for ten awful years but in the end it was not a land that had appeal. This experience, even with the strength of Mao's reputation and Zhou Enlai's administrative ability, proved so wrong, so painful, and so unacceptable to the Chinese people, that it perhaps will be eventually identified by political scientists as the beginning of the end of communism in China. I suspect that the vocabulary and methods of communism have had their best years in China and a moderation to a form of democratic socialism is well underway.

The old revolutionaries, George, Rewi, and Hans, gave all of their years to seeing the reestablishment of China as a world nation and the Chinese—a wholesome, proud, healthy people—"stand up."

But they also saw the flaws—manipulations, the jockeying for power, slander, the justification, rationalization, the cruelness, deification, and desecration. At this point in their long-shared observations they may believe the end justified the means, but they are wise to know now that much of what they were told, and often helped to propagate, was no new, grand approach to solving mankind's problems, but was instead as flawed as all forms of absolutism.

They have lived through a half-century of Chinese history, which on a human's life scale seems significant. But dramatic as this half-century has been, and the characters involved as impressive as they were, Rewi and George have lived long enough to know that what has happened in these fifty years, is but a brief paragraph in the long, continuing history of Chinese civilization.

I offer these two last views. First, the Chinese nation is intact, politically, geographically, emotionally; and we, our children, and our grandchildren will experience the return of the Chinese people to world power. Second, the Chinese civilization is altering the communism of Marx, Lenin, and Mao.

This is not to say that the Communist party of China, by name and fact, is about to fold up and leave the scene. The changes are in interpretation and implementation. Somewhere within Mao's writings will be found any needed justification for a change of direction, even previously cited Mao Thought. The steady, patient, yielding but unyielding Chinese people have begun the process of absorbing, changing, and sinifying an invader. The lasting "ism" will prove to be patriotism.

George is a happy, peaceful man. At the moment he is engaged in a major public health project—the elimination of leprosy.

Are there any lessons in the story of Doctor Horse? There are several, and one can choose the chapter to fit the lesson. *Tenacity:* The immigrant's son who salvaged a medical education from the great Depression. *Imagination:* The young adventurer with his new medical degree, who sailed off to the exotic excitement of the international settlement of Shanghai. *Commitment:* The physician who decided the problems of China could be best solved by Mao's Communists, and believed it so completely that he disappeared from his own family's world from 1936 to 1971. *Accomplishment:* The American doctor who saw the elimination of venereal disease, narcotics, and prostitution from the entire China world. *Compassion:* The physician sent suddenly, dramatically, by Mao and Zhou to give succor to dying Snow. *Love of family:* The family black sheep, an unacknowledged embarrassment from 1936 on through the McCarthy Era, who finally returned, still a Communist, but now respected and honored. *Courage:* The dying man who serenely, even happily, brought his wife on a farewell return journey to his family and roots in 1978.

But there is another, larger lesson that Hatem poses to all of the American people and their sequence of·governments and foreign policy. George can be seen as a single human experience of the China Policy of thirty-five years spent "containing Chinese communism." His complete commitment to China put him beyond the reach of the McCarthy Era, but the pathos of the Snows, Service, and others needs to be remembered.

American-Asian foreign policy from 1945 to 1971 was based on the logic that China had been seized by a dictatorship unwanted by the Chinese people, that the true and respected government was temporarily in Taiwan. It was feared that the Chinese Communists would expand into other countries, and we therefore fought an extremely long and bloody war in Vietnam. Very experienced people such as Edgar Snow, John Service, John Carter Vincent, Evans Carlson and others, had repeatedly warned their government that the China Policy was wrong.

As a result, all of them were harmed, not only by congressional attack, but by negative comments in the press as well. Even as late as the fall of 1971, when it was obvious that the Nixon administration was changing our China Policy, Snow's articles were turned down by the *New York Times*.

Beginning in 1971 and continuing to the present, thousands of Americans—presidents, senators, congressmen, cabinet members, business leaders included—have returned from visits to China and almost uniformly recited the merits of what they had seen. Our determination to save Indochina from China's Communists and our complete dedication to the true China government on Taiwan has now been replaced enthusiastically, almost without a negative voice, by a new set of facts. Vietnam did fall, not to China, but to a government that China itself militarily attacked in 1979. Suddenly the United States and China had a common enemy in Vietnam. The confusion grew when the China we kept out of the United Nations for thirty-five years quickly became one of our most sought-for supporters on the Security Council.

Russian forces pour into Afghanistan as the American secretary of defense is warmly received in Peking. Almost instantly it is accepted by the American public that China is our logical ally, and that the answer to the Russian hazard is a United States-China accord. The United States puts a moratorium on the SALT treaty; the true salt seems to be on the bear's tail . . . the awful risk to Russia if it should foolishly invade western Europe, with a billion Chinese waiting for the right moment to reclaim Chinese territory. Chinese time is measured slowly but accurately. Regaining the land lost to the Russians in the past century is still on the list of things to be done.

The same American skill and logic that kept China out of the UN also shut the door to her participation in the Olympics. Now resistance to competing with athletes from Communist China is gone, and instead China finds itself vigorously encouraged to join the United States in boycotting the Olympics. The Chinese leadership must look with wonderment on the changes in their reputation. To be removed from a designation as "nothing but Mao's faceless blue ants," with Zhou Enlai unworthy of a handshake by our secretary of state, to a role as our most sought-for tourist attraction, our friend at the UN, our cultivated partner in a "free world" Olympics, and our potential ally for containing Russia must occasion a few quiet smiles over cups of jasmine tea.

For George Hatem, a man of peace and a healer, it all adds up to a wonderful completion, even justification, of a career. Yet for Ed Snow's reputation and for his wife, Lois, and for all the others who told the truth, suffered, and endured, it is perhaps all too personal to be seen objectively. The world seems explosive, almost on the brink of a third world war. If the American government will hold a steady course, cultivate fully the potential of its China ally, then the brink may not be reached but instead, a level of world stability found. This is the delayed stability that somehow survived thirty-five years of confrontation. George Hatem, Ed Snow, and the old China hands have made their point.

An honest means of concluding this book is to turn back to Ed Snow and his friendship with George Hatem. Writing in *Red China Today: The Other Side of the River,* Snow said:

"Talking to George Hatem was more illuminating than I am able to convey here; he helped me understand the logic of some things that had puzzled me in China. He knew the faults and failures of the regime, but he also knew the misery of Old China and the enormity of the problems it presented. Because he is the one American who has for twenty-five years intimately shared the ordeals of the men and women who fought for the responsibility to bring China to her feet, his continuing faith in what they are doing merits attention.

" 'China simply could never have stood up any other way', he said. 'Nearly everything done has been necessary, and nearly everything necessary has been done. And, all in all, it is a success.'

". . . From afar China's failure seemed more evident than its success. It was seen abroad as a land of starvation, overwork, commune blunders, cultism, belief in 'inevitable war', shrill propaganda reflecting the fears and tensions of a harassed leadership, forced labor, brainwashing, and persecution of individualism. American cold-war propaganda overstates these charges, but perhaps no more than Communists' propaganda distorts its picture of the American scene by over-emphasis of news on crime, racketeering, government corruption, racial oppression, narcotics addiction, juvenile delinquency, and commercialized pornography.

"But in the quiet of Dr. Hatem's tiny garden beside the still lake, I was reminded of something . . . That is the simple fact that behind all the propaganda stand millions of unknown, unsung men and women who have successfully and devotedly carried out the real work of releasing half a billion people from a heritage of dense ignorance and superstitution, widespread disease, illiteracy and universal poverty. The task is far from accomplished, but the foundations of a modern civilization have been laid, with little outside help, and against handicaps to which Americans have made heavy contributions. These foundations will last regardless of what government rules in the future—unless of course it is destroyed by war and all people perish with it. China is bigger than any government . . ."[1]

Snow made these remarks twenty years ago; they are still true today.

George Hatem long ago made his peace with the world he elected to live in. He is a survivor in a revolutionary society where survivors are few, foreign survivors very few, and where there were no rewards for changing one's mind and "going home." Through these pages, I have hoped to convey the story of a compassionate, warm, human being who is equally a tough, calculating, cautious veteran who was able to navigate safely very close to absolute struggles for power.

How much of this is acquired, learned behavior and what part of it is the original man? Who knows that about any of us? We are all part noble and part imp. George is not larger than life; however, he has brought a very sharp intellect through a half-century proving ground. The proving ground has been one where the ability to survive was the same as the ability to be discreet. Discreet not only in the sense of discretion of conduct, but also an acute discretion to differentiate the shifting of the winds about him.

George Hatem, Doctor Horse of China, will have other biographies. He has maintained that he has no intention of writing his own story; however, the new openness of China and the obvious endorsement of American relationships may change this. It is not difficult to see an official, somewhat noble, documentary about Doctor Horse. Norman Bethune, the Canadian surgeon, and Ed Snow have now been given official places in this foreign friends pantheon. Recent magazine articles from China have taken on this personal, narrative flavor. Anna Louise

Strong and Manny Granich have, among others, been subjects of this respectful handling.

There is undoubtedly a treasure house of Hatem experiences. I have here told of the man as I could verify it: the story of the George Hatem who came to Snow's bedside, who sustained Ed and Lois through the terminal days, who as accurately understood the widow's grief and took every, extra, essential step to bring her and the children through to stability. The George Hatem who spoke at Ed's services at the John Knox Foyer in Geneva: gently, unaffectedly, honestly, remembering a friend; the George Hatem who was told he had an inoperable cancer and free of self-pity, false braveness, and lachrymose farewells, carried out his good-bye trip.

Of course, these emotional trials are not necessarily evidence of capacity, but are what one would expect from a fully seasoned physician. The daily George Hatem, dealing with light conversation, the passing scene, the social moment, is the one I have come to like and enjoy. He is witty, serene in repartee, and always looking for a pun in a turn of a remark. There is just a nice edge of sarcasm and jest, a willingness to turn a question back to the asker with a sharper question. He is no man to debate unless one's ammunition is very dry.

In any roster of remarkable lives, one needs to remember there is an American named Ma Haide, living by a lake just north of Beijing's forbidden city, whose life has been unique. A society in which venereal disease and narcotics addiction were eliminated is worthy of respect. A man who played a major role in that success deserves honor and recognition. The young physician who went to Shanghai fifty years ago and tried to find some purpose for being a physician succeeded. One billion people are now free of syphilis, gonorrhea, and addiction. George did not do that alone, but the magnitude of this truth is certainly due, in a large part, to Doctor Horse of China.

EPILOGUE

ALMOST everyone, conservative or liberal, capitalist or communist, atheist or theist, would identify peace, world peace, as his genuine hope. I modify "every" with "almost" because there are undoubtedly some situations in which war is a necessary prelude to negotiation.

From 1949 to 1972, the United States sought peace in Asia by ignoring the existence of the Communist government of China and by war in Korea and Vietnam. Then in 1972 Richard Nixon signed the Shanghai Agreement, and, in 1978, Jimmy Carter completed the full recognition of the People's Republic of China. Which approach has been most successful?

From the day Mao declared the founding of the People's Republic of China, October 1, 1949, to the day that President Carter officially recognized that government's existence, December 14, 1978, an average of twenty-eight American soldiers died each day in combat on the edges of China.[1] In the years since 1978, there have been none. And there are other facts of significance:

In the twenty-nine years of nonrecognition, no students came to the United States from China; in the first three years since recognition, there have been twelve thousand.

From 1949 to the visit of the United States pingpong team in 1971, the Snows and a very few others were the only Americans to see China or more importantly, to be seen by the Chinese. This tourist year, 1982–1983, 100,000 Americans will visit China.

From 1949 to the 1972 action of President Nixon, there was no economic exchange between the two countries. In the first year of open negotiations, 1972, two-way trade between the two countries was $55 million; in 1981 it was $5.5 billion—a tenfold increase. Since the assumption of relations, thirty-five treaties, agreements, or protocols covering culture, science, technology, trade, aviation, and ocean shipping have been signed, government-to-government, regulating the conduct of one government to the other.

None of these facts will carry the argument with the ideologue who is convinced that communism is wrong and must be attacked wherever it exists. But are not all of these actions the epitome of attacks on communism? To have China's future leadership educated here, to have its people see and speak, this year alone, with 100,000 of our emissaries, to establish legal economic covenants and shared enterprises—are not all of these actions more positive agents of change than military confrontation? Is it not sound foreign policy to stabilize our political relationship, to cultivate the open door for cultural and economic exchanges and allow the internal force of the Chinese civilization to shape the form of government the Chinese people want? And of course, that form of government may never be a two-party democracy, American style. The governments of Taiwan, South Korea, Singapore, and even Japan are not participating, two-party, open democracies; yet we have acknowledged each as appropriate to its culture. Further, each country has had major economic success under its own version of leadership. What we should hope for is a Chinese leadership which is moderate, pragmatic, and reasonably open.

Our greatest contribution toward that goal is cultivation of the greatest degree of open exchange, direct confrontation will only force the Chinese to close ranks and perpetuate Communist control. The welfare of the Chinese people now depends upon production and marketing, not weapons. The same is true for the United States.

A critic's immediate response might be that we should do nothing to foster economic growth and stability of China, and that our own economic survival is jeopardized by the emergence of an immense Chinese labor force. The answer to that argument is that Japan, both Koreas, Taiwan, Hong Kong, Singapore *and* China are already well on their way to international success as giants of production and marketing. Our survival depends not upon containing them but upon a renaissance of our own industries, and marketing the products of our agriculture. There is no possibility of stopping the return of the Chinese people to world eminence.

The Chinese experience is not occurring in a vacuum. An international dependence upon shared resources, the impossibility of censoring world communication and information, and the enduring capacities of the Chinese people regardless of their form of government will bring them the liberties they want. And their definition of liberty may well not be the same as ours.

China is not perfect. Americans must guard against over-enthusiasm—both on their part and in relying on the messages given by the Chinese. For them to announce a goal of world-level modernization by the end of the century is an exciting statement. But as T. S. Eliot said:

> Between the idea
> and the reality
> Between the motion
> and the act
> falls the shadow.

I urge that we all use every opportunity to go, to see, to think, to influence, and to make our own reasoned conclusions. If possible, go again and again. Be modest in your conclusions. Leave room for change. Above all, weigh what you are seeing against the past—against the future—and against the success and flaws of our own society.

NOTES

PREFACE

1. Edgar Snow, *Red Star over China* (London: Victor Gollancz, 1969, 1968).

INTRODUCTION

1. Edgar Snow, *Red Star over China* (New York: Random House, 1938; enl. and rev. ed., New York: Grove Press, 1968).

2. E. Grey Dimond, *More Than Herbs and Acupuncture* (New York: W. W. Norton & Co., Inc., 1975).

3. Lansing Lamont, "China Once Over Lightly," *Harvard Magazine* 81 (1979): 37.

1 DOCTOR HORSE

1. Snow, *Red Star over China,* 1938.

2. Snow, *Red Star over China,* enl. and rev. ed., 1968.

3. Edgar Snow, *Random Notes on China 1936–1945* (East Asian Research Center, Harvard University, 1957). Huang Zhen, now minister of culture and first ambassador from the People's Republic of China to the United States, told Helen Foster Snow in 1973 that he was one of those who went out to meet and welcome Snow. He also told her that as the Chinese ambassador to France, he had earlier gotten Snow his visas for his 1960 and 1965 trips to China.

4. Edgar Snow, *Journey to the Beginning* (New York: Random House, 1958).

5. Edgar Snow, *Red China Today: The Other Side of the River* (New York: Random House, 1961).

6. John K. Fairbank, "Introduction" *Red Star over China,* 1968.

7. In Snow's biographical notes published at the end of *Red Star over China,*

rev. and enl. ed. (Bantam Books, 1978,) p. 534, he tells how his manuscript became the vehicle for telling the Chinese of Mao's story. "In June, 1937, I gave a copy of the completed manuscript which they smuggled to Shanghai . . . I gave translation rights . . . their volume was called . . . *Travels to the West.* It was the only authorized Chinese version of Mao's interviews . . . Later on, various chapters and biographies were printed . . . and reprinted in pamphlet form, in both English and Chinese . . . In 1960 . . . Mao . . . told me that he had never written an "autobiography" and the story of his life as told to me was the only one of its kind.''

2 LEBANESE-AMERICAN IN MOTION

1. Maronite Christians are a tough, enduring people. Some part of them can be traced back to the Phoenicians and they have remained a cohesive, surviving, wily people. The high Lebanese mountains, timbered at one time, protected them from the myriad invaders who came along the Mediterranean coastal route.

Their stubborn vigor made possible their successful resistance through the centuries to efforts by the Roman Church to latinize their rites, and they continue a church liturgy in ancient western Syrian. Census figures (*Encyclopaedia Britannica*) register 600,000 in Lebanon and Syria, 15,000 in Egypt, Israel, and Jordan, nearly 500,000 in southern Europe, and the Americas. As one travels, whether in Khartoum, the Sudan or Lagos, Nigeria or Manuas, Brazil or in almost any city, one notes a cohesive, clever, prosperous Lebanese merchant-trader group. They truly are a surviving people.

2. Rewi Alley, "The Ma Haide I Know," *China Reconstructs,* Spring 1981.

3. George Hatem wrote his own version of this original journey in *China Pictorial,* no. 4, 1982: "I came to know Edgar Snow back in 1936, a decisive year for China, when her political situation changed drastically. One day in June, the Chinese Communist Party underground notified me through Honorary Chairman Soong Ching-ling and some international friends that I could go to the Red Army area in the Northwest—and that I was to meet a friend along the way. This 'friend' turned out to be Edgar Snow.

". . . We met on a train in Zhengzhou and journeyed west together. . . . Braving many hazards we passed Xian and entered the Soviet area in northern Shaaxi.

"He interviewed Mao Zedong, Zhou Enlai, and other Red Army leaders . . . I was present during his discussions with Mao Zedong and others. I still remember the many sleepless nights the two of us young men spent together discussing the things we saw and heard. We were surprised at the firm dedication of these people and their magnanimity. Through this practical knowledge and a variety of other activities, I began to understand China, communism, and proletarian revolution.''

After Soong Chingling's death, Hatem wrote two eulogies and each contains bits of autobiography. These were in *Beijing Review,* 15 June 1981 and *China Reconstructs,* September 1981.

4. Snow, *Journey,* p. 152.

5. Nym Wales, *Inside Red China,* (New York: Doubleday and Company, 1939; Dacapo Paperback, Double-Doran, 1967).

3 SORT OF AN ETERNAL OPTIMIST

1. Snow, *Red China Today.*

2. Dick Wilson, *The Long March* (New York: The Viking Press, 1941).

3. Harrison Foreman, *Reprint from Red China* (Henry Holt & Co., Inc., 1945).

4. Foreman, *Reprint.*

5. Ted Allen and Sydney Gordon, *The Scalpel, the Sword: The Story of Dr. Norman Bethune* (Toronto: McClelland and Stewart, Ltd., 1971).

6. Joshua S. Horn, *Away with All Pests: An English Surgeon in People's China* (Monthly Review Press, 1969).

7. Agnes Smedley, *The Great Road* (New York: Alfred A. Knopf, 1956).

8. Agnes Smedley, *Battle Hymn of China* (New York: Alfred A. Knopf, 1943).

9. Li Teh (Otto Braun) was the German Communist military advisor who was the principal underground agent of the International Comintern. He was the only European to make the Long March. It is an interesting minor historical point that Mao, Hatem, and Braun all married Chinese actresses who joined the Communists at Yanan. Braun divorced the wife who had made the Long March with him and married the actress. He left her behind and left on the last plane that came to Yanan from Russia.

10. Evans Carlson, *Twin Stars over China* (Dodd-Mead and Co., 1940).

11. Nym Wales and Kim San, *Song of Arian* (Ramparts Press, 1941 [renewed 1980]).

12. If one laid George's career on a time-scale, it would approximate this:
 1910-Born Buffalo, New York.
 1926-Premedical education, three years, University of North Carolina, Chapel Hill.
 1928-Scholarship to American University, Beirut.
 1933-Medical degree, University of Geneva.
 1933-To Shanghai, met Rewi Alley, Soong Chingling (Sun Yat-sen's widow), Agnes Smedley, Manny Granich, Talitha Gerlach.

1936-To Paoan to Communist headquarters with Ed Snow and Wang Jumei (Huang Hua).

1936-Article published on chromium poisoning in Shanghai.

1936–39-At Yanan with Communists.

1938-Received Norman Bethune at Yanan.

1939–45-At Yanan, Anti-Japanese War. Spring 1939 received delegation of Indian doctors coming to help at Bethune International Peace Hospital.

1940-Married Zhou Sufei (Chou Su-fei).

1940-Evans Carlson at Yanan, met Dr. Ma Haide.

1944-United States Army Observer Group to Yanan sent by General Stilwell met Hatem.

1944-In November, Patrick Hurley sent to replace Stilwell. Hatem in party greeting him at Yanan. John Service at Yanan, met Hatem.

1944-Reporters at Yanan, met Hatem (Harrison Foreman, Israel Epstein, Gunther Stein).

1945–47-Coalition government. Hatem in Beijing in 1946 as medical advisor to CLARA (Chinese Liberated Area Relief Association) dealing with UNRRA and American Red Cross. Took part in Marshall Talks.

1946–47-American Friends' Medical Service Teams at Yanan.

1947–49-Final stages Civil War, Hatem with Chinese headquarters.

1949-Communist victory. The Hatems move to Beijing.

1949–57-Campaign against venereal disease. Annual trips to minority areas studying incidence of venereal disease, and leprosy, and setting up of health programs. Elimination of venereal disease in China.

1953–66-Hatem chief of staff, later deputy director, Institute of Venereology and Skin Diseases.

1960-Met Snow in Beijing.

1962-First trip abroad to Moscow, Prague, Damascus. In Lebanon, met his father, whom he had not seen since 1928.

1965-Snow again in China.

1966-Article in *China's Medicine* (no. 1, October 1966) summarizing the venereal disease campaign.

1966-To Fu Wai Hospital, Beijing, as a dermatologist. Experiencing the Cultural Revolution.

1970-Snow's last visit to China.

1971–72-To Switzerland to give medical support to Snow.

1977-Ministry of Health as advisor.

1978-First visit to United States since 1928.

1979-Return visit to United States; to Canada for Bethune Memorial Seminar.

1980-Began full-time work against leprosy.

1981-To Australia and New Zealand, lecturing and attending leprosy meeting.

1982-Led Chinese leprosy delegation on world tour, stopped in United States to attend fiftieth reunion of his University of North Carolina classmates. Working full time on leprosy treatment and prevention.

4 THE HOUSE OF MA

1. Chinese Ministry of Health, Beijing, *Health Newspaper,* February 14, 1980.

2. Zhou Sufei has been married previously, and her daughter is by the previous marriage.

3. Geoff Chapple, *Rewi Alley of New Zealand* (Hodder and Stoughton, 1980).

4. Dancing in China today is reported by the western observer, with a degree of glee, as clear evidence of the beginning decadence of Chinese society. This sheer pleasure of dancing has been misread and it was only during the severe days of the Cultural Revolution that two-by-two, "western" style dancing was not "in." From Hatem and others, one learns that in the early years after the establishment of the PRC as the national government, fox-trot type of dancing was, at least in Beijing, a regular and popular entertainment. Almost all of the reports from the Yanan years report a similar enthusiasm. One of the most entertaining descriptions of the Saturday night dances of the Yanan years was written by Anna Louise Strong. In *The Chinese Conquer China* (Garden City, NY: Doubleday and Co., Inc., 1959, p. 25) she wrote:

"Chou En-lai . . . danced with the grace of a diplomat. He was perfect in the waltz . . ."

"Liu Hsiao-chi . . . danced with a scientific precision in which two plus two inevitably made four."

"Chu Teh . . . danced as if doing his famous Long March. He kept a steady one-step, no matter what the band played."

"Mao Tse-tung . . . took the floor . . . with easy definiteness, as if he "gave the party line" to the band . . . He has a firm and delicate sense, and the only theme is his own."

5 WESTERN ISLAND IN BEIJING

1. Wang Bingnan was the Communists' underground contact man in Sian, working as a private secretary to General Yang Hu-cheng. When Snow and

Hatem came through on their way to Mao's headquarters, they made contact with Wang.

2. Lloyd Shearer, *Parade Magazine,* September 1973.

3. Edgar Snow, "China's Blitzbuilder, Rewi Alley," *Saturday Evening Post,* 8 February 1941.

4. Chapple, *Rewi Alley.*

5. Wilfred Burchett with Rewi Alley, *China: The Quality of Life* (Harmondsworth, Middlesex: Penguin Books, 1976).

6. Burchett, *China.*

6 WHEN THE CHINESE CAME

1. Carey McWilliams, *The Education of Carey McWilliams* (Simon & Schuster, 1978–79).

2. Lois Snow, *A Death with Dignity (When the Chinese Came)* (New York City, Random House, 1974).

3. Sidney Shapiro, *An American in China: Thirty Years in the People's Republic* (New World Press, 1979).

7 LUNCH WITH GEORGE HATEM IN BEIJING, MARCH 1976

1. George Hatem is cautious in conversation and in correspondence. However, in conversation, repartee is possible and useful; enjoyable exchanges happen. In letter writing, he is prompt, accurate, helpful, but cautious. His letters can always be considered as thoughtfully written "for the record." A letter to me (Jan. 20, 1982) contained this paragraph, a benign public message: "Everyone agreed that there are new winds blowing in which the initiative of the people have been fired. The proof is seen in the enhanced record agricultural production of the 800 million people."

2. Dimond, *More Than Herbs.*

3. Lin Biao was designated by the Chinese Constitution as Mao Zedong's successor.

4. This mixture is well known as a shandy, sometimes as a shandy gaffe, possibly popularized in old Shanghai by the British. It is sometimes made with lemonade.

8 CHATTING WITH GEORGE, APRIL 1976, BEIJING

1. Clues regarding Rewi Alley's life during the Cultural Revolution came from Han Suyin's *My House Has Two Doors,* (New York: G. P. Putnam's

Sons, 1980, p. 476), Chapple's *Rewi Alley.* Many of the foreign contingent in China, determined to prove their revolutionary enthusiasm, became such violent proponents of the Cultural Revolution that they were labeled the "300 percenters." This group, more than the Chinese, turned away from Alley, and accused him of faults of conduct and essentially isolated him from their own circles. The support of Zhou Enlai continued, but Alley could not get his writings printed, was prohibited from his usual pattern of wide travel, and for three years was not allowed to go to Beidaihe for his summer holiday. He was provided with a security policeman, both for his protection but also to keep his activities under watch. His adopted son, Allen, was under house arrest for two years, and on one occasion came to Beijing badly beaten and George Hatem took him in for treatment and protection in his own home. The schism between the foreigners continues to the present, and George and Rewi have little regard for some of the others who have spent their lives in China. One senses that these frictions will not heal.

2. Liu Xaoqi was also once considered to be Mao Zedong's successor. He came under criticism early in the Cultural Revolution, was placed under house arrest and died, after several years, of cancer of the lungs. Finally, in 1980, four years after Mao's death, Liu was "fully rehabilitated," posthumously. His wife was rehabilitated also, and by 1981 their daughter was in college in Boston.

3. Paul White and Samuel Rosen were the two physicians who entered China with me in September 1971.

9 *CHINA RECONSTRUCTS*

1. A detailed report on an interview with Zhou Enlai on Lin Biao's death is in *China: Behind the Mask,* by Warren Phillips and Robert Keatley (Princeton, New Jersey: Dow-Jones Books, 1972 & 1975), p. 147. One speculates, now that history has run a further course and Mao's last years and the Cultural Revolution have been faulted by the Chinese Central Committee, that if Lin Biao had been successful in his coup, he might well be today's hero in China.

11 NARCOTICS, PROSTITUTES AND VENEREAL DISEASE

1. Snow, *Red Star over China,* 1938.

2. Dr. Ma Haide, *Mao Tse-tung's Thought as the Compass for Action in the Control of Venereal Disease* (The Institute of Dermatology and Venerealogy, Chinese Academy of Sciences, October 1966). The elimination of venereal disease was completed, essentially in a five-year period. By January 1956, spe-

cialists from eight major cities—including Beijing, Shanghai, and Tianjin, reported only twenty-eight cases of infectious syphilis in the four years between 1952 and 1955, and by 1964 the rate of early infectious syphilis in these same cities was estimated at less than twenty cases per 100 million people, with none at all in Shanghai or Tianjin. At about this same time there were an estimated 1.2 million untreated cases in the United States.

12 A VISIT WITH GEORGE HATEM IN KANSAS CITY, AUGUST 1978

1. Joseph W. Esherick, ed., *Lost Chance in China, the World War II Dispatches of John S. Service,* Vintage Book edition, (Random House, Inc., 1975). An excellent source book of the facts within China between 1941 and 1945.

2. *Wall Street Journal,* June 13, 1978, editorial page.

3. Chiang Shan, "Edgar Snow and His *Red Star over China,*" *Beijing Review,* no. 16 (1978), p. 20.

4. B. E. Read, S. G. Hatem, D. J. Bao, and Lee Wei Yung, *Industrial Health in Shanghai-China II. A Study of the Chromium Plating and Polishing Trade,* Special Report No. 6 (Chinese Medical Association, 1936).

5. Hatem is strengthening his own position here. Snow was well-known in China by 1936 and made his own arrangements for the journey to Paoan.

6. Now Hatem has an assignment as a consultant to the minister of health, a task that gives him complete latitude. He also spends some time at Capitol Hospital, visiting the dermatology clinic.

15 ZHOU SUFEI

1. Dr. Ma Haide, "She Sent Me to Northern Shaanxi," *Beijing Review* 24 (15 June 1981), p. 18.

2. Snow, *Red China Today.*

16 TRUE SCHOLARSHIP

1. Arnold Katz is a professor at the University of Connecticut School of Medicine.

2. Angus W. McDonald, Jr., "Mao Tse-tung and the Hunan Self-Government Movement, 1920: An Introduction and Five Translations," *The China Quarterly* 68 (1976) 751–77. There is another source of western thought that probably influenced Mao more than will ever be recorded in Chinese documents. The father of his first wife (Yang Kaihui) went to school in Edinburgh and taught Mao about concepts of western philosophy and ethics.

3. Shapiro, *An American in China,* p. 68.

17 THE RETURN OF DENG XIAOPING

1. Naranarayam Das, "A Fresh Look at China's Hundred Flowers Period," 12 (1976): 44–53.

2. *Beijing Review* 26 (16 June 1978), pp. 27–28.

3. *Beijing Review* 6 (9 February 1979), 30–31.

18 REHABILITATION—CHINA STYLE

1. Snow, *Red Star over China,* enl. and rev. ed., 1968, p. 451.

2. *Khrushchev Remembers* (Boston: Little, Brown & Co., 1970), p. 559.

3. The culprits have been skillfully airbrushed into de-habilitation in *China Pictorial,* November 1976, pp. 4–5, and *China Reconstructs* 25 (1976): 14–15.

4. Snow devoted entire chapters to Peng Dehuai in *Red Star over China,* enl. and rev. ed.

5. Almost every foreign traveler comes within seven miles of my home. Unfortunately, the distance is straight up, as the jet passes over.

6. The Yellow Emperor, Huang Ti, 2697–2597 B.C.; surely a remarkable effort to establish the primacy of the Chinese heritage among the earth's civilizations.

7. *Message to Compatriots in Taiwan,* 1 January 1979. *Beijing Review,* 1 (1979): 16.

19 A VISIT WITH MADAME ZHOU ENLAI

1. Died 12 June 1978, age 86, in Beijing. At his request his ashes were scattered over the fields of Tachai Production Brigade.

2. Snow, *Red Star over China,* enl. and rev. ed., 1968, p. 500.

21 MAO AND HIS THOUGHT

1. Speech by Ye Jianying, Beijing, 29 September 1979, reported in *Press Release of Embassy of the People's Republic of China* no. 79 / 003, 4 October 1979.

22 THE TEMPLE OF HEAVEN—AND RELIGION

1. Snow, *Red Star over China,* 1938, p. 321.

2. Jacques Guillermaz, *The Chinese Communist Party in Power 1949–1976,* trans. Anne Destenay (Boulder, Colorado: Westview Press, 1976).

3. *Jewish Digest,* March 1979, pp. 19–21. Article condensed from *Jewish Week,* by David C. Gross.

4. W. A. P. Martin, "Visit to a Colony of Jews," in *A Cycle of Cathay* (New York: Fleming H. Revell Co., 1896).

5. Martin, p. 276.

6. Howard S. Hyman, "Is There a Religion After Revolution?," *New China* 5 (1979): 15–17.

7. In September 1978, the Institute for Religious Studies in Beijing was reopened after being closed since 1966. The head of the Institute (Jen Chiyu) estimated that the total number of Christians in China before the flight of Chiang K'ai-shek was four million. The number of practicing Muslims, Buddhists, and Christians is today not a matter of record. The number of declared atheists is not known either, but the minimum number would be at least thirty-six million, the official figure for the membership of the Communist party (*Beijing Review,* no. 6 (1979): 1. The total number of national "minorities" is but fifty million (the remaining ninety-four percent are Han people). Included among the minorities would be most of the active Buddhists and Muslims.

23 SHADOWED CHINA

1. *Commentary* (New York: The Jewish Committee, December 1976).

2. An effective response to Professor Luttwak's article appeared in *China Report* 12 (1977) 37–49, by William H. Liu, "The Other Side of Luttwak's China: An Opposition Review." For several reasons Luttwak's article was widely publicized; Liu's excellent response was passed over by most publicists. To gain a balanced view of Luttwak's article, it should be read along with Liu's.

3. John Cleverley, "Deflowering the Cultural Revolution: Letter From China," *Change,* May 1977, pp. 32–37.

4. Pierre Ryckmaus, *Chinese Shadows* (New York: Viking Penguin, 1977).

5. John K. Fairbank, *The United States in China,* 3rd ed. (Cambridge: Harvard University Press, 1972), p. 31.

6. Fairbank, p. 33.

7. Fairbank, p. 204.

8. John Fraser, *The Chinese Portrait of a People* (New York: Summit Books, 1980).

9. Ross Terrill, "Asia: The Panorama from Hong Kong," *Atlantic Monthly,* 241 (1978): 12.

24 THE NATIONAL EXAMINATION

1. Charles O. Hucker, *The Traditional Chinese State in Ming Times (1368–1644)* (Tucson: University of Arizona Press, 1961).

2. In the years of the Cultural Revolution approximately 17,000,000 city youth were sent to communes under the program requiring all middle school (high school) graduates to participate in constructive labor. The usual period of time was two years. Of this total of 17,000,000 there are approximately 900,000 who found a new life in the commune and settled there permanently.

3. *Beijing Review,* 16 (12 April 1978): 11–12.

25 THE INFLUENCE OF THE OLD CHINA HANDS

1. Snow, *Red China Today* pp. 280–81.

EPILOGUE

1. *The World Almanac and Book of Facts* (1982), p. 335.

INDEX